"Out of the Frying Pan"

Forward by Professor David Wilson

It has become commonplace, almost requi
especially high profile ex-offenders – to write an account of their criminal careers and the time that they spent in prison. Books such as Noel "Razor" Smith's "A few kind words and a loaded gun", Mark Leech's "A Product of the System" and Frank Cook's "Hard Cell" are only the most obvious examples of the genre. The fact that these three autobiographies are also concerned with the time that these prisoners spent – to a lesser or greater degree – at HMP Grendon, the only prison in Europe that operates entirely as a Therapeutic Community, is a testimony both to the power of this remarkable prison to change lives, and the continuing publishing success of the "True Crime" market.

What has been missing from this genre is a staff perspective – specifically the voice of the prison officer and particularly at HMP Grendon.

This work was first published in 2009 (Out of the Frying Pan – Chipmunk Publishing – ISBN 9781849910460) now out of print and at that time included extracts from the authors work outside of the prison service. This reworked publication concentrates purely on his work at Grendon Prison.

At that time, it was my opinion that prison officers were rarely the subject of academic scrutiny (although this is changed of late) but we have seen only a few autobiographies of a prison officer, as opposed to a prison governor – and even these are comparatively rare.

Joe Chapman's original publication admirably filled the gap both in relation to the more general issues related to why he became a prison officer and what it feels like to be on the "frontline" of the latest penological fashion.

More specifically, that work and this re-edited work fills the gap about what prison officers did within a therapeutic community and it solely covers his two periods of service as an officer at HMP Grendon.

Like many prison officers, Joe comes across as someone who will not simply unquestioningly accept what he's told to do (and which therefore provides a general reader with an insight into the complex world of prison industrial relations) and is a perceptive critic of change for changes sake.

As such he reveals the various pressures that HMP Grendon as increasingly come under to be more like the rest of the prison system and less like a Therapeutic Community – pressures which he ultimately felt unable to accept.

In between he describes the characters – both staff and prisoners – who dominated the prison in the 1980s and 1990s, visits by the Home Secretary, media coverage of the prison's regime, prisoner successes and failures, and the major disruption caused when the prison had to be closed so that it could be rewired.

In his early chapters Joe reveals that he applied to become a Prison Officer at HMP Grendon after reading Tony Parker's "The Frying Pan" – a journalistic and largely descriptive account of life in the prison from the early 1970s. Joe's book is in my view better than Parkers in that it truly gets beneath the surface of the prison to reveal the tension, hopes, aspirations and contradictions that all add up to provide the context and background within which the prison operated, as well as one-man's story of what it means to have been a prison officer with a vision for change.

Prof David Wilson
Birmingham City University

Acknowledgements:

I would firstly like to acknowledge my wonderful wife Wendy, who never signed up for any of the extra hours away from home and our family when she met me. She continued to support my desire to work above and beyond that which was expected of me as a serving prison officer, without any extra financial incentive.

Much of my journey has involved travelling around the country visiting ex-prisoners in the evenings and at weekends, this meant sacrificing even more family time and on occasions my professional and social life were entwined.

I could not have done any of this without her encouragement and understanding.

I am eternally grateful to Hospital Chief Officer Pete Barker (Deceased) who was the first to recognise my potential in 1977 and to the late Tony Carter (Hospital Officer) HMP Grendon & Norwich Prison, who gave me much needed guidance in my early years in Grendon Prison.

I have the utmost respect for Mr Michael Selby (ex-Governor – HMP Grendon) for allowing me to break down the barriers and stretch boundaries "in furtherance of therapy" whilst working with some of the most difficult and dangerous men in the prison system.

I am grateful to all my colleagues at Grendon who took over my duties while I pursued a variety of training courses and resettlement trips and for their patience and tolerance during times when I was "experimenting" with a variety of therapeutic skills, some of which did not quite go to plan!

Thanks to Dr Ayesha Muthevelloe (Psychiatrist) for nominating me for the Butler Trust Award in recognition of my efforts and to Hospital Officer John Keen for his support during the return to Grendon from HM Prison Wellingborough in 1991, rebuilding the therapeutic community from scratch and to Prison Officers Derek Francis and Sean Lanfear for their sterling efforts and motivation towards rehabilitation during the period at Winchester Prison in 1989.

If I was to include everybody who had encouraged me during my career, it would fill a complete chapter, I was privileged to work with some of the most dedicated prison staff in the service and honoured to be given the opportunity to enter the lives of prisoners who were motivated to changing their destructive lifestyles forever!

Finally, my thanks go to former prisoner Mark Leech who inspired me to write this book and I am delighted that he has continued to succeed, beyond perhaps his own expectations, which is a fitting tribute to Grendon Prison and its capabilities as a valuable model for change, long after the Prison experiment had ended!

Introduction:

Although this is the second edition of the book that was first published in 2009, it has undergone some changes, with chapters removed completely and additional content added.

In the words of the late Ernie Wise, Comedian "I hope you will enjoy this book what I writ" in its slightly rearranged format.

I had been informed that the book is now "dated" and "not viable in the current market" as it contains "memoirs that students or other academics cannot refer to for text" Prior to writing the original I was advised that it would be "better to write it professionally, referring to current research and changes in treatment methods throughout and to retain my dignity by removing any bad language, examples of bad practice and admittance of personal failure."

I then gave some thought to who my book might be aimed at, what I hoped to achieve by writing it and what was relevant to my journey through quite a demanding, but also unique and rewarding career as a Prison Officer working in a therapeutic prison?

The book is aimed at the public, but also anybody who has an interest in prison life and particularly relationships between prisoners and prison officers.

In 2017, 12 years after I was medically retired from the Prison Service, the UK faces a crisis in jails greater than anything else in prison history and relationships between officers and inmates are strained to breaking point, it would be fantastic if I could achieve, through my book, a debate about Prison Officer training, to debate how we have progressed towards the current desperate situation or whether it is time once again to consider extending the Grendon Prison treatment regime into other jails?

However, perhaps the best I can achieve is to fill the gap that occurs in the written records of Grendon Prisons history by providing my honest account of my life in that prison between 1977 and 2005. At least I will have put the information out there again and having edited the manuscript on numerous occasions, this is the finished work, which includes information relevant to my experience but not necessarily relevant to any research, Psychological theories or Prison Officer best practice.

Having never fully behaved in a professional or appropriate manner with Prisoners, why would I bother to pretend otherwise for the sake of satisfying academics. My successful and satisfying career was due to my being unconventional and stubborn.

That is hardly going to change at this stage in my life!

Chapter 1

The summer of 1976 was one of the hottest in UK records and I was feeling particularly hot and bothered. By the end of May, I had decided to cut off all my shoulder length hair, which I had been growing since 1968. I was tired of it sticking to my face and neck as I sweated; I needed a cooler image, and so, with the new haircut, there came a change of clothing style too.

My shaggy afghan waistcoat, blue and purple two-tone flared trousers and green tie-dye tee shirt, was replaced with smart brown casual trousers and a white casual shirt. I even considered a smart three-piece suit would now be acceptable. My slightly rebellious "hippy" look had finally gone, and with this change of image came a sudden huge change of outlook on my life and career.

As a child of the 60s, I referred to things as being "far out and really free man". It was somewhat ironic that my new career would see me moving from my hometown as "far out" as Aylesbury in Buckinghamshire and my new job would mean that I was not "really free" for the next two decades.

I had spotted an advertisement for prison officers in a national newspaper. It all seemed to make sense, to go for a job that was totally different, working with people and with the bonus of free housing at that time, which meant I could get rid of the mortgage that had become such a millstone around my neck.

It would perhaps have sounded more meaningful to say that I wanted to join the prison service to make a difference to society, or that I had some long-term goal to train in psychology/psychotherapy, but in fact it was simply to get out of a mortgage rut. I knew nothing at all about prisons or prisoners, so it was a complete leap into the unknown, but I had faith in my ability to survive the change.

The career choice had been made easier for me, as a year earlier I had been talking with a friend in a local pub, and he just happened to be on home leave from Stafford prison, whilst serving a four-year sentence for burglary. I shared with him the frustration and boredom I felt working with machinery day in day out, as a Mechanical Fitter, and I wanted to move into a job where I would be working with people.

In fact, the boredom was such that I had taken to leaving my place of work, mainly in the early hours of the morning, scaling a fence into an adjacent office block and upon finding an unsecured window I had climbed inside and took great delight in rearranging each of the offices, just for the sheer devilment, imagining the confusion the next morning when the workers arrived to find their desks and filing cabinets etc. in various parts of the building.

I had always delighted in playing pranks but even by my standards this was a step too far.

My friend explained that I was guilty of breaking and entering, which was a criminal offence and even though I had not stolen anything that would not matter to the police. This little escapade could have cost me my job, perhaps my freedom and most certainly my house not to mention the disappointment felt by my family.

He suggested that if I really wanted to work with people then maybe I should choose a career in one of the caring professions. My first idea was to go into nursing but the pay was not very attractive, even back then. He explained that the prison service employed officers who were trained as nurses to work in the prison hospitals and he felt that I had the right personal qualities for that work.

So, I sent the application form off and waited ---

At that time, I worked at Drakelowe Power Station, as a mechanical fitter, and the reaction to my career change was varied. An old friend, Barry Bradford, who had been a mate for quite some time, thought the idea was totally crazy.

"You must be joking; you're a complete disaster!" He laughed "the convicts will all vote for a return to the death penalty, rather than risk having you looking after them". I was not considered to be the most accomplished mechanical fitter and had created some minor disasters during my apprenticeship and in the five years up until now that I had been working alone.

My dad was similarly unimpressed "You're giving up a good qualification, for a low paid dead-end job like that" he said, "there's no future in it".

However, no matter what anybody said, I had made up my mind and it just seemed to be the right thing to do, although I had no experience to base my feelings on.

So, I began to rise to the new challenge, to focus on a completely different lifestyle even though I didn't really know what the future held. I was very apprehensive but prepared to give it my best shot.

There was one comment, made by a workmate whose name I can't recall. He said "Joe, you're every man's dog, you'll be OK".

He told me "You are the type of person who can get along with anybody you want, and this will be your strength in the future". So, I waited for a response from the Prison Service and eventually, at the end of March 1977, I was called for an interview at nearby Stafford Prison.

Seven other people also attended for an interview, which was conducted by the prison Governor and a high-ranking prison officer, known as a Chief Officer. He was the highest-ranking uniformed officer and wore a cap with a "scrambled egg "type of gold braiding around its peak.

This very stern faced authoritarian figure was my very first close meeting with a prison officer.

"Fasten your jacket buttons up son", he roared, as I walked into the room "There's no place for sloppy dress in the modern Prison Service".

I took an immediate dislike to this man's arrogance and resented being referred to as "son", but I instinctively did as I was told and fastened my buttons, straightening my tie at the same time.

"Well gentlemen" the Governor said "your day will consist of three elements. First, you will all be given a medical examination; then, assuming you are fit and healthy, you will take the new entrants examination. Lastly, assuming you can all read and write we will interview you. Are there any questions?" Without pausing long enough for any of us to reply he said "No, that's good, I will now hand you over to Principal Officer Littlewood, who will look after you for the day, thank you very much gentlemen and good luck".

The Chief then ordered us to stand up and they both left the room.

I wondered if I would be able to cope with the apparent heavy disciplined regime?

We remained with Principal Officer Littlewood, who invited us to take a seat. "Welcome to Stafford Prison lads, my name is Bob" he said, which put us all immediately at ease. He outlined the day's programme and we were sent for the medical examination.

Our Medical examination was conducted by a couple of Hospital Prison Officers and although they were trained and qualified as regular prison officers they were also qualified State Registered Nurses and even addressed each other as nurse.

I was given a blood test, blood pressure test, hearing and eyesight test and then Nurse Edwards asked me to stand with both feet on a white line just in front of the desk.

"Now then love", what's your balance and co-ordination like?" he asked, "would you raise your right leg, close your eyes and raise your left arm to the side please".

I did as he asked!

"Very good, now stick your tongue out as far as you can and hold it there for exactly half a minute" he ordered, so I diligently obeyed. I than felt him rubbing something on my tongue and was tempted to take a little peep. He was holding a sealed envelope in one hand and was rubbing a postage stamp on my tongue.

"Excuse me love," he laughed, "I hate the taste of the glue on these stamps, hope you don't mind?"

His colleague apologised on his behalf "It is just something that we do to break the ice a little. You will soon see that a good sense of humour is vital to your role as a prison officer and don't forget as a recruit there might be plenty of wind-ups along the way."

Before I left the medical room, I asked him how I might train as a Hospital Officer, if I managed to get into the job and how long it would take?

He advised "To qualify as a scab lifter takes about two years. You join as a slope head then ask to go for nurse training when you finish your first year's probation. Concentrate on becoming a good screw first".

A "slope head" is what Hospital Officers called ordinary (Discipline) prison officers. Some of them slash the peaks of their caps, so that the peak falls over their eyes like guardsman, then they must slope their heads backwards to see where they are walking.

In return Discipline Officers called the Hospital staff "scab lifters" for obvious reasons.

I soon began to learn that my new world behind the grey walls of this local Victorian jail was a community with rules and a language of its own.

The Prison Officers exam was basic Math's and English, with a Progressive Matrices Test to finish off with. It was all about reasoning and logic, fitting the right shapes into the right boxes etc. I thought I got through the exams alright and we were asked to queue outside the Governor's office for our final interview.

Only four of us had got through to the final interview stage. Two men had failed the medical and the other guy didn't get through the first exam. I found out that the three other men with me were all ex-servicemen, two from the RAF and one ex-soldier.

We knew we would all be told at the end of the interview if we had been successfully accepted into the service, but I must admit, I was beginning to lose my confidence at this stage. It seemed to me to be a highly-disciplined job and if I was competing against ex-military men, I thought I stood no chance of getting in.

The two former RAF men were called in first and we had been told that we could not speak to each other after the interview, so we arranged to indicate if we thought we had succeeded or failed, by raising or lowering our thumbs as we left the room.

As the 2 airmen came out each of them gave discreet thumbs up.

"Ah well, here goes," I thought, "it look's like my prediction will be right, I won't be changing my career just yet". However, the ex-soldier came out after 40 minutes with his thumb down, which surprised me, as he appeared an ideal candidate.

This gave my confidence a boost and I was determined to go in there and try to impress them, and as I was called into the room I quickly made sure that I had fastened the buttons on my jacket and strode in with an air of confidence, but trying hard to hide my anxiety.

The Governor and Chief Officer sat at the other side of a large desk, and as I was invited to sit down, the Chief Officer seemed to be staring at the buttons on my jacket with a slight smirk on his face.

"Take a seat Mr Chapman", the Governor shook my hand as I sat down, but the Chief Officer's eyes were still fixed on my jacket, or maybe it was somewhere else? I started to panic as I imagined that perhaps my trousers were undone!

As I took my seat, I felt my jacket pull to one side, and realised in my haste I had fastened the buttons wrong. I adjusted them and the Chief Officer smiled and relaxed "Good move son" he laughed "you remembered!"

His attitude towards me seemed to have warmed a little, which in turn relaxed me and my interview was soon in full flow.

One of the questions that I was asked has remained in my mind ever since and it was asked by the Chief Officer. "What are your personal views about men who commit crimes against women or innocent children, particularly sexual offences? How do you think we should deal with them in prison?"

I had not thought about this in much depth but felt I had to be open and honest. "My personal belief" I offered "is that these types of crimes are the worst ones of all. To be honest, men like that make me feel sick and angry, I would consider capital punishment to be a consideration in some cases, but of course that has been abolished."

"I think they deserve to be punished" I continued, but then sensed I was in dangerous territory and thought it best to try to offer a more balanced view.

I added "However, I am open to having my belief changed. They may always make me feel sick but perhaps I must control my anger and any feelings towards them I might have. I don't know enough about these men to know why they do what they do, and I don't know enough about prison to know how they might be dealt with. Perhaps they can change their ways, but I don't know if I can help them. Something has to be done and I suppose it has to happen while they are in prison",

I don't know if this answer was particularly impressive or even if it was one of the reasons that I was finally offered the job, I don't even know where it came from? But the good news is that I was successful and started my training as a prison officer in May 1977.

My training began with a two-week period at Stafford Prison during the time that the 1977 Queens Jubillee celebrations were in full swing.

Entering the prison for the first morning of training was scary. There were lots of iron gates slamming, chains and keys jangling, uniformed officers everywhere and raised voices which echoed around the old Victorian gate lodge.

I had joined with two other guys, although not those who were at the initial interview. One man was a former bank clerk and the other a baker's delivery driver; we were the only people not wearing a blue uniform so we stuck out like sore thumbs. The gatekeeper gave us badges to wear, and warned "Guard them with your lives and if you lose these you will be in serious trouble. If they fall into the hands of the convicts they could use them to engineer an escape attempt".

The badges were only attached by a small safety pin, so I spent most of the first day touching it every couple of minutes to check it hadn't dropped off.

On my badge was written the following "Mr J.H. Chapman - P O U T - HM Prison Stafford."

From this first day, until the end of the 9 weeks training course, we were told we would be referred to as "POUTs" (Prison Officers under Training).

The two-week training course included several tours of the prison, with short periods of work experience in several departments, such as the Main Wings, Reception, Education Dept, Exercise Yard, Canteen, Bathhouse and Gymnasium. In fact, an early morning 45-minute session in the Gym was compulsory each day.

After many years without any structured exercise, I suffered aches and pains in muscles that I didn't realise I had until now. You must remember that these were the days when few people considered exercise to be important in their daily lives and gymnasiums were few and far between.

I thought I was strong and fit, but I hadn't done any sustained exercise for about 10 years - and it really showed. Each day we did a 30-minute gym circuit using weights and medicine balls, finishing off with a game of Basketball, Football or Tennis. This was followed by a very speedy "cold" shower, and then we reported to the Principal Training Officer for the daily programme.

During the first week in the Gym the Physical Education Instructor asked, "Are any of you interested in shooting?" Thinking that perhaps a Clay Pigeon shoot was on offer, or even something more exciting, like training to become an" armed" prison guard, I said "Yes I am, I've always had a bit of an interest". It was a lie and I soon wished I had not spoken up!

"Good", the PEI replied, "Then you can shoot around the outside of this Gym for 10 laps, followed by fifty press-ups before you have a shower".

I had already forgotten the Hospital Officers warning that it was not clever to volunteer yourself for anything as a recruit.

On the second day, I was working on a wing called "Crescent Wing". This was large half-moon shaped building housing several hundred prisoners. In the early morning, I observed prison officers checking the morning roll, to make sure that all prisoners were still in their cells, before unlocking them, and more importantly they were still alive.

"There's nothing more embarrassing than finding some convict hanging by his neck when you open the door in the morning. Filling in the paperwork makes you late for your breakfast". The Senior Officer in charge of the wing laughed.

"What do you do?" I enquired, "If you find a prisoner hanging by his neck Sir?"

"First of all, you hang on tight to his feet to make sure the job's successful, and then you nick him, depending on which way he is swinging". He laughed again.

He realised that I could not understand the joke and explained that "nicking" somebody, means placing them on an official report, this can be for several offences against prison rules. They then go in front of the prison Governor, and could end up having extra days added to their sentence.

"So" he explained "If he's swinging towards you, nick him for assault. But if he's swinging away from you, nick him for trying to escape. It's all a win-win situation. Put it this way son, a convict's suicide is inconvenient but it does everybody a favour, saving us tax payers having to keep them in prison for the rest of their lives. But we don't want too many stiffs, or else you and I will be out of work".

It is somewhat disappointing that this attitude exists amongst prison officers 40 years later but it was never something that I ever subscribe to.

I laughed nervously but could not hide the fact that I was shocked by his attitude towards prisoners, which he also sensed. "Listen son, there is no room for sentiment in this job, the convicts are all here because they have been naughty boys and it is our job to teach them that crime does not pay. Don't lose any sleep over these people because you can be sure they'll lose none over us."

As I walked around the jail there was a discernable tension between the Cons (Prisoners) and Screws (Prison Officers). It seemed that prisoners treated staff with a begrudging respect, each treated the other with suspicion and conversations seemed strained. I was immediately uncomfortable with this.

Each morning, once the total prison roll was confirmed as correct, the prisoners would be unlocked a few at a time to "slop out". Slopping out, consisted of a prisoner bringing his plastic chamber pot, or even a bucket full of last night's waste to be emptied down a nearby toilet. The toilet was referred to as a "recess".

The smell of this operation, particularly first thing in the morning before breakfast, was enough to turn your stomach but was something that prison officers soon got used to. In fact, the smell of stale urine, sweat and cigarette smoke prevailed for at least the first 10 years of my service.

The reasons for only unlocking a few prisoners at a time (Controlled Unlock), was because the early morning was the time when most fights might occur. Quite often prisoners had been threatening each other through their windows overnight or, as I learned much later, they had been provoked by certain night patrol officers and were looking for an argument the moment the cell door was opened.

A fight that took place in a recess was called a "straightener" or "recess therapy". The recess was the area in which convicted sex offenders (nonces) were at most risk of attacks from other prisoners.

Also, if too many prisoners slopped out at the same time the prison drains would soon be blocked solid.

I was later told that Pentonville Prison, in London, once allowed two whole wings to slop out at the same time, and the weight of all the human waste forced the manhole covers up in the street outside.

Another good tip I was given in my first two weeks was to open a cell door but immediately stand to one side. It's possible that the prisoner you unlock might have had a bad night, or was upset for some other reason, and you will find yourself wearing the contents of his chamber pot. This delightful little practice was affectionately known as "being pottied".

Many officers who have ignored this rule have later turned up for breakfast wearing the contents of a prisoner's chamber pot which is not attractive, particularly if you have no change of uniform for the remainder of the shift.

Apart from just observing what goes on we were occasionally given simple tasks, often with little guidance or explanation and my first one was to go outside the perimeter of the prison buildings and look for "parcels" that had been thrown from the cell windows overnight.

Of course, nobody explained what might be contained in such parcels, and I imagined it was maybe contraband, such as drugs.

I was given a plastic bin bag and a pair of rubber gloves and was let out through the back door onto the prison exercise yard. I began to walk around the outside of the cell block and picked up old socks, bits of string, used tea bags and half-eaten sandwiches etc.
Then I spotted my first parcel and was quite excited with my discovery. Whatever it was... it was neatly wrapped in newspaper and tied with green string. It was heavy and I was curious. Perhaps one prisoner had tried to swing it to another during the night?

I had been told that the act of "swinging a line" through a cell window was the way that prisoners passed items to one another when they were locked up.

I quickly unwrapped it, like a child with his first Christmas present. It had several wrappers just like a game of pass the parcel and I felt like a winner as I peeled back the final wrapper. Then I reeled back, as a by now familiar stench attacked my nostrils!

"Feeling lucky guvnor?" A prisoner shouted from a window above.

This "lucky bag" was full of human excrement and I had experienced my very first "shit parcel", thrown out by a prisoner who could not be bothered with the early morning slop out routine, and did not want to keep it in a bucket in his cell overnight. Over the next 45 minutes I collected another thirty or more similar parcels before my job was complete.

The task of collecting shit parcels was often give to new recruits to supervise prisoners who were employed to do it for just over £3 per week.

However, my most memorable incident as a trainee prison officer came at the beginning of my second week of training.

I had been asked to go down to the "Bathhouse" to observe the procedure for the weekly bathing of prisoners. But before this, the officer in charge had taken us down into the basement of Crescent Wing, to show us the original Victorian bath, which still existed as a museum piece. He told us that the bath had been filled to a regulation depth of six inches, and the water was emptied after the fourth prisoner had used it.

"During Victorian times" he said, "any prisoner caught pissing in the water would be placed in solitary confinement and would only be fed on bread and water for a week".

I attempted to be funny and observed "so by the time the third man had gone through, a prisoner might welcome somebody pissing in the bath, as it would raise the water temperature a little"?

The officer was not amused as he retorted, "This is no laughing matter pal. Prisoners take two things seriously, their food and personal hygiene".

Oh dear, I thought, maybe I've got the prison humour thing wrong, as we made our way back towards the main wing.

The Bathhouse in Stafford prison in the 70's was obviously much more modern than its Victorian predecessor, and there were several showers available to prisoners, if they preferred

I witnessed approximately a dozen prisoners queuing to use the facilities and at this point the officer in charge said he had to go away use the telephone for a few minutes.

"It's OK "; he reassured me "you can easily supervise while I'm away. There's nothing to it, just two simple rules. One, the bath is still only filled to a depth of six inches. And two, the water can be changed at every third man".

He added "Oh yes, and most importantly, you can still nick a prisoner for pissing in the water even though you are only just starting your training. If you see it, all you do is say, I'm giving you a direct order not to piss in the bath and then take his name and number."

He then asked if there were any questions.

I asked what I should do if things get out of hand and what if I'm threatened with violence."

"No problems" he replied "that red button over there is an alarm bell. Press it and two dozen hairy arsed screws will be here in no time".

I must admit, during the first week I had witnessed the rapid response to an alarm bell. Officers seemed to appear from out of the woodwork and within less than a minute there would be at least twenty available.

"I think I can cope", I said unconvincingly.

The first prisoner appeared with a towel wrapped around him. He appeared to be over six feet tall, covered in tattoos and was solidly built. He glared at me as he began to run the bathwater. I smiled and nodded nervously in return. Then as the water reached a depth of about six inches, in my best authoritarian voice, I said "Can you turn it off now please". At which point he stared at me for what seemed like half an hour, although really it was perhaps only as much as five seconds.

"You're having a laugh guv", he complained. "There's not enough in there to wash under my bollocks".

I remembered what I had been taught earlier in the week. Prison Officers are always in the right. If a convict argues he gets nicked. The other thing to remember is that even if an officer feels intimidated or scared; don't let prisoners see your weakness, stay calm and assertive.

Trying my best to stay calm I responded to the troublesome convict who was trying to undermine my authority. "You know the rules mate, you have to turn it off now or you'll be nicked".

He screwed the bath tap down with so much force it nearly came off in his hand. And he climbed into the water, casting doubts on my parenthood under his breath. I stood nearby as he took his bath, obviously not a happy man.

However, the reaction I got from him had improved my self-confidence. Perhaps I'm suited to this job after all I thought. It wasn't long before he had finished and climbed out.

He went to let the water out, but I told him to leave it in for the next man.

This time he didn't argue and snatching the towel around him, he left the room.

The next prisoner to appear seemed more powerfully built than the first, and I remember thinking at the time that he must do a lot of weightlifting. At eleven stone two I would be no match against him.

The man stood against the side of the bath, just considering the water. "What dirty bastard's left that in there" he said, reaching over to pull the plug out.

I quickly replied" You're only the second man and if you don't want the water let somebody else have it".

On hearing this he dropped his towel and started to piss into the bath water.

I immediately ordered him to stop, but he just stared at me and continued. I felt a panic setting in. "I might be the second man" he shouted, "but you're the 50th". He laughed as he finished emptying his bladder into the bath.

"50th what" I asked.

"The 50th new screw to be caught out by our little game" he roared. And I realised that the whole thing had been a complete set up, to see how I would react. Peeping from behind the bathhouse door was a handful of prison officers and several prisoners.

My face was crimson as I was told that my "initiation ceremony" was over, but I had a feeling it wouldn't be the last time the laughs would be on me, if I was not careful!

It may seem at times like prison life is just one long joke and quite a cruel regime to newcomers, but of course this is not at all the case.

My short time in Stafford showed me all aspects of prison work and I was fully aware by the time I left, that threats, violence, verbal abuse, intimidation, and tests of will power are a part of everyday life for prison officers but new screws were generally monitored and protected from harm.

The rules and boundaries that are set for the protection of staff and prisoners were stronger than I had imagined in this busy little local prison. There was a strong culture of "them and us", and I suppose the overall teaching after the first fortnight was, to learn to be professional and exercise personal discipline when dealing with prisoners and never drop your guard.

I was told that prisoners should never be fully trusted, and to remain suspicious and vigilant always. For some reason, I struggled to accept this, but it was to be a couple of years later before I would really understand exactly why. As for prison humour, it was obvious that the only way to cope with some of the horrors that are experienced behind prison walls is to find a way of reducing stress using comedy, horseplay and friendly "banter".

I might not have continued training if I had left Stafford prison with the feeling that there was no release from the strict disciplined regime and the constant intimidation from prisoners.

I have previously mentioned Principal Officer Bob Littlewood, who later allowed me to stay with himself and his wife Cathy during my training. They were a loving and devoted couple who both sadly passed away many years ago. I felt that if I had stayed working at Stafford, perhaps Bob and Cathy would have become close friends.

However, little did I know now, I was destined for something completely different, but one piece of advice that Bob offered stayed with me forever.

He told me "Regardless of the amount of training and expertise that the Prison Service will push in your direction, your greatest asset would eventually be your own life experiences and personality. Understanding human nature and your ability to make strong relationships with prisoners would gain their respect. It can help to change their lives".

I wrote this in my training diary, long before I knew where I would eventually be posted.

So, at the end of the initial two-week training at Stafford, I left my family home in Burton on Trent and travelled north to Wakefield, West Yorkshire, to begin the first leg of the formal training at The Prison Service Training College, Aberford Road.

Chapter 2

On the train to Wakefield, I made my way through the packed compartments and found one with just a few people in it. I stowed my luggage and settled into my seat to contemplate the possibilities that might greet me at the end of the journey.

I was a little preoccupied and didn't immediately notice the girl who sat opposite me. She had stunning good looks, well-manicured nails and I remember thinking that she could have easily been a fashion model.

When I did spot her I realised that I had been staring at her for a while and she had noticed. To hide my embarrassment, I took a copy of the training course details from my bag and pretended to read them, glancing occasionally in her direction.

Then she spoke. "You must be heading in the same direction as me" she said, with a soft Welsh accent "I'm heading for Wakefield as well."

"Yeah, that's right" I replied, pleased that she had started the conversation "but when we get there I think we'll be going in opposite directions as I'm heading north to train as a Prison Officer. What about yourself?"

"So am I "she laughed "I noticed your paperwork. We're heading for the same place."

This came as a complete surprise. I knew there were female prison officers but never considered they were trained alongside the males and I commented "You're joking, aren't you?" before quickly realizing I would have to qualify my shocked reaction. "I mean I had been led to believe that female prison officers were quite butch, in fact more like men than the men, if you know what I mean, whereas you are very attractive, if you don't mind me saying and I can't imagine you pounding the prison landings."

She smiled, "my name's Gaynor Evans, I am actually a former Miss Wales Beauty Queen and I wanted to try something completely different".

"I suppose pounding a cell block landing will be a lot different to walking a catwalk" I joked. I then recalled seeing an article in the "Sun" newspaper, about a model training to become a screw! I imagined that it had been a publicity stunt but this was obviously not the case, as here she was.

For the remainder of the journey we compared our expectations and discussed the type of people that choose to become prison officers and why that might be?

It was already obvious to both of us that they come from all walks of life. As the course progressed we would meet men and women who were unemployed, bankers, retailers, plumbers, builders etc, but the one thing that everybody seemed to be looking for was job security with a reasonable wage.

It was the case in 1977 that many Pout's were ex-servicemen and women, many who felt that they weren't't qualified to do anything else, or they liked the idea of staying in uniform in a disciplined service.

Neither of us knew what we would look like in the blue uniforms, but imagined that we might soon be looking, thinking, and probably acting the same, in fact, stereotyped if we were not careful.

Very few people at the start of their training could say where their job satisfaction might come from. Basically, we had chosen a career that would teach us to lock other people behind bars and keep them there, nothing more, nothing less. Oh yes, and to punish them when necessary of course!

Gaynor and I had agreed to go out for a meal in the evening, as soon as we had settled in and I must admit I welcomed that but unfortunately for me the Prison Service had other plans and later on Gaynor had hers, so sadly that opportunity never arose.

The Wakefield training school was a typical modern red brick college building, set back from the main road with a large car park to the front. This was to be our parade ground, for a drill practice every morning at 8.o clock prompt.

There were about 180 people on this course and we were split into smaller sections, with 20 - 30 in each section. Men and women were not allowed to mix, other than at meal times, socially in the evening and occasionally for sports and games. The living quarters were on 3 floors, with men on the ground floor and top and women in the middle.

We weren't allowed to go onto the female living areas and vice versa. Anyone caught breaking this rule would be liable to be thrown off the course, to join the ranks of the unemployed, although some did risk it during the course, including me.

On the very first morning we were all introduced to our separate small groups (Sections) and there were 24 men in mine. Two thirds were ex-military, but I got on with all of them. In fact, there wasn't anybody that I felt uneasy about really.

We were all asked to introduce ourselves, to give a little information about past histories, family etc and then to say what anxieties we might have. At this stage, there was nothing that I was over anxious about, but I decided to make a bold statement about how I felt to be wearing a uniform for the first time.

I declared "I value my independence and think that we all might have something to offer the prison service, but how much of our own characters can we keep as we work behind the prison walls? I suppose I'm saying that I hope the training and wearing the uniform won't make us exact copies of each other?

Without meaning to, I had upset some of the ex-servicemen, who thought I was devaluing the uniform. I quickly said I wasn't. I just wanted to know how much we could be ourselves. How much our individual personalities would be affected?

The school's Principal Training Officer answered my question adequately.

"You have got to understand that during the course we will be looking for teamwork and it's important that you prove you can be part of a team. But we are also looking at each individual's strengths and weaknesses. There will be some of you who will have outstanding personal qualities, and yes, the prison service will value these. But you will have to follow strict rules and regulations, which won't be easy for those of you who are not used to being given orders."

I knew I would struggle with the heavy disciplined, authoritarian side of the job. I decided not to prolong the debate and thanked him for putting my mind at rest. What I failed to realise at this point, was that the tutors were constantly making notes on each of us from day one, and this would eventually influence their choice of prison we were best, at the age of 25, suited to. At this point, I felt that I would be returning to Stafford Prison if I got through successfully but this was not guaranteed.

Surprisingly there was very little work required of us in the evenings and we could go into town for a drink. Many decided to use The Royal Oak pub, on the Aberford Road just outside the college gate. The younger element, which included me, went into town most nights.

On top of our decent weekly wage, we also got £37 per night (living allowance), which obviously amounted to a fairly large bit of cash for pubbing and clubbing. The college staff gave us a complete run down of where to go and where not to go at night, including free tickets to some of the nightclubs. There was no strict curfew, but we were told that the main doors to the college would be locked at midnight. Anybody who arrived after that time would have to contact the night porter and a log would be kept for our tutors to examine.

It was clear to me from the first trip into town that Wakefield would provide more entertainment than I could cope with. The days were long and information packed but we didn't have to make many notes as they provided handouts for each topic. This meant more time could be spent propping up the bars in local nightclubs. Some men and women had not been away from their families for years and this was the first time I had lived away for more than a night or two.

During the daily programme I found there was more to prison work than I had witnessed at Stafford and I was soon working my way through reams of paper, official forms and court documents. Each element of a prison officer's work was covered in complete detail. We would also do role-plays, which suited me fine as I was also a semiprofessional entertainer (and a bit of an exhibitionist).

In the first three weeks, we made two study trips to Wakefield Prison and Wakefield Crown Court, both of which I thoroughly enjoyed.

The court experience was rather boring, as it was a fraud case. However, it was my first experience of justice in action, and witnessing the pomp and splendour of a serious trial and seeing the barristers arguing their case, as the elderly judge seemed to fall asleep, was just like I had seen on TV.

Prison Officers were responsible for running all of the courts and producing prisoners for trial. So it was important to learn the role of a Dock Officer. For instance, when a Judge passes sentence, the Dock Officer had to accurately record his exact recommendations, in the exact words used. In the case of an appeal hearing, a Judge could order a prisoner to be freed directly from the courtroom, so it was important to get the facts right or very serious mistakes might be made. The prisoner could be released by mistake or even kept in prison by mistake.

The role of a Prison Gatekeeper was another important job. It was not just about handing over the correct keys and unlocking or locking doors. It was also about correctly recording people, transport, and goods in and out of a prison.

The Gatekeeper is often the first person a member of the public meets, so he had to possess good personal qualities such as, courtesy, tact and diplomacy etc.

Through the course, we were reminded "You all represent the Crown. You represent the Prison Service at all times and must behave in a manner that does not bring disgrace upon the service, you or your colleagues."

Fitting words, but something seemed to overcome a prison officer when he or she decided to let their hair down and the Wakefield course was no exception to this rule.

For most the male officers, booze and women, became the prime focus at night and I immediately took advantage of that situation. As I said before, some of the men had not been away from their homes for years and many had never been unfaithful to their wives or girlfriends, but the Wakefield nightspots were a massive temptation that a few succumb to.

The most respectable of the men could become predatory animals, given a few beers, a disco dance floor and an apparently unlimited supply of eager women. We were encouraged by Senior Prison Managers to check out two of the most popular venues at that time, Tiffany's Nightclub and a place called Heppy's Fish and Strip (a place where you could enjoy a plate of fish and chips while watching an exotic dancer remove her clothes).

On Thursday nights at Tiffany's, it was affectionately known to all as "Grab a Granny night."

This was when coachloads of women came into town from surrounding areas looking for an enjoyable time, dressed to kill and ready to cling to any man who showed them enough attention. They invariably got very drunk and were almost queuing up at the edge of the dance floor by midnight.

The place was something of a pervert's paradise and of course I was there on the very first Thursday night.

I thought I could move well on the dance floor but I think the amount that I had to drink influenced that opinion. And as money was no object, I drank much more than was usual.

On one occasion, just after midnight, I saw the girl of my dreams at the end of the bar. She looked like she was dancing, but as I got closer I realised she was struggling to stand up due to the amount of drink she'd consumed. Approaching her, brimming with liquid confidence I gave my best smile, which thinking about it now must have looked like I was suffering from severe wind.

"Would you like to dance?" I asked. She turned to me, attempted to focus and said "Fine" as we both staggered towards the dance floor.

One of the most popular songs in the charts at the time was "So you win again" by a band called "Hot Chocolate" and I really felt like a winner. We moved together for what seemed like hours. At first not touching, but then accidentally (on purpose) my arm would brush against hers. And then my arm would curl around her waist like a Boa Constrictor, pulling her close, then moving in for a smooch.

Just when things were about to get passionate along came a fast dance number and she turned into a woman possessed by the devil. I suddenly realised that I don't even know her name yet, nor her mine, as she threw herself around the floor like a maniac,

She'll wear herself out soon and have no energy for me, I'm thinking, as I stand by, not daring to try and slow her down. The strobe lights give the impression that she is slowing down… but then…. there is flash of white light from the direction of her mouth!

Did she just spit on the dance floor? Had she been sick?

As I pondered what it might have happened, she suddenly made a run for it towards the edge of the dance floor, with me in hot pursuit and another girl suddenly stopped me in my tracks and shouted, "Show me where you and Margaret were dancing?"

"Why do you want to know?" I asked. "Just show me". She screamed.

I took her to roughly where Margaret and I had been dancing, and she began to frantically search the floor. "It might help if I knew what we are looking for" I pleaded. As she was now on her hands and knees, "It must be valuable".

"It's her teeth" the young girl exclaimed, "Somebody might tread on them ".

Even though I had been drinking heavily, I suddenly sobered up.

Oh dear, Margaret was shaking her head so violently her teeth couldn't cope! Anybody who has tried to do the "bikers dance" (Head banging) will know how easy it is to lose your glasses, but it must be a first for somebody to lose their dentures?

We searched in vain so I decided to do something drastic. I approached the DJ and asked him to stop the music.

" Can you stop the music for a minute, and put the house lights on, it's a matter of life or death" I shouted. He was very puzzled but readily agreed. He also asked the crowd to search for the dentures, and amazingly they were found in no time at all, still in one piece.

"Just rinse them under the tap and they'll be as good as new" I said. "Then I'll return them like a knight in shining armour". But, there was no chance of that. Unfortunately, Margaret was well on her way. She refused to see me or to return to the club. As for the chances of a night of passion, I had somehow lost interest and settled for chicken in a basket and a taxi back to the college.

During First Aid Training the next day, our tutor asked me to step forward and said "Gentlemen, Mr Chapman will now demonstrate what to do if some old biddy you are dancing with loses her teeth on the dance floor." He then warned "The college tutors will not miss anything that goes on in town".

The truth was that our social life was scrutinized as much as our performance on the training course. I decided to give the night clubs a miss for a while, mainly because I was becoming physically exhausted with the training, as we had done quite a bit of sport each day and a couple of sessions of Judo a week, which was then a Prison Officers only form of self defence.

The restraining of violent prisoners was a bit underdeveloped the 1970's and I remained unconvinced by some of the techniques we were shown.

When being trained how to cope with a violent prisoner who is refusing to leave his cell, we were told "Gentleman, you have ordered him to come out and he tells you to fuck off" the instructor advised "One officer will go and collect a handful of dried peas or rice and will stand just to the right of the closed cell door. Then another officer will collect the restraint cushion, (a large cushion, with two leather straps at the back) and he stands just to the left of the door. The third officer is responsible for opening the cell door on my command".

He continued. "As the cell door is opened, the officer with the peas/rice throws them in the direction of the prisoner's face, thereby temporarily distracting him. At the same time the officer with the cushion will rush towards the said prisoner, followed by four or five other officers". He then reassures us "The prisoner can then be carried, kicking and squealing like a little pig, to the punishment block.

In the 70's and early 80's a lot of prison officers received injuries when dealing with violent prisoners, some of those injuries being caused by their own colleagues.

It would be a few years before the Prison Service would adopt a more effective method of Control and Restraint. For now, we were simply being taught, MUFTI (Minimum Use of Force Tactical Intervention)

We were also taught Man Management, the subtle art of communicating with prisoners and dealing with potentially violent situations. The work of the Landing Officer was the key to good prisoner/staff relationships. The Landing Officer was responsible for all of the prisoners in the cells that he was patrolling.

He would answer any questions that they might have, supervise the work and escort them to various places around the prison.

The role of the Personal Officer was one session that held my attention, because it became the reason that I would remain in the prison service, I already felt I wanted to be involved somehow in rehabilitation and to look after the prisoner's welfare. But this was also the session that began to set me apart from the rest of my colleagues, and it happened in quite a dramatic way.

Many my section seemed to adopt an air of superiority over the prisoners in their charge, an attitude of "do something because I said" with no room for communication or explanation of the task.

In the role-play situations, their manner was abrupt and quite abusive and I felt this very strongly when I played the role of the prisoner. I wanted to be "asked" to do something, not "ordered" all the time. And the constant use of my surname seemed to endorse the feeling of intimidation and control. "Chapman, get your cell tidied and the bed made. Chapman, get down to lunch. Slop out Chapman." etc

What made matters worse for me was that our Tutor continued to remind us that convicts were inferior to us as officers. "Don't try to relate to con's, they're in prison for good reason, they're there because they deserve to be."

In the discussion that came at the end of the session, I offered the opinion that I thought some of the officer's manners were a bit harsh, that they could have communicated in a more humane way.

The tutor was clearly rattled by my suggestion that we should treat them humanely, and suggested that the word should be "fairly" and stated, "I think it's fair enough to let them know who's boss, it's fair enough to provide food and clothing, and it's fair enough to remember to lock their cell door at night", he said sarcastically.

However, "as for treating them like humans, they lost that title when they raped and murdered innocent people".

Although, he was clearly not happy with my attitude I continued to argue "Not everyone has raped or murdered and I just think it's reasonable to ask somebody to do something, rather than demand it" I declared "You have to earn respect, you can't automatically demand it and everybody deserves a second chance."

On that note, the Tutor decided the session had ended. We all left the classroom and headed for the dining hall. At this point I was beginning to doubt my ability to become a Prison Officer. Simply locking people up seemed pointless to me, even in the early stages, I felt I wanted to do more, but was not sure how that would work.

Before the course ended, we would all be told where we were to be posted to and we could choose three options in order of importance.

Before my personal choice was made, another person made an important contribution to my life and future career.

A Chief Hospital Officer visited the college from HMP Wormwood Scrubs, in London and gave a talk on the value of training as a Hospital Officer. He also spoke about the Therapeutic Community within that prison. Following his talk, I approached him and said I was seriously considering the hospital training.

The man's name was Peter Barker and he advised, "There is a prison in Buckinghamshire called Grendon. It is listed under Special Hospitals but don't let that put you off, they are always looking for Prison Officers." He added "Try to find a book in the college library called "The Frying Pan" it's written by a man called Tony Parker and it's all about Grendon. See what you think?"

I managed to find the book and read about the work of this unique prison. There were plenty of quotes from prisoners and staff and not only was I surprised to find that they all used each other's first names but, more importantly, the whole prison regime was about helping prisoners to change their lives through Group Therapy.

The more I read, the more I felt that this would be a great place to work and having finished the book; I approached the tutor and asked for his advice.

He confirmed "We have all been watching your progress since you started the course. It's clear to me that you want more from this job than just locking people away, you have some interesting, but some might say strange views on the role of a Prison Officer.
I think Grendon would be a good first posting for you, so go for it."

He also said that he was sure that if I put Grendon as a first choice I would get that posting, "Most prison officers think that Grendon is a nuthouse so they never choose it, I know it isn't because I have worked there."

I decided to take his advice and listed my choice of suitable prisons as firstly HM Prison Grendon, secondly HMP Prison Shepton Mallet and lastly HM Prison Exeter.

A week later, the postings arrived in plain brown envelopes and we opened them together in the classroom.

There were various reactions to the contents of these envelopes. Those that lived in the north of England could easily find themselves posted to a prison in Cornwall or the Isle of Wight. Those who lived on the Isle of Wight could find themselves and their families posted to Wakefield.

There were no guarantees given by the prison service and the postings could not be swapped.

Prison Officers had to accept them and then apply for a return transfer after their first years' probation, or else give the job up entirely, thereby wasting the training, they had just been given.

I would be lying if I said I wasn't anxious. I had read so much about Grendon that I wanted this more than perhaps most did. With shaky hands, I opened my envelope and quickly scanned the letter.

At the very bottom of the letter was the instructions that I was to report to HM Prison Grendon, an August 10th 1977.

There were fellow trainees that believed I was crazy to start my work in a Psychiatric Prison (a loony bin) but Tony Parker's book had got rid of most of my fears, I somehow knew it was the right choice. Of course, there were plenty of witty comments aimed in my direction. One of the tutors said that Grendon prison officers didn't get issued with Truncheons, "they are given long party balloons ". And "Instead of a whistle, you'll be given a plastic trumpet." he continued "Oh yes, I nearly forgot, you're even allowed to take prisoners home for tea sometimes".

There was actually an element of truth in his last wisecrack, and I turned my back on the Wakefield training experience and nervously contemplated my posting to Grendon Prison.

Chapter 3

Grendon Prison is unique with a remarkable history, although it had only been open for 15 years when I started there.

In 1977 HM Prison Grendon was listed under prison psychiatric services (Special Hospitals) and was referred to as a psychiatric prison, with a strict medical referral process, called a 1080 referral. Any prisoners who volunteered for treatment in the therapeutic community had to be assessed by the prison doctor, at the prison they were coming from and would then be assessed again for their suitability for treatment on arrival at Grendon.

There was a clear understanding within the criminal justice system that a prisoner requiring psychological/psychiatric treatment could benefit from the unique Grendon regime and some judges would therefore recommend a referral at the point of sentencing.
Those offenders who might benefit from treatment in a mental health facility (those with a certified mental illness, would not get into the therapeutic community but there was a cross section of offenders who had a psychiatric history, but no current psychosis, who could benefit.

A referral from the trial judge carried an enormous amount of weight and some offenders would ask their defence barrister to ensure that the judge made a recommendation, so that they could immediately set the ball rolling for a transfer at the very beginning of their sentence.

Before I began my first day of work, I read about the development of psychiatric services in prisons, which had been an interesting journey.

In 1774, the prison reformer John Howard investigated the state of English prisons, which resulted in the passing of an act "For preserving the health of prisoners in Gaol and preventing the Gaol distemper".

Gaol fever, which was form of typhus, affected people other than prisoners as it was carried into the courts and was responsible for the deaths of judges, advocates, jury members and witnesses. The alarm caused by this disease was the reason that the medical profession became involved in the prison experience.

Not only did this act legally require prisons to be cleansed regularly, but it ordered that prisoners should be washed regularly and separate sick rooms had to be provided in each prison. The act also provided for a surgeon or doctor, paid for by the state, to attend each prison on a regular basis and report quarterly on the health of prisoners under his care.

John Howard's research interestingly concluded that even now prisons were a profit-making private enterprise run by the Gaolers and the only way they could make money, was by avoiding expenses. For instance, they would use iron chains for safe custody, rather than spend money on secure prison buildings.

The public were concerned about the appalling conditions that prisoners were held in, which led to further legislation, but the problem was not easily solved, because although Parliament would pass a law, nobody had the ultimate responsibility to ensure that changes were being made.

Each prison was under the management of the justices and local authority in each county and therefore standards differed from county to county, but the result was that prisoners remained a low priority for expenditure.

The 18th-century prisons were not used as a penalty for crime alone, but will also places where people awaiting trial all were awaiting punishment and now the punishments for major offences were death or transportation. Minor offences received either fines or corporal punishment.

The American War of Independence put an end to transportation of prisoners to America and this forced England to reconsider its policies and the government was forced to supplement local prisons by providing establishments under government management.

It was decided that prisoners could be confined temporarily in prison ships at Woolwich, London and these ships were used for more than 80 years, but in 1779 there was more legislation giving the government responsibility to set up State Penitentiaries for prisoners who would otherwise have been transported to America.

Transportation to Australia became possible in 1780, which meant that the need for penitentiaries was less of a priority. It is worth noting that the first penitentiary to be built in England was Millbank, which only came into use in 1821.

The rules and regulations for this penitentiary referred to the provision of a Prison Medical Superintendent and a Surgeon. The superintendent oversaw the Prison Medical Department, which he had to inspect monthly, as well as visiting the patients in the infirmary twice a week. The surgeon was required to work solely in the prison and was not allowed to have any practice outside. He had to examine all the prisoners on reception and to attend to any who were unwell. Notably, the rules made no mention of any mental health provision or of how to deal with prisoners who were certified insane.

It was the prison chaplain's responsibility to facilitate rehabilitation or reformation.

When the government took over the local prisons, it made a body of commissioners with responsibility for the running of centralized Convict Prisons and local prisons as well.

Mr Edmund du Cane was Chairman of the Directors of Convict Prisons (state run) and Chairman of the Commissioners for Local Prisons (run by local authorities). His aim was to ensure that prisons became an effective deterrent to crime.

The government wanted state prisons to be used as a means of reforming prisoners, but this had no appeal to DuCane and in 1863 the House of Lords committee on prison discipline developed some punitive measures.

The recommendations referred to "hard fare, hard labour and hard bed". The prison diet was intentionally made poor and unpalatable, hammocks were removed from the cells and substituted with planks and the crank and treadmill was first introduced. In local prisons (where the maximum sentence was two years) solitary confinement was strictly maintained throughout the whole sentence and in the convict (state) prisons it was the rule for the first nine months.

Silence at all times was enforced by the use of punishment and Du Cane made sure that these policies were implemented throughout both systems. In his own words the object was to make sure that "punishment should be carried out so as to make imprisonment a terror to evil doers". (Du Cane, 1874) and in the words of a later Commissioner of Prisons, he achieved a system which substituted "for death itself, a living death". (Fox - 1952).

In the prisons of the 18th and early 19th centuries, visiting doctors made no recommendations for prisoners with mental health issues and it is difficult to imagine the plight of prisoners, who were certified insane, being forced to endure the harsh punishment or indeed, the plight of prisoners who were locked in daily with prisoners suffering severe mental illness. Extreme violence and murder were widespread.

In 1808, the County Asylum Act came into force, which empowered local justices to set up asylums for the care of the insane, which included the insane offender. This was the first piece of legislation that gave the Home Secretary the power to transfer offenders from prisons to asylums. The insanity had to be certified by two justices and two doctors.

This legislation directed the attention of prison surgeons to the question of insanity amongst the prisoners they were responsible for and from the 1840s at least, they were required to make note of a prisoner's liability to be affected by mental ill health as well as physical disorders. The doctor was required to inform the Prison Governor if he had reason to believe that either the mind or body of the prisoner was likely to be badly affected by prison discipline or treatment.

This requirement has been incorporated in all subsequent versions of prison rules to this day.

The prison surgeon was also occasionally called to court as an expert witness in trials where the sanity of the prisoner was in doubt, as it had been held for quite some time that insanity would exempt and offender from ordinary punishment. So historically the prison doctors concern with mental health was for diagnosis rather than treatment.

Diagnosis of mental health was important for three reasons: for the unsentenced, if their sanity was in question it might determine guilt, or liability to capital punishment. For the convicted, it might secure their removal to an asylum, or failing that it might mean that they would not receive the harsh treatment that normal prisoners were used to.

If a medical officer found that imprisonment was adversely affecting the health of the prisoner, the governor was bound by the rules to take appropriate action.

Regarding corporal punishment, the prison surgeon was required to be present when this was administered and the governor had to obey his recommendations, if he considered that the prisoner's physical health was at risk. Therefore, the prison surgeon was the referee in cases where prison punishment was being administered and generally speaking his relationship with a prisoner was much different than the usual doctor-patient relationship.

Prisons were highly punitive in the 19th century and doctors saw their role as an important one. If they felt the prison diet was poor, they could order extra food or if they felt that solitary confinement was affecting the prisoner's sanity, they could order this to cease. It became clear that prisoners who were diagnosed as suffering from insanity would be made worse by the over punitive prison regimes.

Over a period it was realised that prisoners who were known to be mentally infirm, would benefit from free association with prison staff and other prisoners.

One of the prison ships (Hulks) was set aside as an "invalid depot" for "weak minded" convicts as well as those who were physically ill but the conditions remained deplorable.

Due to the very loose regulation of prisons, there were many failures in the duty of care to prisoners and in 1835 the government introduced the first Inspectors of Prisons and local authorities became subject to government inspection and control.

In 1852, Dartmoor prison was designated as an invalid depot for both physically and the mentally infirm and by 1855 the Medical Officer in Dartmoor, Dr John Campbell, had 100 "weak minded convicts in his care and was advising that they should be segregated from the other prisoners and placed under the care of officers having some experience in the management and peculiarities of the insane" (Campbell, 1856).

Obviously, the insane were not intended to remain imprisoned and were supposed to be transferred to asylums but there were difficulties about security and the lack of vacancies elsewhere. Therefore, the need for a State Asylum for insane offenders became a priority and Broadmoor hospital was opened as a Criminal Lunatic Asylum in 1863.

Interestingly, the 19th-century lunacy laws described persons as "lunatics, idiots, insane, or of unsound mind". These terms were used somewhat indiscriminately to cover the major forms of mental disorder.

Even though local asylums and state asylums, such as Broadmoor were opened, it did not mean that insane prisoners were necessarily removed from the prison system completely and in fact Broadmoor Hospital found that transferred convicts were more troublesome and escape minded than its other patients and in 1874 the transfer of insane male convicts to Broadmoor was stopped.

It was decided that they could be cared for within the prison system in a wing at Woking prison in Surrey.

The final centralization of the prison system came about in 1877 when the local administration of prisons became the responsibility of the government. By this time, the government had considerable experience of running its own prisons and when transportation to Australia stopped in 1840, the government developed a prison building programme for the next 10 years

John Campbell became the doctor in charge of Woking's criminal lunatic wing.

He recorded some of his experiences and views in his book called "30 Years' Experience of a Medical Officer in the English Convicts Service" (Campbell, 1884).

He regretted the need to conform to standard prison regulations such as denying prisoners privileges such as tobacco, which they were allowed in asylums and Broadmoor. He did not think that most his patients were dangerous but remained worried that the "bad" should escape punishment by deceiving the authorities into treating them as "mad". He felt the caution was required when discriminating between those who suffered real mental illness and the more cunning prisoner, who would use mental illness to hide their criminality. He felt that the latter belonged to the worst description of criminals and work therefore worthy of the most deterring punishment.

Woking stopped being used as a criminal lunatic asylum after 11 years and transfers to Broadmoor were resumed. However, prisoners still had to cope with the many insane prisoners who did not warrant transfer to Broadmoor or could not be placed in local asylums. Around 1890, prison medical officers were encouraging the lower courts to remand prisoners for psychiatric reports to try to reduce the supply of insane persons to the prisons system.

There remained a group of offenders which the prison authorities could not hope to divert or transfer from their prisons and who were not covered by the lunacy acts. Therefore, the prison authorities came to use the phrase "feeble minded" to cover a wide range of mental abnormality, falling short of insanity and the most numerous prisoners in this class worthy mentally defective.

There was no systematic provision for the care of those considered mentally defective in the 19th-century and so many got into trouble with the law and were being sent to prison repeatedly.

The medical officers who dealt with them in prison emphasised the importance of segregating them and treating them separately. This protected them from the consequences of the ordinary prison discipline and from incurring repeated dietary and other punishments for unwittingly breaking prison rules, such as the rule of silence.

It was generally accepted that imprisonment for men who were classified as feebleminded was unsuitable and did little to improve their offending behaviour. By the end of the 19th century Parkhurst prison on the Isle of Wight had been designated as the establishment for prisoners who were unfit for ordinary prison discipline due to some mental disability other than insanity. The prison regime made some allowance for a prisoner's mental condition and certain rules were relaxed e.g. prisoners could talk whilst on exercise.

In 1873, if a statement by the Directors of Convict Prisons concluded that if "by punishing those who have an incurable tendency to crime, we can deter fresh recruits joining the ranks of the criminal class, and the whole object of punishment is affected, and obviously if we could possibly arrive at the result that all convictions were re-convictions and none of them first sentences, we should be in a fair way to putting an end to crime altogether."

This simply showed that little value was placed on the effect that imprisonment might have on an individual.

As this system was intentionally organise for inflicting deterrent punishment and suffering of prisoners, prison doctors could scarcely find a therapeutic role beyond their basic task of looking after the prisoner's physical health and trying to protect at least some of the mentally disordered from the office aspects of prison. Carrying out any rehabilitative treatment in prison now was impossible.

The prison authorities felt that treating some prisoners differently from others would not only cause trouble and discontent, it would destroy the discipline of the prisons and that the government accepted that to introduce individualized treatment into the prisons regime now would destroy Du Cane's ethos that all prisoners were treated exactly alike and that the previous career and character of the prisoner should make no difference to the punishment to which he is subjected.

But, a turning point for the prison regimes was not far off and in 1894 the Home Office appointed the departmental committee, called the Gladstone committee to review the state of prisons. At that time, the Permanent Secretary at the Home Office, Sir Godfrey Lushington, said it would be impossible to introduce an effective reformatory element into the prison regime, but the committee recommended that an attempt should be made to devise a system that aimed to turn prisoners out of prison better men and women physically and morally them when they came in.

And so, at the beginning of the 20th century prison diet was improved, talking as a privilege was introduced and the treadmill ceased to be used. In fact, the idea that prisoners might respond to rehabilitative rather than punitive treatment was put into effect in the new Borstal system, where offenders were thought to be young enough to be amenable to good influences.

From 1902 onwards, some prison reports continually drew attention to the lack of suitable provision and control for the mentally deficient prisoner. The reports called for this class of prisoner to be subject to non-penal compulsory control, to be properly cared for and prevented from coming into repeated conflict with the law.

The prisons commission accepted this need and made recommendations that he could be met perhaps by the establishment of mental deficiency institutions.

The prison authorities supported these recommendations. The commissioners of prisons in 1910 referred to "the clearing out from prisons of the drunkard, the tramp and the imbecile, which would at long last enable prisons to be used exclusively for the treatment of the criminal". (Commissioners of Prisons and Directors of Convict Prisons, 1910).

The first to be removed from prison were the drunkard's and courts would be given powers to commit drunkenness offenders to special inebriate institutions and the Inebriate Act had been cast in 1898, to confine drunkards to special reformatories for a maximum period of three years.

Two classes offender were covered: those convicted in the High Courts of offences caused by drink and habitual inebriates who had more than three drunkenness convictions in one year. However, the reformatories were to be as free from restriction and as little like prison as possible and they were unable to manage or control some of the most intractable and violent offenders.

The special state reformatories were therefore set up in 1901, one performing at Aylesbury and one for men at Warwick, to cater for the cases which the other institutions could not manage. At this point the medical expert came to be regarded as the appropriate person to manage this type of institution. It was decided that the state reformatories should be conducted on the same lines as prison but only so far as is necessary to provide control. They would be run on strict asylum principles in all matters referring to the treatment of prisoners and the medical aspect to control the application of restraint and punishment.

Exceptional care was taken to place the immediate control of affairs in the hands of the medical Governor and a Medical Officer.

The reform system for inebriates ran into to severe administrative and financial difficulties and was finally abandoned in 1921. The drunken offender has remained a mainstay of the prison population ever since despite a widespread view that they would be better dealt with elsewhere.

In 1927, the very important Mental Deficiency Act came into being and it redefined a class of "moral defectives", who had a mental defectiveness coupled with "strongly officious or criminal propensities and who require care supervision and control for the protection of others". The act was mainly used for cases where moral defectiveness was coupled with subnormal intelligence.

In the 19th century, prison doctors had to consider the progress of psychological medicine, rather than simply referring to psychiatry and there emerged a fundamental difficulty in separating the mad from the bad. It was a challenging task, but they felt it could be achieved by a sufficiently skilled and experienced medical officer.

Once psychiatry entered the era of Meyer and Freud, the possibility of clearly separating the mad from the bad became more and more elusive and it was because of this difficulty that psychotherapy got its foot inside prison gates. It became evident that psychological factors could be the root of some "bad" behaviour that there were no suitable institutions which non-certifiable prisoners of this type could be transferred.

At this stage, the prison authorities started to look at the possibilities for the psychological treatment of offenders.

Ideas about the psychological and psychoanalytical treatment of offenders began to penetrate the English system, from America in the 1920s. The Americans had been applying this to the treatment of their juvenile delinquents. The local justices were being increased to look not just at a psychiatric diagnosis on sentencing but also any mental condition that might warrant a more careful investigation to ascertain whether the accused was insane or mentally defective and most importantly whether delinquent conduct would benefit from treatment of an underlying psychological disorder.

The first investigations of this kind were carried out in Birmingham prison hospital by its full-time Medical Officer Dr M Hamblin-Smith. However, he concluded that prisons could not be used for the effect of psychological treatment of offenders, due mainly to the prison systems punitive ethos. He felt that the deliberately imposed deprivation and hardship were anti therapeutic and the prison regime bore no relation to the prisoners needs.

He paid tribute to the prison officers at Birmingham Prison but he doubted whether prison staff were really the right people to carry out treatment. He would have liked a different method of staff selection, one that ensured the officers would be of higher educational status, young and enthusiastic, free from any inclination to blame or adopt any other attitude of superiority.

He firmly believed that an unwilling patient could not be helped by psychoanalytic means and treatment was only possible when the offender himself wanted to change.

This constituted a fundamental difficulty about the use of psychological treatment in prisons, which are places to which offenders sent against their will.

Quite often people talk as though some special form of institution was able to reform by itself and quite apart from the co-operation of the subject.

Over the years, professionals agree that reformation is the result of the mental process within the man or woman and there is something wanting in any scheme which assumes that all the value is contained in what is done to the prisoner and which overlooks the vital function of change, which must come from within the person themselves.

Dr Norwood East became Medical Commissioner in 1922. In his report of that year, he recommended that abnormal prisoners could not be reformed by normal means and required curative treatment.

He suggested a separate establishment from a prison with "special staff". He referred to such prisoners as "non-sane non-insane" and felt that they all exhibited three main characteristics, such as those who were subnormal is, ranging from near normal to near mental deficiency, those who had psychopathic personalities and those who were neurotic, ranging from near normal to near insanity.

Therefore, once prisons were no longer taking prisoners with certifiable mental illness they were left with the problems of the remaining abnormal prisoners who were attracting the attention from medical staff.

Norwood East referred to a variety of medical opinions that psychotherapy could be relied upon to "cure" many prisoners who found themselves constantly in and out of jail and most first-time offenders. However, there were no statistics available to show how many lawbreakers in this country had been treated in such a way and as far as he was aware there was no medical psychotherapist with any extensive experience in this method of dealing with crime.

The claims that psychological medicine could be a cure for crime were further examined in 1932 by the Home Office and evidence was taken from many experts who specialised in methods of psychological examination and in psychotherapy, which included prison medical officers but no witness was able to give any precise information concerning the value of psychological treatment for many prisoners.

They believed that the application of psychotherapy was in its infancy and likely to remain the case for many years to come and to test thoroughly the value of this treatment a systematic follow-up of cases needed to be done over a prolonged period of time and all of the results, which included failures as well as successes had to be published at some point. There were very few outpatients' clinics and it was recommended that if this work were to be carried out it would have to be in a selected prison or even a Borstal.

A year later Dr W H de Hubert was appointed to carry out psychological treatment of selected prisoners at Wormwood Scrubs prison and it was to be a four-year investigation to find out how for psychiatric and psychotherapeutic experience in the management and treatment of psychotic and Psycho neurotic illnesses, and various forms of behaviour disorder could be applied with some efficiency to prisoners.

He decided to use to methods of treatment, one which gave the prisoner (patient) a better intellectual understanding of his problems, through one-to-one discussions and secondly to develop the use of the analytical therapeutic method and medical officers in prisons all over the country were invited to suggest suitable cases for treatment.

At this point in time the criteria was broad, but prisoners had to be under 40 years of age, willing to have treatment, serving at least six months and convicted of offences which were due to some remedial condition. Unstable adolescents were also potential candidates, but no prisoner with a certifiable mental illness was eligible. 406 cases were referred to Dr Hubert and 214 were approved for treatment.

A report was completed by Dr East and Dr Hubert, which gave case histories for many of the referrals including those found suitable for treatment and showed their response to psychotherapy whilst in prison, but there was no follow-up data because at the most any of the treaty cases could only have been out of prison for four years, at the time of the report, and the majority had been released from shorter periods.

Some were still serving their sentences so it wasn't possible to show the result of the investigations accurately. The report failed to fulfil the requirements of the persistent offender's committee but Hubert and East felt justified in reaching certain conclusions.

One of the conclusions was that psychotherapy completed as part of an ordinary prison sentence appeared to be less effective in preventing or in reducing the chance of future antisocial behaviour and they felt it was more than probable that skilled direction, management, specialised training and other general psychiatric methods of treatment were applicable to a much larger number of cases and to a wider range of conditions than psychotherapy alone.

The main recommendation of this report was that the most satisfactory method of dealing with abnormal and unusual types of criminal would be by the creation of a prison of a special kind, which would serve three functions firstly as a clinic and hospital, where cases could be investigated and if necessary treated, and where criminological research could also be centered. Secondly, as an institution in which selected prisoners could live under special conditions of training and treatment.

The aim would be to give them a psychiatric experience, to achieve alterations in their lives where future behaviour was concerned. It was recommended that the medical staff at the proposed prison should be psychiatrically trained and that the superintendent should be a prison psychiatrist and they recommended that the proposed new prison should be part of the prison system.

The East-Hubert report marked a turning point in history of British prison psychiatry and it defines the objective for treatment to be a behavioural objective rather than a medical one and the main purpose of psychotherapy in criminal work was to prevent crime being committed or repeated by individual offenders.

The outbreak of the Second World War put a stop to any further progress, but it was once again examined by the Commissioners of prisons in 1957 and the government produced a White Paper in 1959 (Penal practice in a changing society) which announced that work on a psychiatric prison hospital would soon be started at Grendon Underwood in Buckinghamshire.

It was recommended that as soon as Grendon prison was ready, the major psychotherapy work carried out at three existing clinics in Wormwood Scrubs prison Wakefield prison and Holloway would be concentrated in that one place.

It is worth noting that Holloway prison housed female prisoners, but in fact no female prisoners were ever referred for therapy at Grendon, for a variety of reasons.

Grendon prison was finally built and opened by Home Secretary Rab Butler in July 1962.

Chapter 4

I had made a significant effort to educate myself as much as I could for my work at Grendon but the truth was all of the theories and academic studies that have been written about the prison cannot prepare anybody for a role as a Prison Officer there, and in fact, even the Psychiatrists, Psychologists and civilian workers only had a small understanding of the difficult role officers performed there on a daily basis.

My first brief introductory visit to Grendon prison came at the end of July 1977. Grendon is situated close to a small town called Bicester in Buckinghamshire, which is about seven or eight miles from the village of Grendon Underwood.

I had to take a taxi from Bicester town centre as the local buses were very infrequent and the driver joked that there was a stagecoach that passes through Grendon once a week as it's a bit out of the way.

Grendon Underwood is just off the A41 main trunk road and the prison is situated on the top of a hill at the far end of the village.

On the map that I had been given it showed a small store/post office about a mile and a half from the prison living quarters with a pub called "The Swan" opposite. And that was all, apart from another pub called "The Fox" in the nearby village of Edgecot. There were no shopping facilities on the housing estate where many the prison staff lived. In fact, all the houses on Springhill estate were prison officers rented quarters.

The area was very rural and very pretty. The main entrance to the housing estate consisted of a large pair of red brick pillars with ornate iron fencing to either side. Just inside this entrance, to the left, was an early 19th century gatehouse, which I later discovered were the living quarters for one of the prisons long serving Principal Officers.

On the hill leading towards the prison there was a large housing estate to the right, with what looked to be at least 200 or so 1960's style semi-detached houses. These were the Prison officers living quarters and they seemed quite impressive from the outside.

At the top of the hill, on Springhill Road, I was stopped by a prison officer, who was operating a wooden barrier across the main road.

"Where are you heading?" he asked cheerfully.

I told him I was here for my first visit to Grendon, I said I would start working there in August and I handed him the letter that confirmed a meeting with the prison Governor Dr Barrett.

"Blimey, they'll be pleased to see you" he declared "We haven't had a recruit for over a year now. Nobody wants to come to Grendon; they think it's a loony bin but then you have to be a bit mad to work there," he joked.

"I'm beginning to wonder if I've done the right thing now", I said.

"Nah, I'm only joking mate, you'll be fine. It's just very different from other jails. If you drive straight on you'll see the big wall and main gate on your right, I'll tell them you're coming." He directed me through the barrier.

As I drove through, there was a large mansion house on the left, which was apparently the offices and staff living quarters for Springhill Open Prison. Grendon Hall had been home to the local clergyman prior to World War One. Then during the war, it was developed as a training ground for British Spies. When the war ended, the hall and grounds were converted for use as a low security (D Category) Open Prison. Apparently, the local villagers protested when the Home Office decided to build the higher security Grendon Prison on the same site. They feared that there would be plenty of escapes. But in fact, by 1977, there hadn't been any in the whole history of the prison, which was very impressive.

In stark contrast to the neat hedgerows and cultivated lawns and flower borders of Springhill prison, the high grey walls of Grendon loomed above me to the right with razor wire on top and a large expanse of green security fencing to the right and left of the main prison.

The prison gate was like Stafford's. Two large doors made of solid oak about fifteen feet by ten foot each, with shiny brass hinges but no handles on the outside. In the right-hand gate was a smaller door, about six feet by two with a small observation hatch in it. I later found out that this was known as the "Wicket Gate."

I rang the doorbell and waited.

After a few minutes of door slamming and keys rattling from within, the Wicket Gate was opened and I was greeted by a very smart looking officer, wearing a crisp blue uniform. He looked to be a couple of years older than me and had a dark Mediterranean appearance.

"Welcome to sunny Grendon" he said, shaking my hand vigorously. "You can report to the gatekeeper next but I want to give you a kiss first" he declared and suddenly grabbed me and planted a wet sloppy kiss on my cheek. I was so shocked I was unable to resist. (At least that's my story and I'm sticking to it)

I was taken back by this unconventional welcome but then the young officer gave his explanation.

"My name's Dave Hill" he offered. "I was the last recruit to arrive at Grendon about 18 months ago. Now you've arrived I'll go up from the bottom rung of the ladder. You'll find that a new screw gets all the crap jobs for a while, so now you're here my life should improve greatly."

Later on, that day I was shown a large board in the Governor's office that listed all of the uniformed staff currently in Grendon. The names were in order of the length of time spent working in the jail, with the longest serving at the top.
Interestingly, I noted that most of prison officers at Grendon were Hospital Officers and I still felt I wanted to do the training at some point.

The Gatekeeper had introduced himself as Bob Greaves and he spoke with a broad Yorkshire accent. "I look after the staff hostel and it looks like you might have to stay in there for a while until there is a staff quarter available."

"Just go straight down the drive to the double gates, somebody will meet you on the centre" Dave said, as he slammed the heavy iron gates behind me.

I made my way down the short tarmac drive and noticed a group of prisoners working on the flower borders and lawns.

I made eye contact with one of the prisoners and said "Hi, alright mate?" He responded with a very polite "Afternoon guvnor" as I entered through the wooden gates in the centre of the Administration Block.

Surprisingly these gates gave access to the prison "centre" and remained unlocked and wide open all of the time, unless a large vehicle was coming into the prison. When this happened, the Control Room would give the command by radio to "Freeze the Centre" any prisoners who were working freely within the prison grounds would be temporarily called inside and the gates were secured.

Once the vehicle had gone, they would be unlocked and remain open again until the next vehicle arrived. In Stafford prison, it was the golden rule that no gate or door should ever be left unlocked whilst the prison cells were unlocked, so this felt very strange.

Grendon had its own unique "Open Door" policy.

Wherever possible, doors throughout the prison were left open for the free access of staff, prisoners and visitors. One thing that the Governor insisted on was that everybody (including prisoners) had the right of passage through Grendon's Centre.

Even though this gave unescorted prisoners clear access to the stairs which led to the main offices, but there was none who would abuse this trust.

I was informed later by the Governor "Just as the Ravens disappearing from the tower of London would signify the death of our monarchy. Locking off these centre doors as well as several other gates within the prison would signify the end of a truly therapeutic prison community".

The large element of trust afforded to Grendon's prisoners was proof of the jails effectiveness and set it apart from every other prison in the country.

I was shown into the Governor's office where Chief Prison Officer Ken Debenham greeted me. He was a large elderly man with a very stern overbearing appearance.

However, although he spoke with an absolute air of utmost authority, there was a hint of compassion in his voice as he confirmed that there were no living quarters immediately available for me or my family, he apologised for this.

"We are expecting two officers to move out before the end of the year. That means that two houses should be available before Christmas. Until then you will be in the staff hostel which I think you'll find to be very comfortable." I told him that I had spoken to Officer Greaves and he will show me around later.

"That's good," he said, with a smile "Bob Greaves is our landlady at the staff hostel." This friendly banter made me feel comfortable to start my work at Grendon

He gave us a little bit of information about the daily programme of activities for prisoners in Grendon and told me what I should expect as a new officer, and of course what his expectations were of me. Then he organised a short tour of the prison.

I left the office feeling that Mr Debenham would be a very firm but fair boss and over the next couple of years I was not to be disappointed.

I had the prison tour and was impressed by the welcome I got everywhere, from staff and prisoners. The one thing that impressed me most of all was the very relaxed and friendly atmosphere, with the use of first name terms for all prisoners, and the prisoners were encouraged to address the staff on a first name basis. Once again this was also unique to this jail and it enhanced the prisoner staff relationships, in my opinion.

By the time, I left the prison I felt that this posting had been a good decision. I couldn't wait to start working there.

Before leaving to travel home I collected my new uniform from the stores and Bob took me to see the staff hostel.

The hostel was comfortable, although quite empty. There were about 12 rooms but he said that only two or three staff and the odd visitor used it. However, as it was only temporary I felt I could cope.

I drove back to Burton-on-Trent, sure that this would be a good move and a completely fresh start. I would return to start work at the end of August.

Because Prison Officers at Grendon can openly challenge prisoners Offending Behaviour, giving them insight into their past behaviour, and helping them to change their lives (for the better) in the future, this was exactly what I was looking for when I joined the service. I realised that this was the best start I could have had. It was all very exciting stuff.

I had ample opportunity to try on the new uniform for the first time prior to my first day.

It was a strange feeling, bearing in mind that less than a year ago I was dressed in the "hippie" fashion and was a bit of a non-conformist. However, whereas the ultra-smart blue uniform may have given the impression that I was conforming on the surface, underneath I had a feeling that I would struggle to conform to every single rule laid down by the prison service.

At least this jail gave me the opportunity to retain some of my individual character traits and I knew from the beginning that I could experiment with my communication with prisoners far easier at Grendon than anywhere else.

I arrived at the Grendon hostel on the Sunday afternoon and I was due to report to the prison at 9am on the Monday morning for the first day of a two-week induction. Bob Greaves was there again to welcome me and I was shown to my room, which was on the first floor to the rear of the hostel.

The rooms were quite small, with just a single bed, wardrobe, chest of drawers, desk and chair. However, as the Chief had said, they were comfortable and of course only temporary.

I didn't sleep much at all on the Sunday night. My mind was racing and I still felt tired when my alarm clock went off at 7.30am.

It took me ages to wash and dress. I wanted to give a good impression on my first day, so the uniform had to be just right. The fitting wasn't too bad but the boots were brand new and squeaked as I walked. I hadn't noticed the right-hand pocket until today and apart from the usual pocket there was also another one about 12 inches long and 3 inches wide. "Word must have got around to the tailors that I was very well endowed" I thought optimistically.

This was wishful thinking, of course, as this pocket was designed for my stave (truncheon). I had previously been informed that there was a local agreement at Grendon that Prison Officers should not carry staves. All members of staff accepted this and having questioned what might happen in cases of extreme violence? I was told that prisoners and staff worked together to deal with such violence.

This sounded very vague but within less than a month I would witness how effective this was on two occasions.

Physical violence was a rarity at Grendon but verbal abuse could be an everyday occurrence.

On my first morning, the walk from the hostel to the prison was really pleasant at this time of the year. It was still warm, the birds were singing and the air seemed very fresh when compared to Stafford prison, which was in an urban area where the air was always choked with exhaust fumes.

When I reached the gate, I was issued with my key chain on which there was hanging a circular brass tally. This was engraved with a number, in my case -130. This was my personal number and I would hand the tally in each day when collecting a set of keys.

The gatekeeper said that I could not be issued with any keys until I had my security talk which would be sometime later in the day. Another new Officer, Bill Chilvers, had arrived the same day. He was already an experienced prison officer; in fact, he had recently been promoted to Principal Officer so of course he was allowed to collect his keys immediately.

"Your keys are more valuable than the Crown Jewels" the Gatekeeper said. "If you lose them, not only will it cost a large fortune to replace all the locks in the prison but you could find yourself out of a job".

"What a nightmare" I exclaimed "when I think of the amount of times I've lost a set of keys at home it will be a miracle if I get through my first year without losing them,"

I had been asked to report to the Chiefs office, so I introduced myself to the officer in the Centre and he directed me upstairs to the administration block. I would have to wait outside his office for a short while, because all of the Senior Managers had a meeting with the Medical Superintendent for the first hour each day in the boardroom.

I had expected to be greeted by Ken Debenham, but instead another Chief Officer was at his desk. He introduced himself as Mr Lee and said he had organised for somebody to show me around the prison. "We were going to give you two weeks' induction and the second week would have been a therapy training course. Unfortunately, that course is cancelled so you can go straight onto your wing at the end of the week. You will be working on G wing, which is a young offenders wing."

There was a knock on the door and Officer Dave Hills walked in "Blimey, I didn't recognise you with your clothes on" he joked, referring to my uniform.

The Chief raised his eyebrows. "Mr Hills will be your guardian angel today, Mr Chapman. Sorry we couldn't find a proper officer to show you around the place. "

Dave and I left the Chief's office and started the tour around the prison. Everywhere we went I was overwhelmed by the greetings, but these were always followed by an element of humour. It appeared that this friendly; some might say inappropriate, banter was very much a part of healthy communication. I certainly felt comfortable with it.

First of all, Dave took me through another set of centre gates into the main prison.
Straight ahead there was a long corridor that seemed to be going underground. In fact, it reminded me of the sort of long walkways that can be found in the London Tube system.

"That's what we call the M1 corridor. It's the main route to most of the wings and we'll go down there later. It doesn't actually go underground, that's an illusion because the jails built on a slope." Dave explained.

I noticed that the walls were painted a distinct colour every couple of yards, and I wondered why that was? Did they keep running out of paint?

Apparently, the Medical Superintendent ordered it to be done. "Psychologically it's supposed to give the impression that the corridor is shorter than it is. I don't rate it much" Dave smirked "When you've got to run from C wing at the bottom of the corridor to an alarm bell in the prison Hospital (at the top) it still feels the same length to me."

To our left and right was another long corridor that was called the M2. This led to the prison Hospital and Education Department one-way and the prison Library, Chapel, Gymnasium, and F Wing the other. "We'll go left first, and pay a visit to the A P U. (Acute Psychiatric Unit) It's our prison Hospital and there are some right head bangers in here." he warned.

On the way along the M2 we passed a couple of classrooms on the left, an art room, ordinary classroom and a woodwork room at the far end. The rooms were all full of prisoners who appeared to be working hard. An officer appeared from a small office no bigger than a broom cupboard, in the middle of the Classroom block.

"Hey, Hills, you dosser, how did you get a cushy job like that?" he shouted.

"Alright Bootsy, just get back in your hole and keep polishing," Dave replied, "We'll be back to see you later, you twat." Dave told me that the officer (Bob Bracey) was called "Bootsy" because he must polish his boots and belt at least ten times a day. He said he was a good officer to have around. He likes the job done properly and "you know where you stand with him."

Apparently, there are two types of staff at Grendon, those that believe in the therapy and care about working closely with the prisoners, and those that don't and would rather just do the usual prison officer stuff. Obviously, on my first day I wasn't able to judge any real difference between the two?

We turned left at the end of the M2 corridor into a smaller corridor with a gate at the end, above which was a sign A P U (Acute Psychiatric Unit). As we entered the prison hospital it looked and smelt just like any other hospital I'd been in. There was a staff office on the right with about half a dozen men in it. They were all wearing prison officer's uniforms but each had a white jacket on. I noticed that on each shoulder they had an epaulette with a large silver H on it.

In a raised voice, Dave announced "I will leave you with these scab lifters. Can one of you girls put your knitting away and give Joe a tour of the funny farm please?"

A very tall quite distinguished looking officer stepped forward and shook my hand. "Good morning, pleased to meet you, my name is Mike and I work in the EEG department, allow me to show you around Joe."

Mike Storm was a Hospital Principal Officer, apparently well respected by most staff because he had been at Grendon since the prison was built.

He had managed to get into a unique position in the EEG department and it was a job that gave him the opportunity to work in other prisons from time to time. Mike struck me immediately as being very educated, experienced and quite a gentleman.

He took me into a building at the rear of the hospital which was full of medical equipment of all descriptions. In one room was a large machine next to a couch. From the machine came dozens of wires which Mike explained were electrodes for the measurement of a patient's brain activity.

EEG stood for Electro Encephalograph, a method of checking for areas of abnormality in the brain. Mike explained its basic operation but I only remembered a fifth of what was said. The whole works looked like something out of Baron Frankenstein's laboratory.

I spoke to Mike for about ten minutes, during which time he impressed me a great deal.

It was clear that he fully believed in the work that Grendon did and was in the job because he cared about the prisoners. He wanted to help them as much as he could.

Before we left the EEG department he said something that I felt was quite inspirational.

"The prison system is overloaded with prisoners who suffer from very severe personality disorders but they are not mentally ill, that is something distinctly different." He added, "In the case of our Grendon men, some have suffered from mental illness but the majority have been affected by dysfunctional family lives. We can affect change through personal example, showing them how to behave correctly and what the rewards will eventually be."

But the most important comment that registered with me was "If you can obtain a good relationship with prisoners based on good trust and confidence, you will get a lot of satisfaction from working at Grendon." This in fact became the blueprint for the work that I was to eventually do and I was thankful to Mike for his guidance in my early years at Grendon.

But for the moment my experience was only just beginning.

On the way back into the hospital Mike visited a prisoner in one of the hospital cells; he was just packing his personal belongings into a bag in preparation for leaving.

"Thanks a lot Mike!" The prisoner shook his hand. "I'm happy that there is nothing serious going on, I've just gotta get the drinking sorted out. It was a bit of a nightmare but I've got something to work on and I won't be coming back for more, I promise."

"That's good" Mike said "because you won't be getting any more. You can't afford to touch a drop in the future. Take care Bob." Mike shook hands with the man and we left the cell.

The prisoner was on his way back to one of the wings. He had been in the hospital for the weekend, undergoing tests, to decide how much the use of alcohol affected his brain and to determine if any permanent damage existed.

The prisoner had been linked to the EEG machine and had been given increasing units of alcohol until he was completely drunk. At each stage his brain activity had been recorded. Through this and linked to talking about the issue of excessive drinking, the prisoner gets the ultimate benefit from Grendon's treatment.

The assessment of suitable candidates is very important as there are obvious risks involved. To observe a prisoner recovering from an authorised drinking session within a prison is a novelty. I had spent so much time with Mike Storm; I didn't have time to see the rest of the hospital unit which had a working Operating Theatre, Dentist, Opticians and X ray department. It seemed a very expensive facility for such a small prison. Grendon only housed 230 prisoners at this stage but I was informed that if you calculate the cost of taking prisoners out on escort to the local hospital, a lot of money is saved.

Dave and I left the hospital through the back gates and he announced, "We'll have a look in on the baby burglars in Workshop Two it's like a toy factory."

Workshop Two was in a line of buildings at the back of the Hospital which looked to be quite close to the prison wall. The other workshops in this block housed the Main Stores, Clothing Stores, Works department (Painters & Plumbers) and Garden Party.
Dave also told me that when Grendon was built it had its own Morgue, as the authorities imagined that there might be a lot of deaths, "It doesn't inspire confidence in the system if they thought that prisoners would want to top themselves on a regular basis?" I remarked.

"That's right, but I think it was built for the staff", he laughed. "Anyway, it's never been used. The only dead things in there now are the old prison records and the odd cockroach."

There was a lot of noise coming from Shop Two. It sounded like kids shouting, and loud music echoed through the main gate. "You're going to G Wing, aren't you? Well fuck your luck, these little darlings are yours, and you're welcome to them," he nudged me through the iron gates of the workshop.

There was about twenty or so teenagers' busily packing things into cardboard boxes and the air was thick with the smell of fresh paint. This was the second of two operational industrial workshops, the other one being Shop four, which was much larger, across the road. Its employees were Young Prisoner's, aged 17 to 21, some of whom were serving life sentences for murder. All of them were in prison for serious crimes such as Rape, Armed Robbery, GBH, and Burglary.

The level of noise dropped as we entered the shop and all of the lads stared at me for a second or two before going about their business. Some of the lads chatted in small groups, glancing at me occasionally. My ears were definitely burning.

A man who wore a white coat over his civilian clothing approached us. I was already getting used to distinguishing Prison Officers from Civilians (Civvies). Prisons are very good at putting people into little tidy boxes. Ray Cooper was classified as a Workshop (Civilian) Instructor and it was his task to come in each day to run the light assembly lines. The contract was with a company called Dekkertoys and G Wing lads were putting together and packing toy Punch balls.

For this the prisoners earned from £2.90 to £3.75 a week.

"Magic us up a cup of tea Ray," Dave joked, apparently referring to Ray's part time occupation as a children's entertainer and Magician. I found out later that Ray was also a former Policeman but he never wanted the boys to know this in case it affected his relationship with them. Ray was obviously well respected by all. Even though his role was to supervise the workshop, I realised that his input was very important to the staff as he got to know the prisoner's very well indeed. He saw many things that prison officers working on the Wings didn't.
"Get your own damn tea; you know where the kettle is. Or else get Cookie to do it, he's doing now't", Ray replied. Cookie was the Prison Officer who was working in the shop with Ray today and I was told that there would always be an officer there, for discipline reasons in case of any trouble. But trouble was quite rare.

Bob Cook (Cookie) came over and introduced himself. He brought with him three prisoners and introduced them. "This is Hayden, John and Harry".

We shook hands and I introduced myself "My name's Joe, pleased to meet you."

"You won't be saying that in a weeks' time, when you get to know this lot" Bob suggested "especially the skinhead over there (pointing to the prisoner called John) he's a pain in the arse". John squared up to Bob. "Oi, screw, I'll fucking do you in a minute".
He then responded by starting a play fight with Bob. Picking the officer up, he threw him into a pile of empty boxes at the back of the shop. The other staff simply stood and looked on and the rest of the prisoner's cheered.

This was not exactly the text book behaviour by staff that I had been taught to expect at the training school, it looked much more fun. "As they say, you don't have to be mad to work here Joe but it helps," Hayden advised, "You're coming to G wing I hear, where are you from?"

I must have looked a bit awkward; as I wasn't sure how much information I could give to a prisoner? Shaun immediately sensed my unease "Don't worry, I don't want to know where you live, I meant which nick?"

"I was at Stafford for a couple of weeks and then the Training School so this is my first permanent jail". I relaxed a little and Shaun continued, "You'll soon get used to things, it's a bit strange here at first but you'll like it I'm sure." Shaun then said he had to get back to work but looked forward to seeing me on the wing soon.

This seemed rather surreal to me. I had just received advice and support from a prisoner. Not only that but he also looked forward to seeing me again. I was told to expect Grendon to be different, but at this rate I might have to flush the prison officers training manual down the nearest toilet.

We stayed for a further half an hour before Dave announced that he would show me the gymnasium and then we would go to "The Greasy Spoon Canteen" (Staff Mess) for a sausage sandwich.

On our left as we walked from the workshop were two large tarmac exercise yards. The one furthest away was marked out as a basketball pitch. The prisoners came out to exercise at 12pm for one hour. At Grendon the inmates didn't simply walk around in circles as I had witnessed at Stafford. Instead they enjoyed a game of 5 a side football or Basketball and there was an inter wing league table. The Young Prisoner's (YP's) had their own exercise yard but they did play games against the adults occasionally. Apparently, this was also unique to Grendon, as YP's and adult prisoners were normally not allowed to mix in all other jails.

As we made our way to the Gym, Dave pointed out a building on the left with steam rising from its windows. It was the prison laundry. "I think we'll give that a miss today, it's too bloody hot to stand around in there but don't worry you'll be spending a few hours on that job over the next couple of months." New screws get stuck in the hot steamy laundry in the summer.

Three prisoners appeared from behind the laundry and acknowledged us as they passed by. Dave pointed out that the man in the centre of the group had only just been "taken off the books". He was a short spindly character, not unlike the Hunchback of Notre Dame. "What does taken off the books mean?" I enquired. "It means he was a category "A" prisoner who always had to be escorted by one or two staff. The staff carried a log book of his movements and when he was handed over to another officer, the book was signed and passed on."

A Cat A man was a very high-risk prisoner.

He was either at risk of committing violence to staff or other inmates, or, as was the case for this man, being assaulted by other prisoners.

"How come he can walk around without any staff now? I thought prisoners needed a Red Band to show that they were trusted. None of those inmates had one on?" I queried.

He explained that in Grendon prisoners could go from point A to B unescorted. It's part of the regime to give them that amount of trust.

He explained, "The three we just met were on their way to the CES (Clothing Exchange Stores). Probably they would have been let out through the door in the M1, and then the officer who let them out would ring the CES to say that they were on their way. `When they reached their destination the Storeman would then contact their Wing, to confirm that they had arrived".

This was yet another example of a basic prison rule that was blown apart by the Grendon regime. "It's a golden rule in the prison system" I offered, "that all prisoners, except Red Bands should be escorted by a Prison Officer. How can Grendon be so different?"

Dave advised "It's simply because Grendon has permission from Prison Service Headquarters to do things differently. It doesn't matter how hard you argue, the truth is it works. Very few prisoners try to take advantage of it." The other Golden Rule that worked in this jail was the "No violence" rule.

"Another thing that will blow your mind" he added "is that the man I pointed out to you is serving life for the rape and murder of a four-year-old girl. After raping her, he then mutilated her body. Apparently, his final act was to place a long stick inside her vagina and he then kicked it, so hard, that it almost disappeared. The two men walking with him are in for burglary and armed robbery. What about that then?"

I told him I couldn't believe how a man who had done something like that could walk around the prison in complete safety?

He informed me that Grendon has produced its own rules, as well as the usual prison rules. The Golden Rule here is that there will be NO VIOLENCE. The prisoners have volunteered to come to this prison to do group therapy and to sort out their problems.
If anybody commits an act of violence towards anybody else they could be transferred out immediately.

I started to realise how powerful the therapy must be if hardened criminals are controlled by it?

As we walked along the M2 towards the Gym my mind was still focused on the Sex Offender and how happy he looked to be out in the warm sunshine with two of his mates. Surely this wasn't justice, I pondered.

The Gym was situated next to the prison Library opposite the Chapel; it wasn't just a Gym but was also used as a theatre. It was like my old-school hall, with a large stage at one end. There were some weights and an exercise bike on the stage and some scenery was being painted for the Christmas pantomime.

Dave told me that Grendon always produced a pantomime each year for charity. Old people from local homes were invited in for Christmas dinner and a panto, some staff even brought their kids to see it. The actors were a mixture of prisoners and staff and the Medical Superintendent played a lead role in last year's production.

At the back of the hall opposite the stage was a large balcony which was where the prisoners from nearby Springhill Prison would sit. They were not allowed to mix freely with Grendon men. Last night had been the regular Sunday Cinema Night when 70 or 80 inmates came to see a film. It happened every Sunday and the prison Library Officer was the projectionist. Two or three staff would come on duty to supervise, sometimes without any pay, just to see a decent film for free.

Dave introduced me to Peter Alland. He was a Senior PEI (Physical Education Instructor) who had been at Grendon for quite some time. Peter talked about Grendon for at least twenty minutes and like Mike Storm who I met earlier, he was very enthusiastic. It was obvious that here was another man who could give me some sound advice if I needed any. It was clear that he not only cared about his work but he also cared about the prisoners. He believed that PE was an important part of the Therapy programme.

When I left the Gym, I could see the benefits of being "sound in body, sound in mind" and Peter mentioned that quite often, former drug addicts gained the most from physical fitness and a healthy diet. And on that note Dave and I made our way down the M1 corridor for a big fat sausage sandwich with loads of brown sauce!!

"The Greasy Spoon" was situated opposite the gates to G Wing. It was a very small cafe style set up, with a long row of soft chairs on the right-hand wall and two or three tables and chairs on the left. In the corner was a large one-armed bandit with a £100 jackpot. "That's Jock's machine. I don't think he's in today so I might drop the jackpot, that'll really piss him off" Dave joked.

The Jock he referred to was Jock Shillinglaw a Hospital Principal Officer who was rumoured to spend £10 to £20 a day on the machine. He would stand there for his whole lunch hour in the hope that the god of fortune was smiling down on him

The cooking was done by a couple of prisoner's who were classed as mess Red Bands.

Although all the meals were basic, from beans on toast to bangers and mash, at least you could get a hot meal without having to walk from Grendon to the "Big House" at Springhill. Dave said he was on an E shift (which stood for an Early Shift) so he would be off duty at 1pm. I thanked him for the morning's tour and a quick glance at my Induction programme told me I was on G wing after lunch.

During the lunch hour prison officers occupied all the soft chairs in the mess.
They lay down in a long row with their feet up on several coffee tables and slept soundly, almost snoring in unison.

This must be the lunchtime fitness session Pete Alland mentioned I mused, as I read through some of the information the Chief had given to me.

From what I had seen already, it looked like the training and background of prison officers at Grendon was no different from staff in other jails and the Chief had confirmed that officers are not especially selected to work here.

The Kitchen staff, the PE department and Works Department are just as likely to be actively involved in therapy alongside the Psychiatrists, Psychologists, Hospital officers or ordinary Prison (Discipline) officers.

The prison accepted convicts who want to modify their behaviour and stop doing crimes. Some of the info says that their attitude in prison changes for the better, but more importantly they behave better when they get out. The prisoners volunteered to come there and they can stop the therapy and go back to the prison they came from at any time. I also read that other cons and staff can also vote a prisoner out. If he breaks any of the Grendon rules or he isn't doing anything to change his ways, he is moved swiftly.

In the past Grendon had been described as a Psychiatric Prison but the Home Office now called it a Therapy Prison. Although it was still managed by the Medical Department, it was not run like a Psychiatric Hospital, apart from in the APU.

The prisoners were an important part of the management process and had a say in how things were done, but it was not a soft option! Prisoners were challenged about their faults and weaknesses and it would get very uncomfortable.

I knew nothing about the therapy process before I arrived which was quite frightening as I did not know how I might be personally affected.

Reading through some of the rules that the prisoners had made for themselves, I could see how difficult it might be for them. They had to take responsibility for their own actions and couldn't blame anybody else, not just for the crime they were in for, but past offences as well.

Grendon made them aware of their victims and how they and their families also suffered.

As well as the No Violence rule that I mentioned earlier, there was also a NO DRUGS rule. Not just drugs like Cannabis or LSD but also prescribed medication such as Valium, Anti-depressants or sleeping tablets.

A Prisoner also had to agree to reject the sort of behaviour that goes on in other prison's that was called "Nick Culture". They were encouraged to give information on anyone who was not working within the rules or who would not take responsibility for themselves. In the rest of the prison system it was called "grassing somebody up" but at Grendon it was called "Therapeutic Feedback".

It is important to note that aggressive men, who have caused problems everywhere else, learn to change that behaviour without being placed in a "Segregation Block". Grendon's block was hardly ever used. It was a powerful treatment programme and I could not wait to see how it worked in practice.

Following my lunch, I was escorted by Bob Cook to G wing.

Just inside G Wings gate was a large square entrance hall covered in highly polished red lino. This was appropriately named "The Red Square" and in the middle of the square was a pool table. Bob pointed out that on the right was the staff toilet and on the left a washroom with a twin tub washing machine and an ironing board. The young prisoners did all their own washing and ironing. There were five or six prisoners on the Red Square who all carried on their activities as Bob led me into the staff office.

G Wing was a strange shape, as there were two corridors running parallel from the Red Square and each had doors at either end. So from the office you were only able to view a brick wall and from a security point of view this was a bit alarming, as you could not see any prisoners.

Bob explained that the wing used to be G & H Wings and obviously was separate, but now it was all classed as one unit. It was still possible to isolate one half of the wing from the other within minutes if necessary

In the office, I was introduced to three more staff, Officer Cliff Pitwell, Officer George Prosser and a rather elegant lady called Eileen Ogden, who was the wings Social Worker. They all gave me a very warm welcome.

The lunchtime "Patrol Period" lasted from 12 until 2pm. Bob explained that the prisoners remained unlocked all day but nothing happened during this period as there were only two officers around, George was just going to lunch.

As we sat in the office, various prisoners came in, politely introduced themselves, and then left. One or two stayed as Bob explained the G Wing system. There were thirty prisoners on the Wing, all aged between 17 & 21 years.
The shortest sentence was six years and about half a dozen were lifers, which Bob suggested was a low figure.

Normally lifers numbered about a third of the population.

They normally stayed in therapy for 18 months to about 2 years, but a couple had been there just a bit longer. These were lifers awaiting a move. When the boys reach the age of 21 and they still need to continue their therapy, they can be moved onto one of the four adult wings.

I looked at the wing roll board and saw that their crimes weren't listed and I asked if this was for their own protection, suddenly realising what a stupid question that might be.

Bob realised my embarrassment and answered sympathetically, "The boy's wings are the same as the adults, and everybody gets to know what each other's crime is so we don't need to advertise them. Lads are protected by the non-violence rule; the only difference is that the men on the other wings are assessed before they arrive on their wing but the boys aren't. So, we have to be a bit more cautious when a new lad arrives".

Bob explained that young boys tended to be more volatile than adults. So, the G wing staff used a slightly different approach and the therapy was different. "On G Wing, we use the T.A he said.

"T. A ... hmm" I pondered for a few seconds. That stands for the Territorial Army. "It teaches them to communicate better with each other" Bob added. "And they learn how to be more adult."

"I don't suppose they're allowed to use real guns though, are they?" I asked. "Guns?" Bob looked puzzled, "What guns?"

"You know, like the old 303 rifles or stuff like that" I replied. Bob looked even more puzzled and the same look appeared on the prisoners' faces also. "You've fucking lost me now" he exclaimed!

Trying to make myself better understood, I explained. "As a kid, I was in the Army Cadets and we used rifles that fired blanks. I thought the Territorial Army still used the same sort of thing?"

The whole office suddenly erupted into roars laughter and one prisoner was holding his sides with tears streaming down his face. Bob was in bits himself as he screamed "Not the Territorial Army you twat, I'm talking about Transactional Analysis, the type of Therapy we do."

My embarrassment this time was so strong it made my head ache and my face and neck glowed fiery red.

"Sorry Mate, I should have made myself clearer. I can just imagine these psychos on the loose with a loaded gun" he smirked.

Once everybody had regained their composure he explained what Transactional Analysis was all about and this was where I got my first insight into the world of Psychotherapy.

Chapter 5

In my first few weeks it was explained to me that Transactional Analysis is a form of therapy that was developed by an American Psychologist Dr Eric Byrne. Basically, he said that we all have three main parts to our personality and these are called Ego's. There's the Parent Ego, the Adult and the Child. We are always in one of these ego states at any given time.

Bob Cooke attempted to simplify it for me. "While I am explaining this to you I am in my Adult Ego" He said "and while you are listening to me like you are, in an adult way, you are in your Adult Ego. Are you with me so far? He asked.

"I think so" I replied, a little unconvincingly.

"Good. That means that we are communicating together in the same direction, in parallel. ... Have you got that? We are talking adult to adult".

He then explained that this was called a good or "Positive Transaction" between two people. He continued "If you then decide to take the piss out of me while I'm talking, that means that you will have changed from your Adult Ego to your Child Ego. You're being childish. ... OK so far?"

"Yes", I nodded.

"Right, so the moment you start taking the piss, I start to get angry. This means that the transaction between the two of us, as gone from a good to a bad one, or a Negative Transaction, and a fight could develop. ... OK?"

"This means that the good Parallel transaction has become a bad Negative transaction. Which means we have had a Crossed Transaction? So that's what Transactional Analysis is all about. ... See what I mean? In very simple terms" he asked

"Sort of, but I suppose I'll see things better when I've been here a bit longer" I said. But where does the parent bit come into it?" I enquired.

"Just take one step at a time" Bob advised "It's really not that hard. There you go; I have answered in my Parent state!"

For the time being, it felt that the therapy on G wing might take a lot of understanding. My brain was already beginning to explode and this was in less than half a day.

In the afternoon, there was to be a full wing meeting (called a Community Meeting), where I would learn even more about the weird and wonderful world of Grendon.
The meeting included 35 prisoners and 6 prison staff. 5 prisoners did not attend as they were out of therapy and awaiting transfer to other jails.

These prisoners would be locked in their cells for the duration of this meeting.

The Community Meeting began at 2.15pm prompt and anybody who arrived later would not be allowed to enter the room. The idea being that this is therapy time and there should be no distractions. Equally, nobody could leave the room at any point, for any reason, even to use the toilet!

I met several other staff members just before the meeting and would have the opportunity to get to know them better later during a short meeting of staff after the Community Meeting. This was referred to as the "Staff Feedback Session".

Chairs were arranged around the sides of the room and across the corners so that they formed a large circle. Staff would disperse themselves around the room rather than sit together, and the prisoner I had met earlier, called Hayden chaired the meeting. He held the title of "Wing Chairman ".

Hayden called the meeting to order and there was complete silence. "Before we deal with the business we have a new officer with us so we will introduce ourselves". He said "I'm Hayden and I'm serving 8 years for Burglary."

There then followed a round of introductions that was reminiscent of televisions popular game show, at that time, University Challenge.

"I'm Pete, doing 6 years for Rape." and "I'm Gary, doing Life for murder" or " I'm Barry, doing 5 years for Robbery" and so on around the room. When it came to my turn I said, "I'm Joe, looking forward to a new career at Grendon and I will be working with you on G Wing."

Once the introductions had finished, Hayden announced that there were "Group Backings" to be done. He asked the candidates to put their cases forward.

Backings were a form of voting process, whereby prisoners would be considered for job vacancies on the wing. Some were paid jobs but others were voluntary, taken for therapeutic reasons. There were three jobs available, two paid and one voluntary.

A prisoner called Chris G spoke first and announced that he was going for a job "behind the hotplate". Another boy by the name of Terry J said he would also like the job and each candidate was invited to put their case forward.

Working behind the hotplate meant that they would be involved in the serving of all food, washing up, returning all trays to the kitchen, and cleaning the dining room area after each meal. It was considered to be a job with a lot of responsibility and one that often led to violent confrontations. Food was very precious in a prison environment.

Chris began by saying that he had been at Grendon for nearly a year and his group felt that he needed a job with more responsibility. He felt he could do the job well.

He was interested in hygiene and thought that he would treat everybody equally and fairly.

A prisoner at the other side of the room questioned him "Chris, I reckon you could do the job but how would you handle the arguments over food? Do you think you're strong enough to cope?"

Chris replied nervously "I have a problem with saying no to people, that's true, but that is why I am going for the job. I think it will teach me to stick up for myself and become stronger, more assertive." He glanced around the room nervously as he spoke, searching everybody's face for approval and continued "One of the reasons that I commit my offences is because I can't say how I'm feeling, I let it all bottle up and then explode and light fires."

He was serving a Life sentence for a series of Arsons mainly on Industrial buildings, but his last offence was on a large children's home which was fully occupied.

Another prisoner spoke" But how can we trust you? What if somebody upsets you? Supposing it was John, how will you tell him?"

John B was the prisoner I had met in the Workshop with the shaven head, I learned later that he was doing time for football violence (GBH) and had the reputation of being a bully. He was a strong muscular lad compared to Chris, who was small and skinny.

Chris looked over at John as he replied, "John's been OK with me. I don't think it'll be a problem but if I do have one, with John or anybody, I'll bring it to my group and talk about it." There were about half a dozen more questions and then it was Terry's turn to put his case across.

Terry was self-confident "I just want the job because it's more money, with Christmas coming up and all that. I want to buy some extra stuff. I could give you all a load of old Psychobabble bollocks but the bottom line is I want the extra dosh. "

He smirked and shot a glance in John B's direction, before adding, "I could do the job stood on my head and nobody would give me any hassle. ... Easy as that."

"Has anybody got any questions for Terry?" Hayden asked.

There was a long silence, before one of the members of staff spoke up.

Bernie Marcus was the wing Therapist, a very well spoken, smart, cultured man, in a pin striped suit with a very colorful tie, which he rolled around his finger as he spoke. "Terry, can I ask you if you take your therapy seriously, and if so - is there anything that you think you would get out of the job other than extra money?"

"Yeah" Terry replied, "Extra chips!"

He laughed, and again looked towards John for approval. Once again there was a silence. It was obvious to me, even though this was only my first day at Grendon, Terry was a powerful character and he seemed to have a grip on the whole community.

I sensed myself getting angry but I couldn't be sure where it was coming from. Was I angry at Terry for trying to mock everybody? Or was I angry at the other prisoners and staff, who seemed to be letting him get away with it?

Hayden broke the silence and asked, "Has anybody got any comments? If not we'll take a vote. But remember, nobody can abstain, it's either for or against." he called for "Votes for Chris?" There was a show of hands and twenty-six prisoners voted that he should get the job. Eight thought that he shouldn't and only one abstained.

Terry was the abstention and Hayden asked him why he hadn't voted for himself?

"Because it's all a load of bollocks" Terry snarled "If I gave you a load of crap like that little prick, I could have got the job.
At least I'm honest."

Hayden calmly announced that Chris had got the job but it still had to go to the staff group later for their decision?

This was my first taste of the Grendon way of doing things and I ended up feeling very confused?

Obviously by the way the vote went, Terry wasn't holding the other prisoners to ransom, but why had nobody argued with him? And if Grendon was a democratic community and the prisoners had voted for Chris to take the job, why did it have to go to the staff group for a final decision? Also ... why hadn't the staff voted during the meeting?

I held on to these feelings throughout the rest of the meeting, which was conducted fairly well by Hayden. The other jobs were for a Cleaners Foreman (the prisoner who was paid to supervise a gang of cleaners?) and TV Rep (who volunteered to control the TV channels that were being watched?) ... this was all mighty strange stuff!

But the latter was an important role as there was only one TV to share in the evenings between 40 young prisoners, so the vote to change channels became crucial!

During the remainder of the meeting a boy called Mike E talked about his recent Home Leave. He had been allowed to go home to stay with is parents for two nights and he told everybody how successful it had been. He said that he felt he could now live without using drugs and was looking forward to working with his dad, as a Painter and Decorator. Mike was being released within the next few weeks.

Just before the meeting ended, Hayden announced a five-minute period called "The Quickies". This was the time for anybody to make one quick comment before the meeting ended.

There were various comments but a prisoner called Barry said, "I've got one for you Terry. I think you're behaving like a prat at the moment and you should seriously look at your attitude."

Terry immediately tried to argue with Barry, but was cut off abruptly by Hayden who said -

"Leave it out Terry; you know there are no comebacks in the quickies."

The meeting was ended and the prison staff came out of the Community meeting, and gathered in Bernie Marcus's office for the Staff Feedback session.

As happened in the prisoners meeting, everybody introduced themselves again and welcomed me to Grendon. "Well Joe, what did you make of the meeting?" Bernie asked.

I said it had been interesting but I was still confused about the situation with Terry. I told him why and asked if somebody could explain it for me?

A Hospital Officer called Tony Carter began to explain. He said that Terry was a member of his small therapy group and was going through a tough time in therapy. His father had died recently and he was deciding if he should stay or go from here.

"Unfortunately, his closest friend on the wing was John B who has not been at Grendon very long and isn't the best one to advise him. Terry is looking for a fight with anyone at this time and nobody wants to give him the chance. The vote was a fair one and it was perhaps more in Chris's favour than we imagined. Most of the boys who had voted for Terry had done so out of sympathy, which is no reason to give anybody the job.

Staff members do not vote on meetings, just in case they may influence the outcome. The final vote by the prisoners is a recommendation only.

The Staff have the final word. However, we would rarely turn somebody down unless there was a good reason and we always explain any decision to the prisoners."

I was satisfied by the answer Tony gave and added his name to the growing list of people who I could turn to for advice.

My duty ended at 4.30 pm and I was very tired, there was so much to take in. I knew that I would have to make regular notes rather than try to remember it all. I left G wing at 4.30 and retired to the Officers Mess to reflect on the experience.

It was a pity that the "Introduction to Therapy Group" had been cancelled for next week, it was already obvious that I would struggle without it. Little did I realise at this stage that my work with young prisoners was to last for a total of 7 years. During which time, I was to learn a great deal about the psychology of offending behaviour, and almost as much about my own faults and weaknesses.

I found myself to be in a position of some considerable authority at the ripe old age of 25. I was taking responsibility for the welfare of some very disturbed young men, some only 5 years younger than me, at a time in my own life when I could hardly take responsibility for myself.

At this stage I still could not afford to buy a car, so in my first month I was isolated to the life on the prison estate but that was not such a bad deal. Although life in the hostel was mundane, I took up jogging with Bob Greaves each evening, which was good for my overall fitness. I was also using the prison gym at lunchtimes, mainly for weight training.

However, the thought of being confined to the hostel every evening was just too much to bear so the Prison Officers Club became my regular haunt.

The officers club was reasonably well attended so it was an ideal opportunity to meet other officers and their families.

Eventually the invitation came to join the committee and I agreed to become Entertainment Secretary.

As I viewed life on the Prison Officer's estate the more interesting it all became. Many families got on with their lives in an uncomplicated way. Dad worked at the prison, mum either stayed at home to look after the kids, making the daily trip into the village store to pay extortionate prices for family provisions or else she travelled to work from 9 to 5 in an Aylesbury factory or office. They sat and watched TV most evenings and attended the Prison Officers Club on special occasions, especially at Christmas time for the annual kid's party.

Those that stayed on the estate all day might get an invitation to the regular coffee mornings with other bored wives and mothers, to share the local gossip and tear apart the lives of those who chose not to accept the invitation. What they didn't know they would often invent, just like tabloid journalists - no matter how damaging the juicy gossip might be to the victim of their fantasies.

These were the days of plenty of overtime. Officers would fight each other, (on occasions physically in the club car park) for the opportunity to do up to seven 12-hour shifts in a row, which was worth between two to three hundred pounds a week extra.

These regular "Overtime Bandits" could afford to party every night of the week but they didn't because they were always at work and were too tired on their days off. But their wives could enjoy themselves and often did, arranging babysitters for some late-night knees up at the club or a house party.

A few of the officers gave up the temptation of regular overtime for the pleasure of entertaining a mate's wife. One or two would offer the overtime to the unsuspecting husbands, who would sometimes buy them a pint as a gesture of gratitude.

It seemed remarkable to me that these apparent pillars of the local community were able to cope with the pressures of late night/early morning drinking sessions, fighting and debauchery.
Going into the prison the next day to take on the role of group therapy facilitators for some of the country's most violent and disturbed offenders.

Such was the nature of the work that I undertook, and it didn't take long before I felt settled into the regime on G wing. There was always a new experience just around the corner. No two days were ever the same, even though the daily/weekly routines seldom varied. It would be impossible to present every single occurrence, so I have chosen those which I feel accurately portray the atmosphere in the prison now.

I got my first experience of an early morning start in the middle of the third week.

The routine was simple enough. A single prison officer would arrive on the wing at 7am and he would take over from a Night Patrol Auxiliary. The Auxiliary was in uniform but was not a fully trained prison officer. Therefore, his duties were limited to the operational part of the work. He would not be required to supervise any prisoners and would not be allowed to carry keys to the cells.

The prison officer would first ensure that the roll was correct and of course that all prisoners were alive.

The auxiliary officer could then leave the wing and the roll would be reported to the Centre Office before any of the night staff could go off duty. It was always the first responsibility of any officer to confirm the number of prisoners that he was taking charge of and he would then countersign the daily occurrence book (logbook).

Unfortunately, my first early start was not without incident.

I was awakened from a deep sleep as my Big Ben alarm clock threatened to shake the hostel out of its foundations. Last night had been a heavy drinking session in the club and I had the mother of all hangovers. My mouth was as rough as the bottom of a parrot's cage and there was a pounding in my head like a dozen hammers.

One eye refused to open as I struggled to focus on the clock face. The time was 6.30 am. ... "No problem" I thought, just lie here for a few minutes and then take a nice refreshing shower. Then 5 minutes later I remembered that this was to be my first early morning start and I had to be in the jail by 6.45 am.

I flew out of bed, heart pounding heavier than my head, adrenalin rushing like the Niagara Falls. As I stumbled into my uniform there was no time to wash or shave. I gathered my senses together and rushed out of the hostel.

The morning air was heavy and it was already quite warm as I attempted to run up the hill. I don't now how much I drank last night but I still felt quite pissed. I would have to pull myself together before I reached the prison gate.

A quick glance at my wrist as I arrived outside the prison gate told me that I had left my watch behind in the rush. I could hear voices in the gate lodge so hopefully I was still on time.

The gatekeeper greeted me with a cheery smile and I attempted to return the same, but the muscles in my face hadn't fully woken up yet.

"What's the time?" I asked feverishly as I tumbled through the Wicket Gate.

"Slow down and relax pal" the gatekeeper said "You don't get any medals for rushing around like that; you'll be giving yourself a coronary. You look as rough as a bears arse. A good night at the club, was it?

"Never again" I swore as he let me through towards the Centre Office.

I was carrying my hat underneath my arm as it made my head ache worse if I wore it, but besides that, I was sweating so much it might not stay on my head anyway.

Who's going to bother about silly rules now, I thought?

Then a broad Scots accent boomed from within the centre office. "If hats were meant to be carried they'd have handles laddie!" It was Principal Hospital Officer Jock Shillinglaw, glaring at me through the office widow. He had a face like an eagle with piercing eyes and in my early days he always appeared to me to be cold and unapproachable. But later on, I was to learn that he had another very gentle side, but for the time being I felt very intimidated by him.

"Sorry Sir" I apologised as I hurried through the gate onto the M1 corridor. "Good afternoon Officer Chapman - nice of you to join us" Jock said sarcastically, "We hope we haven't interrupted your beauty sleep young man. It is clear that you need plenty of it"

Hurrying down the M1, I couldn't wait to get onto G wing and eventually relax with a soothing cup of coffee.

As I approached the wing office there was a radio playing and the pleasant smell of pipe tobacco. Although I had always been a non-smoker I found pipe smoking to be quite acceptable.

Ernie Gostellow was G wings regular Night Patrolman. He had worked in Grendon for many years and was well respected by all staff but more importantly by all of the prisoners on G wing. And there was a very good reason for this.

Ernie took his night duties very seriously. When he started his duty at 8.45pm he would ask the day staff if any of the inmates were feeling low or particularly depressed. He would complete a thorough roll check, and before settling down to the shift, he would speak to every single prisoner for at least 4-5 minutes each.

He could spend up to an hour talking to any prisoner who was feeling very upset.

In contrast to the other night patrols, who would merely ensure that each prisoner was in his cell, some people might have felt that Ernie was taking things a bit too far.
However, he had very good personal reasons to be so thorough.

A few years previously staff had not told him that one of the prisoners was depressed.

When Ernie did his rounds, the boy had appeared to be OK. However, during the night a cell alarm bell had sounded and Ernie went to see what was happening. As he approached the landing he could hear several boys screaming. As he got closer to the cell in which the alarm bell could be heard, he could smell smoke.

Looking through the spy hole he could see that the boy's cell was well and truly alight and he could hear the young boy's blood curdling screams pleading with Ernie to get him out. But unfortunately, the Night Patrol staff didn't have keys, and even if they did they could not unlock a cell without being given the authority by the Night Orderly Officer.

By the time help arrived the young man had burned to death in cell eight feet by six, which at the height of the blaze resembled a blast furnace. The fire brigade told the staff that the heat was so fierce it had warped the cell door and had even melted the vinyl record collection belonging to a prisoner in the cell above.

This terrible incident had been etched permanently into Ernie's mind. It was why he always spent some quality time communicating with them and if any boy didn't respond positively he would ask for him to be unlocked and examined.

Night staff had since been issued with cell keys in a sealed pouch but not to be opened unless it was an emergency.

It is difficult to say what age Ernie was when I first met him and I might have done him a disservice to guess, but he was very much a kindly Grandfather figure to the prisoners and another great inspiration to me. I remain eternally grateful for the support and advice he gave in my early years.

So, returning to my first difficult early start……..

"Blimey boy, you're looking a bit rough around the edges! Wouldn't she leave you alone last night?" Ernie joked.

"A chance would be a fine thing; I'm still living on my own." I replied. "Well perhaps you should leave yourself alone then" he responded, "It'll make you go blind in the end you know."

I assured him that it was all down to drinking too much, nothing more sinister and immediately set out to check the wing roll. I was looking to count 30 prisoners.

Ernie left the wing and headed for the Centre Office to await my confirmation.

Counting the prisoners wasn't as easy as I had expected. Some of them were tucked right underneath their blankets so I needed to get some sort of response from them? I had seen the officers at Stafford prison kick the cell door to get a response and so I imagined this to be a tried and tested method.

The first door I kicked obtained a definite response "Fuck off, you noisy bastard there's no need for that" was the shout, followed by "Piss off back to the system."

I got a similar response from every landing, which was a bit of a traumatic experience. Never mind - at least I finally counted 30 prisoners all alive and well. I got back to the office to ring the numbers through to the Centre.

"Thirty boys on G wing all present and correct" I announced confidently.

"Oh, thirty is it officer. Are you absolutely sure?" It was Jock's voice and he was even able to intimidate me over the phone. This was where I made one of the biggest mistakes so far when I replied, "Yes sir - I think so."

"Oh, you think so do you? Well I suggest you check again young Mr Chapman if you are not altogether sure?"

Why on earth did I say I think so, when I was so confident? But perhaps there weren't thirty? I'd better do as I'm told. So, off I went again to repeat the body count, this time causing more uproar than before. And this time I only counted twenty-nine?

"Shit, I had been wrong the first time around - what an embarrassment" I thought.

"Twenty-nine correct on G Wing Sir" I said, trying to sound confident for the second time.

"Oh dear - are you really sure this time?" Jock asked. I immediately replied, "Yes sir, I'm fully confident."

"Well that is a shame, because that's not the number on my board up here. Can I suggest you check again officer?" Jock ordered.

I was just contemplating the possibility of causing Grendon's first riot by going back onto the landings to cause more mayhem, when Hospital Officer Tony Carter walked in. I told him what had happened and he offered to check the roll for me this time.

"You were right first time" he said, "there are thirty." He called and gave the numbers to Jock without any questions being asked.

He could see that I was totally fed up and anxious about the whole incident but reassured me that everyone makes the same mistake at some point in their career, but not everybody has to put up with Jock Shillinglaw, and his silly pranks.

He told me that Jock enjoyed a joke and in a way, he wanted me to face up to him and build confidence in my decisions. It may have seemed a little cruel but it kept me on my toes.

Tony was the person who gave me the most advice during the formative years at Grendon. He wasn't afraid to speak his mind and he taught me to value my own opinions.

If I wasn't rude or intimidating in my approach then others would be prepared to listen.

He told me that Jock always liked to play games with new staff and Dave Hills had confirmed this, Jock respected those who could stand up for themselves and the time soon arrived when I had the opportunity to try this theory out.

You will recall that Jock's favourite phrase was "If hats were meant to be carried they'd have handles." well, Tony advised me, the next time Jock says this I should hold the hat up by the chin strap and simply smile at him.

So, sure enough, when the next occasion arrived, I nervously did as he had advised and Jock simply smiled back at me and said, "Hey, you'll do for me son." From that moment on I had no further troubles and in fact Jock became one of a few officers that I greatly respected during the rest of my time at Grendon.

I recall that when he was on patrol as Orderly Officer during the evenings Jock would creep around the outside of the building and spy on staff and prisoners through the windows. He would occasionally catch officers dozing in a chair or playing cards with prisoners and would tap on the window and wag his finger in a disapproving way, with a broad smile on his face.

Those who got wise to him would close all of the windows and draw the curtains on the ground floor whenever he was on duty.

I remember I was in an office on the ground floor of G wing and had spotted a cockroach under the desk. A young prisoner was bending down trying to get it into a jam jar so that I could take it home to show my son, I was leaning over him with a torch.

"Is it in yet" I asked the young lad, and then glanced up to see Jock's face framed in the window. "Well, well, young Joseph, I think I have seen and heard it all now?" he laughed. "I hope you and that boy will be very happy together, but there is a law against it you know!"

I tried to explain that I was trying to get a cockroach into a jar, but all I got in return was "So that's what they call it these days, I will bid you a good evening."

It remained a not so private joke between us for a couple of years but it did not stop him from asking my wife if I had tried "the old cockroach in a jar trick on her lately" when he eventually met her!

For the first couple of years I made many mistakes. Some of them could have cost me my career; if it wasn't for the support I received from certain Chief Officers, Governors, fellow officers, but more importantly prisoners. Like many fresh staff, I was meddling with people's lives through the Grendon process with insufficient experience and very little training and these were people were very disturbed in the first place.

The learning process was trial and error and I would cause distress for quite a few people before I could finally get it right. It is not something I am proud of but it more common than some people realise.

The therapeutic theory of Transactional Analysis, which was the backbone of G wings regime, was an ideal foundation to build on and well chosen by Bernard Marcus as a vehicle for young boys to learn about the psychology of relationships. But the most important vehicle for change was their practical experiences of the world they lived in, not simply behind the prison walls but on their eventual return to society.

The jargon used during the therapy meetings was strange but after a short while it all began to make sense.

For a healthy transaction between two people, the responses should be matching and the relationship will be healthy.
If responses become crossed then confrontations will develop. It was that simple!

The prisoners and staff would be analysing each other's conversations on a daily basis, pointing out when things go wrong.

This in itself is an enormous pressure, which affects prisoners and staff in much the same way. Prisoners in therapy will be encouraged to talk about that pressure. However, for Prison Officers, particularly the new and inexperienced, this did not come easily.

The staff held their own support meetings, called "Sensitivity Groups", whereby they could (in theory) talk about the pressures they were under and anything else that they might be struggling with, in complete confidence.

The problem with such groups within an hierarchical system such as the Prison Service, was that your manager/supervising officer would sit on the same group and a genuine fear for some staff was that the exposure of their faults and weaknesses might be recorded in Annual Staff Reports (ASR's). This could be referred to for future promotion.
It is traditionally very difficult for Prison Officers to admit their own faults and weaknesses, especially to Prisoners, but again, at Grendon, this happened daily.

In the early days, my own faults were brought into the open in quite dramatic ways and the first major learning curve for me occurred during a Monday lunchtime exercise period. It appeared to come from nowhere.

The young prisoners were playing a game of five a side football on G wing exercise yard, Tony Carter and I were the supervising officers. However, Tony liked to join in the game, which meant I would stand by the alarm bell.

During the game, which was quite rough at times, I watched prisoner John B tackle a smaller boy on several occasions in an aggressive manner.
He was also pushing and threatening him, when he thought nobody was watching. It became obvious to me that John was a bully and he was using the game to get at the weaker kid.

As I watched this, I became aware that my own anger was building up and the whole focus of my attention was on John B. As he came towards my side of the yard I suddenly shouted at him, "Why don't you pick on somebody your own size - bully boy?"

John stopped in his tracks and said "What did you say to me? Who are you fucking talking to? You prick."

There was no turning back for me now - "Are you fucking daft as well as deaf" I responded. At this stage I was aware of nobody else but John and me.

John started to walk towards me shouting abuse and threatening to do me in but several other prisoners held him back. I still continued to shout at him "You don't like your own medicine, do you pal?"

Then I became aware of Tony Carter who stood between me and John, and told me to back off, I realised immediately that I had allowed my own feelings to get the better of me, but still felt that I was justified to say what I had.

After all, this is Grendon and people can share their feelings.

Fortunately, the exercise period was over in the next couple of minutes and everybody returned to the wing for lunch. John glared at me as he went in but we stayed out of each other's way for the remainder of the lunch period.

The regular Community Meeting was being held at 2.15pm, and the usual staff were present.

Hayden opened the meeting but announced that he was not going to deal with the usual business, due to a serious incident that occurred over the lunchtime. I wondered what he was referring to, as I had been away during the second half of Lunchtime Patrol.
Then.... to my surprise, he turned to me and said "This is difficult for me Joe, but you are being brought to the meeting to explain why you threatened John B during today's exercise period. So perhaps you can tell us all what happened?"

I could feel all eyes were on me but particularly John's, who seemed to love the idea that I would have to explain my behaviour to the whole community.

I decided not to give him that pleasure and said, "There's nothing to explain. John was acting the big bully and I just let him know how I felt, that's about it - he knows the score."

And then I added "Anyway, I'm not here to look at my behaviour."

This proved to be my downfall as the whole meeting erupted, and at least a dozen people criticised me, not only for the comment I'd just made but also for the original incident on the exercise yard.

I stubbornly refused to budge an inch and argued my case for just over half an hour, occasionally glancing towards the staff for support, although none was forthcoming. Eventually Hayden spoke again, "It's obvious that you are not prepared to accept the blame Joe, so I am calling for a wing vote that you should be transferred from the wing for provoking violence and then let the staff group deal with it."

"This was stupid," I thought to myself and laughed out loud. Any moment now a member of staff would back me up and stop the process. But all the staff remained silent as the vote was taken.

It was unanimous that I should be considered for transfer and Hayden asked Bernie Marcus to consider the vote seriously, Bernie agreed and the remainder of the meeting was concerned with general business.

When staff feedback began, I expected to get the support that I was hoping for in the prisoners meeting but this was not the case.

Everybody felt that I had handled things very badly and the vote was deserved.

I continued to argue my case. The most crucial factor for me was that I was a member of staff, I didn't come to Grendon for therapy but the prisoners did and I wasn't prepared to accept the "stupid vote".

Bernie advised me "As a member of staff we all have to set a good example for the lads and if you can't see what you are doing wrong - well perhaps you should be working elsewhere" He added "If you were at Springhill prison that sort of behaviour could have cost you your job How would you have felt about that?"
I remained stubborn and said that if the staff felt I didn't deserve to be here then that was fine. They could do whatever they wanted.

Before I finished work that day Tony Carter asked if I would like to join his family for tea. I thought this was his way of saying he was on my side, so I agreed, besides, it was always nice to have a home cooked meal rather than something from the Greasy Spoon.

During that evening, Tony spoke to me in a way that made everything fall into place. I had not been prepared to listen to anybody, which was a common fault for me and I was always more reasonable in a one to one situation, I tended to play to an audience, regardless of the consequences for me.

"But this is not just about you" Tony urged "The rest of the staff would lose all credibility if they allowed you to behave the way you have today and we try to lead by example. We are only human and we can gain respect from prisoners if they see this side in us." He added "Your feelings about John may not be wrong but you cannot criticise him while you are behaving as you are."

He suggested that my profile with the prisoners and with the staff group would be improved if I could admit that I was wrong. I should apologise to John and move forward. But I could only do this if I genuinely thought I was wrong. "Sleep on it." He advised.

I did sleep on it and decided to go back to the next Community Meeting and apologise to John. Not only that, but I also asked the prisoners to vote that I should stay on G wing and explained why I had reacted to John so strongly.

To cut an extremely long story short, my respect from prisoners grew overnight and I decided to cultivate every opportunity to better my relationship with them. I was able to offer advice where I felt it was appropriate and was willing to accept their views about me from time to time. As I began to understand myself, then the more I could offer to the prisoners in my charge.

Chapter 6

I put all my efforts into learning as much as I could about the therapeutic programme, although there still weren't any training courses available, I read as much as I could and sought the advice of Bernie Marcus as often as possible.

I had been placed on a small Therapy Group with Tony Carter, which was a bonus, because he could also offer guidance from time to time until I had found my feet. Whatever the future might have in store, I was determined to find a way of working which would give the most scope for using my personality as well as the theory.

As I stated earlier, the therapy on G Wing was very structured and I soon found the confidence to facilitate the bits that were most useful.

There were full Community Meetings on Monday and Friday afternoon, and the smaller group, that Tony and I ran, was on Tuesday and Thursday morning and also on Wednesday afternoon, so I was actively involved in therapy every day of the week.

In the smaller group, prisoners would talk about anything they wanted to. Sometimes they spoke about difficulties they were having in prison or perhaps family problems, but more importantly they would have to discuss their offences in great detail. The main aim was to get them to examine why they had behaved in the way they did and to learn how to behave differently in the future. I almost used the term "to act differently", but purposely avoid using it.

Behavioural change must be real and never an act, but of course over the years there were many prisoners who were able to "act" their way through the process.

I quickly began to understand that offenders are quite often skillful actors. They have used the skills to avoid detection, although some might argue not so skillfully or they wouldn't have ended up in prison? However, they have developed a strong ability to deceive the closest members of their own family.

So the Therapeutic Programme had to take into account the fact that the prisoners may not be behaving honestly, particularly in the very controlled environment of a prison.

The fact that the Grendon policies state "there is to be no confidentiality and inmates can be open and honest with each other "doesn't mean this is ensured.

It wasn't difficult for me to understand how easy it became for prisoners to practice deceit, but I needed to build a personal strategy to check out the information being given to me was accurate and to ensure a prisoner had the commitment and motivation to change, which was a task.

It was also important that this commitment and motivation continued, otherwise they would be wasting their own time as well as everybody else's.

Transactional Analysis used techniques to assess the game playing that goes on between individuals. In fact, Eric Berne wrote a famous book called "The Games People Play" which highlighted the problems of "crossed transactions" which were sometimes purposely misleading, but very often subconscious.

In other words, there were prisoners who genuinely did not know the damage they had caused, but also did not realise how damaged they too had become. I started to find similarities in my personal life. In group therapy, we would watch for the signs and symptoms of game playing and would also recognise the individuals who used it, using jargon to describe the process.

For instance - playing the "Little Professor" describes somebody who uses big words and complicated phrases to mislead the discussion or to hide their true feelings and emotions. In this country, we refer to this as "being blinded by Science".

Another person may be described as playing the game of "Uproar" which means purposely starting arguments within a group to hide what they are really feeling.
They will then sit back and enjoying watching others argue between themselves.

Again, we refer to this as creating a "smoke screen" or offering a "red herring" in order to mislead. Somebody described as using "a wooden leg" is merely using an excuse for bad behaviour.

During one of my first meetings the following scenario developed.

Mike E was being questioned about why he had threatened another prisoner with violence, simply because the other boy had wanted to turn the TV channel over. Especially when Mike wasn't really watching the programme himself?

Another prisoner asked the question, "Mike, it looks to me like you've been collecting stamps?" and others in the room nodded their heads in agreement. I was totally puzzled by this comment, particularly as Mike also agreed and he added, "Yes, I cashed them in and I am sorry."

Following a brief discussion within the group of prisoners and because "Mike had recognised his stamp collecting" the recommendation was that he should be allowed to stay in Grendon and should talk about it further on his small group?

Not wanting to interrupt the meeting or to appear thick, I waited until the staff meeting and said, "I am a little bit confused but where did Mikes interest in Philately (Stamp Collecting) fit in with the argument about the TV programme?"

Tony Carter explained "The phrase Stamp collecting refers to the collecting of feelings. In this case stamps are feelings and they can be either Red Stamps which are bad feelings or Gold Stamps which are good." he continued "So Mike admitted that he had been saving up bad feelings (Red Stamps) against the other boy and had cashed them in when he threatened him over something as simple as a TV programme."

"So, collecting Gold stamps is OK?" I asked.

Tony shook his head "Not necessarily. We all like to receive compliments, which are nice, but if we collect the compliments (Gold Stamps) and then cash them in the moment we do something bad, we are using them to justify the bad behaviour. It means that we just have to recognise when we are doing it."

I thought it was a good description but felt the point could have still been made in simpler terms. For the time being I was content to use the phrases, if that was what was expected?

Other interesting developments in the first year was my Introduction to the use of "Role Playing" whereby prisoners would be able to reconstruct situations that they had found to be difficult, in order to play them through again but to get it right this time.

This was fun, and gave me the opportunity to put my own acting skills to the test.

We also played "Group Games" as a way of building confidence and trust, and although prison officers are usually not encouraged to take an active part in them, I decided to join in.

I went through two very interesting scenarios.

In the first, I had to stand in the middle of the room and the group of prisoners formed a circle around me. I was then blindfolded and turned around several times so that I was unaware of which prisoner was immediately behind me. The room went quiet, then on an instruction from a member of the group; I placed my hands firmly by my sides and fell backwards, expecting that the prisoners behind me would catch me.

I had to be confident enough within the group to feel that they would not allow me to hit the floor.

The second scenario was the "Obstacle Course", which involved pairing up with one prisoner, again allowing them to blindfold me and then being led by voice command around a room full of various obstacles. This included climbing over tables and chairs and stepping over sweeping brushes and fire extinguishers.

I decided very early on to participate in activities on equal terms with the prisoners. This included sessions in the gym, volleyball, circuits and weight- training. A few of the other officers did the same, although it was frowned upon by some others who felt we were there to supervise and any distraction from our duty was a security risk.

There was also a rule that staff shouldn't eat the prisoner's food but once again I felt that the sharing of a meal was an ideal opportunity to communicate on a less formal level, as was playing cards, pool, scrabble and darts. All such activities were encouraged throughout the jail but particularly on the boy's wing.

The wing also organised a Social Evening every three months and invited professional people, visitors from local churches and villages and more importantly we invited our wives and families. My wife and my sister Cathy attended three socials in the first year including a concert in the prison Gym.

By now you will have gathered that sharing a social scene with prisoners was considered just as important as sitting in the structured therapy groups. Therefore, the traditional professional boundaries were stretched to a limit far in excess of those which existed in normal jails.

We also held Family Therapy Meetings on a regular basis, which gave staff and other prisoners an insight into a boy's family relationships and staff were given the authority to attend family events outside of the prison "in furtherance of a prisoner's therapy". This was a mark of real progress, of trust and confidence, if a prison officer attended a wedding or christening.

I have been a best man to prisoners on four occasions and a godfather on three other.

Another form of alternative therapy offered to them was the "Psychodrama" sessions.

The G Wing Psycho dramatist was Jinnie Jeffries who came in to work with prisoners assisted by a prison officer. Officers were actively encouraged to participate in this form of therapy and this also enhanced their relationship with certain prisoners.

Psychodrama enabled prisoners to act out events from past history, current situations and possible future happenings. They could examine in great depth how they related to each experience. This was very powerful therapy and on occasions prisoners would re-enact their offences in front of a group of fellow prisoners.

In a couple of sessions Jinnie played the victim of a rape, serious sexual assault and a murder, in order to bring to life, the events surrounding an offence. This helped the prisoner to connect once again with the feelings they had at the time the crime was committed.

The group would examine these feelings, feed them back to the offender and support him through some very painful experiences. One important aspect of her work was to promote victim awareness.

I thought this work was extremely valuable, as it got underneath the surface and prisoners' raw emotions were exposed. There would be plenty of anger and tears.
During the sessions, it was not unusual to hear loud screams or furniture being smashed around.

Whatever happened, other prison officers would never intervene, and the important thing was, nobody got injured. This was a salute both to Jinnie's professionalism and the dedication of prisoners and officers who took part.

I became really hooked on Psychodrama but still felt there was something lacking on occasions, particularly when some of the factual/forensic information did not make sense. There were times when I was very suspicious of the prisoner's account of events leading up to the crime.

Contact outside of therapy, with a prisoner's family and friends, proved to be very valuable but I developed a strong urge to go even further in my quest for information. I was beginning to realise that certain aspects of it could never fulfil my original ambitions.

The tedious operational role of a prison officer didn't excite me at all. I could do the work well enough but felt no job satisfaction from this alone.

Simply keeping prisoners in safe custody was not very rewarding. I concentrated my efforts on learning as much as I could about the therapeutic process and read several theories which related to the work that was being done at Grendon. I soon realised that a combination of psychiatric and psychological interventions provided the fullest approach to understanding criminal behaviour. But I also saw a weakness in the treatment programme.

Something seemed to be lacking? I didn't think that the information we were given about a prisoner's social history was ever accurate enough.

There were loopholes that any intelligent offender might find his way through and far too much was left to assumptions. It was too easy to accept a prisoner's description of his life outside of prison and the events leading up to and including his crimes. In my early days, we could refer to evidence from the prisoner's record, if problems arose in the groups but by the start of the 80's there was no cross-referencing of forensic evidence and it occurred to me that involvement with the prisoner's family and friends was vital to the rehabilitation process.

Of course, the Probation Service retained very useful contact with the family and knew the problems that the offender could face on release. This information was available if there was good liaison with the probation officer outside, but in situations where the prisoner was refusing contact or the probation officers workload was too heavy, then accurate information was limited. All too often valuable information was missed or arrived too late.

One scenario highlighted the problem for me and I began to think of ways to resolve it.

I had been invited to a prisoners wedding in South London. Several of the G wing staff group had attended for the reception in the evening and we had stayed until the early hours of the morning, arriving back on the prison estate at about 3pm.

I had been watching the ex-prisoners' interaction with his close family, realising how difficult it had been for all of them whilst he had been inside.

One of the most powerful experiences was to hear how grateful his mother was that the Grendon staff had helped him to change his ways. However, as she spoke I also realised that there was a whole load of information that he had not disclosed to the staff group or any of the other prisoners.

By all accounts this boy was going to succeed and he had all the support he could ask for from his own family, his new wife and a very nice group of in-laws. However, there was something inside me that said all of this is not going to be enough for him.

Having listened to his account of his crimes back at the prison, he had convinced everyone that he had got into burglary to provide for his family. He had described an invalid father and alcoholic mother who struggled to make ends meet. The first burglary he did (according to him) was encouraged by a friend who had always been in trouble with the police.

Watching his father throw himself around on the dance floor it was difficult to see how he could possibly be described as invalid? And later, hearing him boast about the success of his building company was even more confusing? As for mother's alcoholism, she was still on her feet at midnight having consumed only minimal amounts of sherry.

When speaking to his older brother I discovered he had a gambling and drug habit which had certainly not been examined as an issue at Grendon. The family had visited the prison regularly but had not had the opportunity of meeting any of the wing staff. When it had been suggested that he could arrange a family therapy group meeting, a last-minute excuse had prevented it from going ahead.

The other factor that concerned me was that the boy's outside probation officer had shown very little interest in the case. He claimed budgetary constraints and a heavy workload made regular visiting impossible. Significantly the probation officer had not been invited to the wedding.

In a nutshell, we were celebrating a success story having worked with only 50% of the available information. Some pretty important facts were missing. I did question this at the reception but of course his wedding day was not an appropriate place to talk about his failings.

Several staff had doubted his ability to stay out of trouble, so what were we doing here, pretending that he had done all the work he needed to do, undoubtedly endorsing some of the stories that he had given his parents about his time spent in Grendon, which were also inaccurate.

It all seemed so false and the prison had even donated money to buy him a wedding present!

In fact, the boy stayed out of prison for less than six weeks and his new bride was soon visiting him every fortnight in another jail, as he began a six-year sentence for Aggravated Burglary (A burglary where violent force is used), to fuel his drug habit.

This first experience and one or two more that followed made me determined that no matter who it was that I worked with, I would go out of my way to make sure I had as much information as possible. It was never going to be sufficient for me to simply take the prisoners word for it, or to accept that every piece of information that lay on our files was accurate.

In certain cases, if the family or friends couldn't come to me then I would go to them, sometimes very discreetly, to check things out for myself. This was way over and above the normal call of duty but I personally felt it was necessary.

This was the point at which my working life began to overlap into my social time and on many occasions the "professional boundaries" ceased to exist. I made a conscious effort to have as much contact as I could with ex-prisoners and their family and friends, in their home areas if possible.

This was not always to check out the accuracy of information. Often I was invited and the social contact was allowed by the Governor "in furtherance of his therapy". I was given permission in writing, so there was never any come-back on me.

I had enjoyed several days and nights out with ex-prisoners and their families, so it didn't have to be just a tiresome chore. Over the years, I would enjoy attending birthday parties, weddings, christenings etc. It was never all work and no play.

The young prisoners were not assessed prior to arriving at Grendon but we would receive a large amount of information from the sending prison. Boys were referred through Prison Medical Officers or Probation Officers. There was a reasonable amount to begin with and I would always cross reference this information with accounts from close family and friends, during prison visits or in the community.

Each boy was assessed as soon as they arrived on the wing and then again, every three months. A small reception group was set up to welcome them onto the wing. As soon as the vacancy arose for a new staff member I put my name forward to run it. The advantage here was that I could assess their motivation and commitment from day one.

I was also the first officer they would meet on arrival so it was important that I was able to give the right kind of encouragement, able to send out the right signals. The main advice I gave was that Grendon will be a difficult place to be. If they had come just for a comfortable ride then they'd be better to leave right now.

Most of the lads came from local catchment areas such as Aylesbury, Oxford, Swindon, Milton Keynes, London and Northampton. Therefore, a reasonable amount of contact following their release was not too difficult for me. I felt it was rewarding for me to witness their success and a mark of respect for the prisoners I had a working relationship with and had formed friendships with.

Many professionals will no doubt condemn me for pushing the boundaries as far as I did but that has never concerned me too much. I believed all of my additional contact placed me in a position of being better informed than most others.

I am writing this book almost 40 years later and I believe my efforts have been rewarded many times over.

The first prisoner that I can say I really got along with was Paul T.

Paul came from Northampton. I knew from the first day he arrived on the wing and before he started his assessment process, he would fit in well with the other lads on the small therapy group that I ran. I had not read any of his prison record or pre-sentence reports but it was obvious he was well educated, and had a strong motivation to work on his faults and weaknesses. He had a real motivation to change.

Paul's offences were interesting. He had done a series of burglaries in and around the Northampton area, but the most surprising fact was that the burglaries had been done whilst he was a serving Police Officer. He had reported each crime and had been assigned to each case as the first on scene, investigating officer.

What struck me immediately was that his upbringing and school achievements were much the same as my own and he came from a very normal middle class background.

He had been bored on the night shifts and had committed some very petty crimes in order to go through the process of investigation. As the person who had done the crime, he got to meet the owners of the property (the victims) and very few burglars are ever in that situation.

He claimed that some of his excitement came from the fact that they didn't realise that he was the offender. This makes his crimes even more deplorable not simply because he was employed in a position of great trust but also because he had "victim awareness" immediately after the crimes and still went on to commit more.

Eventually the burglaries would also supplement a poor income as a young PC.

I worked with him very closely and although I always believed that he was being open and honest with me, I felt it was worth checking a few things out, particularly his family background and social connections.

He had impressed the staff during his first week on the wing by disclosing that several prisoners were using Cannabis. Given the fact that all the prisoners knew he used to be a copper placed him in an awkward position. He had stated from the outset that he was anti-drugs but I was left wondering if in fact this was a way of trying to convince us further. However, he coped with the pressure of being labelled a "grass" and continued to work on his own issues.

I met his mum and his sister on the first visit and was really impressed by their attitude, their willingness to help the staff to help Paul, but also the deep sadness and shame they felt to see him in prison clothing having destroyed a valuable career. I continued to pop up to the visits on Paul's invitation each time they came in but was surprised that his father didn't visit?

"Dad's struggling to cope with me being in prison," he said sadly "I know he will support me but he still thinks this is just like any other prison."

"Perhaps we should put in for you to have a day out with me" I said, "so that you can talk to him on home territory, I could convince him that this place is different but also it would be useful to have a family group at some point." Paul thought this was a great idea and eventually I managed to get permission to drive him to his family home.

It was relatively easy to arrange for a visit to strengthen the family ties, depending on the distance involved and the overall cost. As this was almost on the doorstep, I didn't get much resistance.

The meeting with his father went very well and he agreed to attend for the next visit at the prison. I was made very welcome at the house and we talked openly about how it had felt when Paul was first arrested.

There was a photograph of him in his police uniform above the fireplace and his father joked that perhaps they could stick his prison mug shot alongside it?

Before we left to go back to the prison they asked if I would like to meet up with them for a drink at some point and I said fine, I would bring my wife with me also. In Paul's case, there were no future problems and he went on to build a successful future as far as I am aware.

But, of course, for every successful story there were always half a dozen or more failures.

Rob H arrived from Aylesbury Prison and was assessed as a borderline case for therapy. He had been involved in fights and the information from the Security Department was that he may have been responsible for bringing drugs into the previous prison.

When I interviewed him on reception I was not impressed with his motivation and felt that he showed little commitment to change his ways.

A report from a Landing Officer at Aylesbury said "this boy is a thoroughly bad lot and is responsible for most of the problems on the wing. Having spent the past 3 months in and out of the block (Segregation Unit), his only chance might be a period at Grendon Prison."

This was often the sort of recommendation for therapy that we received from Prisons who simply wanted to get rid of a thorough nuisance. Dr Snell (Therapist) had warned, "if the prison is used as a dumping ground for troublesome prisoners, the therapy will fail".

The Medical Officers report was even more conclusive "A young man who has an extremely serious addiction, having used Heroin since the age of ten. Any form of therapeutic intervention will not work until he has undertaken a period of detoxification in a specialised unit. At this stage, he is refusing to accept that he has a problem."

I told him that I was prepared to help him, but first of all he had to want to help himself. Was he prepared to work hard enough to change his offending behaviour? His response was "All I have to do is stop fucking robbing that's my problem, nothing else" Rob said, and he added "but I ain't gonna be brainwashed."

"What about the drugs" I asked. He replied, "I only do drugs in jail, it helps the bird go quicker and is a nice little earner." Rob was a prime example of a prisoner who had clearly not volunteered to come to Grendon. If he had, it was only for a change of scenery so he was perhaps never motivated to look at his faults.

According to some of the more experienced staff this was a problem that Grendon had suffered since the day it first opened and would be a problem that would continue for many years. No doubt, there are still problems in Grendon, with men who are simply there to play the system or have been told they must do therapy rather than volunteering to do it.

After only a few weeks it was obvious to most of the uniformed staff that the atmosphere on the wing had changed. We all suspected that Rob's arrival was more than just coincidental but we had no evidence that could support moving him, other than he was clearly not interested in therapy. This in itself should have been enough. However, the prison's Senior Medical Officer Dr Barrett felt that he deserved an equal chance and stopped all attempts that were made to transfer him.

Again, this was a frequent problem that Prison Officers faced. Although it was rarely voiced, the opinion of some Psychiatrist's, Psychologist's and other Senior Medical staff was that Prison Officers were not qualified to make such judgements.

It was perfectly acceptable to allow them to run therapy groups with little or no training at all. But it was not acceptable that we can make a final judgement on a prisoner's suitability for treatment.

Officers were not considered to be "professionals" in that sense.

If we were being forced to keep him, Rob was going to be very hard work.

Eventually I met his family in the Visit's Centre and was even less impressed with them, especially by the three brothers who had all served lengthy sentences for drug offences. They ridiculed the Grendon regime and Rob was happy to go along with it all. Our meeting was less than friendly as he had told them that I was always on his case, blaming him for everything.

This was not completely true. I didn't blame him for everything, obviously, but I did let him know that I thought he was wasting his time and everybody else's.

I felt very strongly that he was damaging the therapeutic community. The problem that developed for me was that Rob had made a significant effort to convince other people of his innocence. He knew that the Senior Medical Officer was on his side, so he quickly learned to keep his head down and say the right things at the right time.

Having had some contact with his family during visiting times, I could sense that whatever story he had told them about me it wasn't good. There were the odd comments made under their breath and of course the "evil eye" now and then, but nothing more than that.

What made the situation even more difficult was that I had met up with an ex-prisoner who had been discharged a couple of weeks previously. He confirmed that Rob was bringing drugs into the wing and that he had become "top dog".

I was often given information by ex-prisoners about the stuff that went on up on the landings out of view of the staff.

The prisoners referred to their own style of "Recess Therapy" and although Grendon boasted a strict No Violence rule, now and again lads would fight it out in the toilet areas to prove who was the toughest and this was never openly brought to the attention of staff.

He said that Rob had got himself into the position of top dog very quickly and most of his reputation came from the previous prison. He didn't necessarily have to fight any more to prove his strength.

I asked him to put it all in writing for me but he wasn't prepared to. If anybody found out about it Rob's family would "do him" as they came from the same area of Northampton.

I offered the former prisoner's information to the Security Department but it was not logged. The Security Principal Officer laughed as he told me, "You can't trust the word of an ex con, didn't you now they've all been in trouble with the police."

There was very little gathering of intelligence in the early days of Grendon as the regime generally managed to reveal any important issues, through the therapy process, but sometimes that process would break down.

To satisfy my own curiosity, I decided to take a look at Rob's home area and to judge how influential the family was.

He had talked about a couple of pubs that his family used from time to time and as they were on my route into the City Centre, I decided to drop in. I had been using a nightclub called PJ's, in Northampton, which was owned by a guy who I'd met when he was doing a sentence in Springhill prison. He allowed prison officers free admission and the odd free drink so it was always good to finish the night off in there.

The only obligation was that if there was any trouble in his club, we would assist the door staff.

The visit to Rob's home area just confirmed everything I had suspected. He was only using Grendon as a means to a more comfortable prison experience rather than any personal journey of change.

Over the next couple of weeks my feelings about Rob was justified by an incident on the wing.

The prison had been forced to take in a group of nine prisoners from Feltham Borstal, even though we had protested that this amount of new arrivals would further damage the regime. Our pleas were ignored and about half a dozen of these prisoners caused total mayhem.

They threatened violence towards staff and prisoners, particularly those who were in for sex offences. They armed themselves with pool balls and large PP9 batteries in socks and went on the rampage one evening, also setting fire to a settee which was in one of the dormitories.

Eight prisoners were escorted out to Glen Parva Borstal and amongst this group was Rob H, who had quickly allied himself to the newcomers.

He did return to Grendon later and as a much older prisoner for a fairly successful period in therapy, and looking back, I suppose he was just not ready in 1981.

However as soon as he and the others had gone, normal service was resumed and other prisoners revealed the full extent of his bullying and intimidation

In the aftermath of the G wing unrest the staff were blamed for the breakdown in control, even though our concerns had been well documented when the troublemakers first arrived.

In what I considered to be a very unfair move, the entire community of staff and prisoners on G wing were exchanged for their counterparts on F wing. However, for me and the rest of the team, this bizarre move proved to be a valuable bonus.

Chapter 7

F wing had been originally intended to house female prisoners but the Home Office had decided not to proceed with this. Instead, it was used for young male prisoners.

It was a smaller unit than G wing, housing 30 inmates. This included a small dormitory which was converted into a bed-sit for boys who were approaching their release. It was called "The Discharge Flat" and boys were taken into town, to shop for themselves and to learn to cook prior to release.

We only had a total of twenty-five boys who were split into four groups for therapy purposes, so this allowed the staff to devote more time to each individual. I ran a group entirely on my own to begin with, which allowed me to develop my own style of working within the new therapeutic structure that the prisoners and staff had developed.

The new regime gave me more scope to continue to work and to socialise with ex-prisoners and their families, so I suppose the work with offenders still occupied 60 - 70% of my life.

Prison Officers are forced to leave their personal problems at the prison gate on the way in but now and then they must cope with all manner of personal problems whilst trying to support prisoners and this can be an extremely frustrating process. Eventually emotions are bound to rise to the surface.

I have always been far from perfect and occasionally my personal feelings overshadowed my work. Over the years of working in therapy I had gained some valuable personal insight but my anger had always been an area of concern to those who knew me well.

Fortunately, I am older and wiser now but 40 years ago it was a different story and on this occasion, I was not coping with problems outside of prison very well at all and one particular prisoner became a target for my frustration.

For about a fortnight a prisoner called Pete H had been purposely trying to wind me up by reporting late for roll calls and hiding away when it came to lock up at the end of the evening. I had strong words with him on a couple of occasions but he continued to ignore me.

On one evening, everybody else was locked away by eight thirty and Pete, as usual, was nowhere to be seen.

I could have used the prison disciplinary procedures and placed him on a charge for "not being in a place where he was required to be". However, it was the tradition in Grendon to deal with difficulties by using the therapeutic process. This means asking a prisoner to talk to his group about the problem, or else to bring the problem to the attention of the whole wing via the full Community Meeting.

A special meeting could be called in emergency situations and of course I should have been keeping my colleagues informed about my personal issues, instead of allowing them to become worse.

I felt my anger increasing as I searched for him around the wing then I heard him call from his cell. "Ah, ah, I'm in here, you mug."

I told him that I had looked in his cell a few seconds earlier and he wasn't there then, so where had he been? "Why didn't you look under the fucking bed?" he smirked.

This triggered something powerful in me and I grabbed him by the neck and threw him against the wall, spilling the jug of tea he was holding all over the cell floor. "Listen to me, you fucking little shit" I raged "carry on taking the piss out of me and I'll smash you all over this fucking cell."

I turned and slammed the cell door behind me, shaking uncontrollably and made my way up the landing towards the office. As I passed the prisoner in the last cell, he shouted "Nice one Joe, it's about time the little twat got a good dig."

Then the enormity of what I had done hit me.

I had committed an assault against a prisoner and risked losing my job.

The Officer who was on duty with me had heard the commotion and asked what had happened? I knew if I told him the truth he would also be compromised, so I said it had just been a bit of horseplay. We were always play-fighting with the boys so it was nothing new to hear raised voices on the landings or even the odd threats of violence.

I didn't sleep at all that night worrying about what I might face when I arrived at work in the morning.

I decided to go straight to the Chiefs office on my way in and explain the situation. But then I decided to wait until I got to the wing and tell the staff team before we unlocked.

Whatever happened, I felt I could not keep this to myself, particularly in a place like Grendon.

When I arrived on the wing, the Night Patrol Officer handed me a note which had been handed to him during the night.

The note read as follows: "Joe, I want to talk to you when you come on duty, about last night. Pete.

Two things entered my head, one, it might be better not to say anything to anybody until I had spoken to him, and two, was he still holding some feelings against me and would I be at risk if I went down to his cell alone?

I decided to risk a one to one chat with him and went to the cell straight after we had unlocked everybody else.

What happened next was to mark a huge turning point in my career.

When I entered the cell, Pete offered to shake my hand and said "I'm sorry about last night. I've been thinking about what I was doing and I'm sorry I pissed you off."

I shook Pete's hand and told him that it was I who should be sorry." No matter what you did I had no right to grab you like I did, I should have controlled myself."

Pete then said that nobody had seen me grab him so there were no witnesses and if I said anything he would deny anything happened. He also said that most of the boys had heard me shouting at him but nobody heard a threat being made, so it was no good me making a big issue out of it.

I asked him if he had been threatened by anybody to keep quiet about this but he told me he hadn't. "I see what I do to people and I've gotta sort it out" he added "not only that but the lads straightened me out on a few things about you during the night."

Pete told me that I had gained a lot of respect from the prisoners because of the way I treated them. My friendly attitude and willingness to help anybody was something that most of them had rarely seen in a prison before, "especially from a screw". He had been reminded that for me to be affected like I was last night must mean that he had really pushed me over the edge.

It was good to know that the prisoners felt this way about me, but I told Pete that I did have a few problems of my own that needed sorting out and last night's reaction hadn't all been because of him. However, before I left the cell I said, "Just accept that you are a pain in the arse at times but that doesn't't make you a totally bad bloke."

I did inform the staff team about what had happened and told them that I had lost my temper with him, shouted and pushed him. They were concerned about me and urged me to talk to them about my difficulties.

I felt supported and was also able to share some of my personal stuff on the community meeting, including giving praise for the way that Pete had handled our confrontation; after all he had been more controlled than I had.

This incident, more than other, showed me how unique the Grendon regime was and how valuable the work was to me. But it also showed how I needed to get some professional help for my own demons!

Pete and I remained friends until he moved on from Grendon. I recall he did very well in therapy, receiving one of the first Duke of Edinburgh Awards that was given out and he was visited by the late Sir Patrick Moore (Astronomer) who assisted him towards completing this achievement.

I am thankful to Pete for his ability to turn a disastrous situation into something positive for both of us and I sincerely hope he went on to achieve his goals and stayed out of prison.

The policies that F wing prisoners agreed to were the same as those on the adult wings.

However, there were always differences in the way that each wing implemented them. The Golden Rule was that "a prisoner may find himself being transferred if he commits an act of violence against anybody or if he provokes an act of violence." But on the adult wings the policy reads "a prisoner will be transferred etc .

The feeling behind this was that there are various levels of violence, ranging from spitting at a person, to using an offensive weapon. And because young men were considered to be more volatile and susceptible to violent outbursts, we accepted that there may be regular outbursts and each must be judged on its merits and we would not over-react to any show of aggression. In fact, there were times when aggression in the formal groups was actively provoked!

This was always a difficult call and there were occasions when it took a couple of hours of debate to decide a prisoner's fate.
If we were working effectively with violent young men we had to expect a certain amount of acting out of hostility.

Bearing in mind the prison housed some of the UK's most violent and disturb prisoners, there were very few incidents of serious violence.

It had taken me over three years to grasp the significance of working in Grendon as opposed to other prisons. In this time, I had done numerous detached duties, at prisons such as Brixton, Pentonville, Wormwood Scrubs and Oxford. Grendon's social atmosphere couldn't be found anywhere else in the country and it was due to the relaxed less formal pattern of relationships, which stretched right the way up to the Medical Superintendent (Governor).

As I progressed in therapy and my confidence and experience grew, then my relationship with prisoners was enhanced. It wasn't necessarily the case that prisoners behaved any better but I learned diverse ways of coping with such behaviour. And it wasn't simply due to the small therapy groups, but also because officers and prisoners spent a lot of time together in the evenings and at weekends.

In my case, I had also used my relationship with their families and friends outside of the prison. By the end of 1981 I had produced my own individual blueprint for working with offenders and was testing it out on a regular basis, to reasonably good effect.

Grendon continued to give plenty of scope for officers to be involved with prisoner's outside of the prison environment and The Duke of Edinburgh's Award Scheme was one such example.

The scheme was started in 1977 by SOPEI Peter Alland who ran the prison gymnasium. In 1984, it already had three gold, eight silver and nine bronze awards, so the scheme was very popular with Young Prisoners and the younger more energetic staff, which included me at this stage. Activities ranged from Cooking to Canoeing, Bird Watching to Rock Climbing.

The lads needed to be assessed on the spot by experts, so Prison Staff had to develop their own expertise in a variety of fields to be able to direct and instruct entrants to the scheme.

Grendon's Farm Foreman, Colin Lennox, was so successful in developing his own abilities in Rock Climbing that he ended up in Buckingham Palace to receive his own Gold Award.

I chose to do Orienteering and Mountain Leadership which gave me yet another ideal opportunity to work with offenders in the community, literally out in the wilds.

By the summer of 1983, I was looking towards a change of direction. I had been working with Young Prisoners for almost six years. I had been spending more and more time in the Gym involved with the Weight-Lifting and the Boxing Club. So, it was suggested that I might like to consider training as a Physical Education Instructor.

At this stage I suppose I was feeling that something was missing from my therapeutic work and some of the job satisfaction was starting to disappear. It was obvious that Grendon could operate a therapeutic approach to the treatment of prisoners within quite a controlled setting. It helped them to build more confidence, a better attitude towards each other and towards the staff. But my experience was that this didn't transfer very easily to other settings outside of prison.

With many young prisoners, the change was often short lived and Grendon should have been aiming at helping them to avoid criminal behaviour after release.

Unfortunately, there were no resources to do follow up work with people in the community. I had been busy attempting this alone, without any funding, over a four-year period and had worn myself out in the process. Not to mention how much it had cost me to travel all over the country, during my extra-curricular activities and the pressure it had placed on my personal relationships.

The other problem at this stage was that there was too much emphasis being placed on the normal operational duties, with not enough hours in the day to balance them out with the therapeutic role and therefore I was getting no real personal achievement or satisfaction at the end of it all.

Resources had been cut back and it wasn't unusual for prisoners to sit on their own on a therapy group without a member of staff.

I was finding myself regularly detailed to the Operations Group and I found myself to be sitting on a chair some days, and watching scaffolding for a whole shift, whilst there was no continuity on the therapy groups.

Robbie Macpherson a Principal Psychologist put it across well when he said, "As long as therapy remains everybody's business, the business will remain therapy" but for now I was looking for a change.

I decided to take up a training course as a Physical Education Instructor. I had put a great deal of effort into improving my personal fitness levels and Pete Alland felt that I had the right qualities for this role. Furthermore, the work of the PE Department was structured to complement the therapeutic treatment programme.

I was pleased to have passed the Pre-selection course at HMP Stanford Hill on the Isle of Sheppey and while I waited to go to HMP Kirkham near Blackpool, for the second stage of the training, it was decided that I would work full time with Peter Alland in the Gym.

I thoroughly enjoyed the next three months. I was supervising prisoners in small games sessions, such as Football, Volleyball and Basketball. We were also organising the Annual Summer Sports which took place on the large sports field at the rear of the prison.

Dr Ray Gillett was the prison Medical Superintendent. He was an absolute mountain of a man and it was rumoured he had been a competitive weight-lifter as a young man.
Unfortunately, it would appear that he had not trained for many years but had perhaps carried on eating enormous amounts of food, I could only estimate that he weighed in excess of thirty stone.

Dr Gillett had a particular interest in the connection between offending behaviour and individual body types. So, in order to complete his studies, the Gym was required to conduct Samatotype tests on prisoners a few days after their arrival.

The tests set out to distinguish between the three basic physiques. An Ectomorph would be seen to be of large build, pear or barrel shaped and apparently overweight. An Endomorph was the exact opposite, slim build, lean and wiry. Whereas the Mesomorph was of muscular build, strong and athletic.

The theory was that Mesomorphs were more prone to crimes of violence, murder, GBH, or Robbery etc. It was felt that, in prison, they required a physical outlet for their aggression.

It gave us an ideal opportunity to recommend remedial PE or to recommend extra periods of PE for those who needed to control their anger, thus giving them the physical as well as mental outlet for their anger management.

I conducted numerous tests over a period of nine months which proved to be initially a very embarrassing process, for me and newly arrived prisoners.

The process was quite a shock to new arrivals.

On his first day of reception the prisoner would be taken into an empty room and was invited to strip down to his underpants. Using "Fat Calipers", I would take measurements from six areas of the body. Dr Gillett would take a seat behind me and record all measurements, and then I would ask the prisoner to flex four of the major muscle groups.

I would then feel each muscle and rate it on a scale from 1 to 7, seven being hard and one being very soft.
These figures would be once again carefully recorded.

From the information taken, the combined figures would be cross referenced in a book of body types. The book contained hundreds of pictures of naked international athletes.

The conclusion was reached by asking the prisoner to take off his underpants, while Dr Gillett and I compared him, completely naked, against the pictures in the book.

You can imagine the reaction of many prisoners to this very intrusive form of scrutiny within one or two days of their arrival. However, we never had anybody who refused to be tested, but I doubt that this process would be well received by today's prison population or even by other professionals.

But, Grendon was always experimenting with new techniques for the control and examination of aggression, which proved to be highly successful. However, nowadays, in our more politically correct society, with our overindulgence in human rights such methods might now create a public outcry.

For instance, Boxing or sparring in the Gym which led to some young boys competing in outside Boxing Tournaments was scorned by some members of the medical profession. Indeed, many felt that teaching violent young men to continue their violence was ethically wrong. However, we could constructively channel their aggressive behaviour into a recognised sporting activity and gradually through the use of therapy, eliminate it completely.

The Prison Department decided they couldn't risk bad publicity.

Speaking of aggression, another technique that I personally used on occasions was to ask an aggressive prisoner to agree to be tied to a chair during therapy meetings. When restrained, he was not able to hit out or smash up when his personal issues were being examined.

He would learn to verbalise his feelings constructively, in a very caring and supportive environment, eventually learning to fully control the urge to act out hostility. Not one of the boys and men involved in this process said that they felt abused. Instead, they all reported that it was a positive step towards their personal rehabilitation. But of course, this would never be allowed to take place in the Grendon of today or anywhere else for that matter.

I used to meet up with one man who went through this process many years ago and he jokingly introduced me to his wife as "the man who introduced him to bondage".

Unfortunately, over a couple of decades Grendon's approach to dealing with aggression has become more mainstream and it appears that the current policy is to tolerate displays of physical aggression much less. In early Grendon history, a prisoner "smashing up" was not uncommon and the use of restraint during therapy meetings occurred frequently, with the prisoner concerned being allowed to continue his therapy.

Results with violent prisoners were remarkable and it was an area that I received special recognition for, but sadly times have changed and the triggers to anger are not explored in as much depth and displays of aggression are tolerated less.

I failed to make the grade as a PEI because I had very poor ball skills, particularly Basketball and terrible co-ordination. I was invited to improve my skills and return at a later date, but I think it was fairly obvious to me and other colleagues that I was already missing the group therapy work.

So, when the opportunity arose, I applied to return to the therapeutic communities and after very careful consideration chose to go to C Wing.

I quickly settled in to the wing and became involved in the group therapy again, finding that the adult prisoners were much easier to work with than the young offenders.

The majority had come through the Borstal and Detention Centre experience and had an average of about ten previous convictions. Their life histories and experiences provided plenty of scope for examination and many of the men were in their late twenties to early thirty's, which I felt was the age that most people are more susceptible to change.

The regime on the wing was not that different from anywhere else. The policies were similar and the content of the meetings was surprisingly the same.

I met one or two prisoners that I got on very well with and the first interesting character that I came across was a man who I shall refer to as Daniel S. He was younger than most of the other men and I had already been warned about his ability to spin a good tale. I was to be his personal officer, so it was important that I got to know as much as I could about his background.

When we first met, Daniel spent more than one and a half hours telling me about his life story.

He spoke about a very rich and privileged lifestyle; mixing with various film stars and celebrities and being cared for by a nanny, because his parents were very busy media executives. He also talked about a brother and sister who were in the American Police force.

He told me his sister had become something of a local hero, after a grizzly bear had escaped from the local zoo. She had apparently arrived home to find the bear sprawled out on her carpet. She restrained it and returned it safely to the zoo.

His brother had also apparently foiled an armed robbery. There had been a shoot-out leaving three men dead.

I listened to a string of experiences he had with comedy stars such as Spike Milligan, Michael Bentine and Morecambe and Wise, before I finally got him to talk about the offence he was in jail for, which was Burglary & Arson.

Daniel had committed a burglary at the home of a pensioner. Very little of value had been taken. However, he said that he had accidentally set fire to the house before he left and the pensioner who had been asleep upstairs had died in the blaze. It had been classed as manslaughter rather than murder, so he had a date of release after 6 years.

Over a period of time I began to dismantle his stories, to get to the real truth and attempt to find out why he had done what he had. Surprisingly, a great deal of what I had been told was true but the most difficult aspect of this crime had been the lack of apparent motive. But, Daniel did not have any brothers or sisters, so the American tales were false.

He was the only son of two very successful people. His mother was the Editor of a leading women's magazine and his father was a TV executive. His parents had split up a few years previously and both visited him separately. I met them on several occasions in order to build up a complete picture of Daniel's life.

Both parties were thoroughly decent, nice people, who were clearly shocked by their son's situation. Mother wanted to believe that he had been led astray, but father was more grounded and sensible about the situation. He realised that his son may have been affected by their chaotic lifestyles and of course by a reasonably difficult divorce.

It was true that he had been brought up by a nanny in a very privileged household. He lacked nothing materialistically, but it soon became obvious to me that he had little affection shown directly towards him by either parent. The most critical issue was his lack of self-esteem.

He appeared to be an under achiever who was desperate for recognition. Most of his stories were made up to improve his position in the prison hierarchy but sadly he was viewed by many as a bit of an idiot.

Working with him was like working with a child, but he was a likeable rogue and in a very brief time we developed a mutual trust and confidence. I could remind him of his tall tales and would also remind him of the story of "Pinocchio".

In some ways, he was not unlike the puppet in his appearance. Daniel had not been crafted from wood but he had been crafted by two people who wanted a child that they could provide for, who would achieve the success they both had. Unfortunately, Daniel let them down time and time again. He had no Jiminy Cricket or Good Fairy so he had to make his own confused decisions.

There is no doubt in my mind that he did the burglaries as a source of excitement but there was also no doubt in my mind that the fire was no accident. Perhaps he did not know that there was anybody asleep upstairs, but he did know that the fire would get him noticed. This was his way of letting people know how dangerous he could be, if he chose to be.

Another important aspect of his personality was to continuously play the victim. In almost every scenario of his life somebody would pity the poor little rich kid and even in this tragic crime, in which a frail innocent old man lost his life, Daniel was to be pitied.

He didn't know the old man was there, people would say "he must feel awful, he will have to live with that for the rest of his life."

I did not allow him to immerse himself in self-pity.

But, the truth is that people who kill and maim others don't feel bad all of the time and even in therapeutic communities there is plenty of laughter. Daniel always enjoyed the odd practical joke along with others. "Prison Humour" is the black comedy that helps to keep people sane in a world full of tragedy and pain.

Eventually Daniel's good fairy arrived on the wing in the shape of a visiting trainee nurse, who attended one of the C wing social evenings. Helen and Daniel met and fell in love. Then they planned to live together on his eventual release.
And so they did.... Except in this story they didn't live happily ever after.

Daniel and Helen initially lived together in the nursing quarters, in a hospital in Essex. One night Daniel discovered a fire raging in the hospital laundry. He raised the alarm and attempted to put the fire out. He was praised as a hero and gave evidence to the police describing the man he saw running from the scene.

Police quickly realised that the man he had described bore a remarkable likeness to him and later on, when questioned further, he admitted that it was he who started the fire?
This time, for this Arson attack he received a Life Sentence and the undivided attention of his parents once again. Oh, yes and of course the loyalty of Helen, his good fairy.

He was never allowed to return to Grendon - very few people are given a second chance and as Grendon can only accommodate less than one percent of the total prison population spaces at that time were valuable and there was always a waiting list in excess of 200, which is not the case today!

Grendon is all about victim awareness.

One of the main aspects of my own work has been to get offenders to own up to their faults and weaknesses and to change their pattern of behaviour so that there are no more victims.

The truth was, Grendon's track record at this point was not particularly good, with a success rate of around twenty percent, compared to about fifteen percent within the normal prison population. This was based on reconviction rates, but success could be measured on many distinct levels and there were many who we referred to as "Grendon Successes".

A Grendon success was a man who had been extremely violent in his previous prisons. However, having spent only a brief period in the regime and being transferred out of therapy, back to the previous prison, his behaviour was improved one hundred percent.
Other prisons would contact Grendon and say, "We don't know what you've done with this man but compared to the one that left, he's an angel."

The other form of dubious success is a man who was convicted of offences against the person, i.e. Rape or GBH, but is then reconvicted for petty theft or handling stolen goods. This suggests an area of improvement, although there are still victims of course, but at least the offences are no longer directly against the person or as severe.

On occasions the Grendon men would be victims themselves. Indeed, many had been abused as children then went on to abuse others. They were also attacked by other prisoners.

I spoke earlier about some unusual therapeutic techniques.

At times, I would purposely steal a small item from the cell of a man who was serving time for Burglary, who could not apparently understand how it feels to be a victim. Many burglars state that they have no victim empathy because they rarely meet their victims. Once the man realises something has been stolen from his cell he will report the matter to the staff complaining "Some dirty bastards been in my pad (Cell) and nicked my cassette tape. If I catch him I'll chop his fucking fingers off!"

He will of course be advised to talk the feelings through on the therapy group.

At the stage when he is really beginning to know what it feels like to be a victim, I would boldly declare "I'm glad you now know what it feels like to be robbed. Let me put your mind at rest, it was ME who stole it." I would then fetch the stolen item from the staff locker room or office and return it to him during a very animated discussion about the effects of crime.

This method succeeded on many occasions. But unfortunately, on one occasion when I went to retrieve the item from the locker room it had been stolen, obviously by somebody with a key?

I was called to the Governor's office to account for my actions and the prison had to buy the man a new Sony Walkman cassette tape player. Needless to say, I didn't do any more "therapeutic burglaries".

We were also always on our guard for any drug abuse, which was more often than not, Cannabis. Just after my arrival on C Wing I informed the small therapy group I was running, that I suspected one of them, or maybe more, were smoking Cannabis. With confidence, I announced "At bang up last night, I could smell weed on the group landing."

Of course, the men denied it, but I kept bringing the subject up every couple of days. One particular prisoner, Dave B said "Why don't you give it a fucking rest. You're like a fucking sniffer dog and just as useless." I inherited the nickname "Sniffer" and whenever I went upstairs prisoners would shout "Sniffer on the landing."

Totally unconnected to this, I had begun to play practical jokes on one or two of the prisoners that I got on with, especially Steve R. He would continuously leap out at me when I least expected it, following which there would be a fairly realistic play fight.

He would also fall to his knees in front of me, especially when there were visitors around and embarrassingly beg "Please don't hit me again sir. I'll do anything you say Sir."

In return, at lock up, I would sometimes hide underneath his bed and when he entered the cell I would grab his ankles and bark like a dog. On every occasion, I would almost frighten him to death. However, on one such occasion things took a fortunate turn, depending how it is viewed.

One evening, I held my breath as I waited for Steve to enter the cell. Then just as I was about to grab his feet I heard another voice. "I'll look out for the screws. You've gotta work fast how many is there?" This was Dave B's voice, whispering to Steve, who replied, "Just four pieces. Tom and Billy have had theirs."

As I peeped out from beneath the bed it was obvious that Steve was dealing Cannabis.

I suddenly began to feel very uncomfortable. What would happen if Steve realised I was hiding under the bed? I froze solid and held my breath for so long I thought I would collapse. The risk of being taken hostage was very real!

Fortunately, within a few minutes the two men left the cell and headed off down the landing. I quickly got out from under the bed and left the cell without being seen. I then went down to the staff office and noted down the parts of the conversation I could remember. I was shaking for some time after, and it was difficult to face Steve when I locked him up that evening.

Having put in a report to the Security Department, I knew that I would have to explain the fact that I was lying under a prisoner's bed at the time. Needless to say, I was given a stern warning about any future acts of stupidity.

I suppose I could have said that I was standing outside the cell door but this would spoil the plan that I had for tomorrow's group.

Next day, the small group therapy meeting began as normal. Then I introduced the usual issue "Let's have another look at the cannabis issue and how some members of this group are dealing it and using it" I said confidently.

"Oh, for fucks sake, don't you get fucking bored with the same old obsession?" Dave B sighed. So, I asked "Do you and Steve deny knowledge of any drugs on the wing?" Steve began to get angry. "What the fuck are you going on about?"

"How does this sound then" I asked. "Last night just before bang up, Dave said, I'll look out for the screws. You've got to work fast. How many is there? and you replied, just four pieces, Tom and Billy have had theirs." The two prisoners stared at me in disbelief and so I decided to force the issue.

"Would you like to hear more of what was said as you dished out the weed Steve?" I offered "it's all well recorded". I made them think that I had recorded the full conversation, which I had, but not on tape but on paper.

"I can't believe you've had the front to bug his cell. Somebody must have grassed us up? "Dave was furious that another prisoner would give the staff information, but he was also worried that he might be transferred out over it. Still pretending that I got the information from another source, I argued "It's not grassing Dave. Let's call it therapeutic feedback, shall we?"

Both men decided to own up to using cannabis and the wing held two special meetings so that others, who were also guilty, could admit to the problem. The staff were happy to grant an amnesty to anybody who would own up to using drugs.

But, it was declared that if anybody was found out after the final meeting, they would be automatically transferred out of the jail.
On the strength of this, fifteen out of the thirty prisoners on the wing admitted their involvement. Seven had directly used it and eight were compromised, because they knew about it.

During the final debate, Steve asked me where I got the information from in the first place. But, I replied by asking him another question" Where should you always check as soon as you enter your cell, especially when I'm on duty?" His mouth dropped wide open and he said "Oh no, I don't fucking believe it. You were under my bed you slimy bastard."

Steve and Dave were given the chance to remain in therapy at Grendon and did extremely well. We kept in touch when he was released and four years later, I got an invitation to his wedding. He became the proud father of twin boys and is still out of prison at the time of writing.

Although, I did ask him to check under his bed on the wedding night, just in case!

Sadly, despite several success stories, C wing soon became another bad experience and I was to face the biggest dilemma of my career so far.

Apart from Jackie Lynch, the wing Probation Officer, there was no other member of the staff team, in my opinion, who showed any real interest in the ethos of the prison. The group therapy was struggling to survive, in a climate of suspicion and mistrust.

For the first time, I felt that I was being forced into the role of custodian and "keeper of the keys".

We had several electrical blackouts over a period of a week and the wing was plunged into complete darkness. Yet there was no trouble and no one was harmed.

On one occasion, Jackie had been led by the hand from her office to an area of safety by a prisoner who was serving eight years for a violent rape. There was nowhere in the prison system safer than Grendon! And yet, the wing management proceeded to tighten the regime and enforce petty rules, which was seriously damaging the relationships between prisoners and staff.

The final straw, for me, came at Christmas time when Jackie bought a box of chocolates for a small group of prisoners.

I made the purchase on her behalf and brought them into the prison, something that I had done every year since 1977.

My manager warned her that it constituted "trafficking of illicit items" and she could therefore not give the prisoners the chocolates. This goodwill gesture was very much a part of the Grendon regime and had been for the past 22 years. Of course, the staff team showed no shame as they ate the chocs she had bought.

I felt it was time to make my feelings known and decided to withdraw from therapy groups completely, knowing that I might be moved to work in nearby Springhill Open Prison.

In a memo to the Chief Officer, I wrote: - Sir, Due to my constant dissatisfaction with certain policies and the administration of our regime at Grendon, I feel incapable of continuing in my present role of a group therapy officer. I will of course perform my duties as a prison officer to its fullest and I also realise that my actions could jeopardise my position on C wing. I do not feel any other reasons are required.

A verbal message came back from the Chief Officer, thanking me for my resignation from the Prison Service and the Wing Manager then gave me a direct order to continue to sit on the therapy group, which I then refused.

I responded again in writing: - I am advised that my memo to you as been taken as a possible resignation from my job as a prison officer. Let me state quite clearly that this is not the case and am amazed that it can be taken as such. Many Officers at Grendon have refused to sit on therapy groups and wing meetings without prejudice, and they are not being instructed to carry out this task as part of their normal duties. I have given you my reasons which are good enough.

For my sins, I was quickly moved to nearby Springhill Prison and the very next day I found myself supervising a cabbage patch on the prison allotments in the pouring rain. Oh dear, what a monumental error of judgement,

Chapter 8

Springhill prison housed about 250 prisoners in D category (very low security) conditions and the majority of the other prison officers had previously worked in Grendon. They had transferred to Springhill either because they needed a break from therapy or they were unsuitable to work in a therapeutic regime.

Here the prisoners required very little supervision and some even worked within the local community or on the prison officers' estate. There were no walls or fences to keep them in, so the majority were there on trust. Anyone who absconded would be arrested and returned to a more secure prison.

Although this was a low security prison, some of the prisoners held were at the end of long sentences for Manslaughter or Murder. But the majority were serving sentences of between eighteen months to six years. There was a small group of men who had committed the so called "white collar crimes" against their companies, mainly Fraud or embezzlement.

One prisoner who made my tea and coffee during the first day was a former Senior Policeman from the Thames Valley Police Force; apparently, he had been taking bribes.

It is quite a regular occurrence for staff to be chasing around the local fields after dark, looking for prisoners who are on the run or have gone to pick up parcels that may have been dropped in the hedgerows by family or friends. The saying goes "Crime doesn't pay," but for many in our Open Prison's at that time, the sentence is nothing more than an occupational hazard. Of course, things have changed now as assets are seized under a Confiscation Order.

I was asked to supervise the Farms and Garden's party, a group of twenty prisoners, who mainly worked inside a large compound next to Grendon Prison.

At 8 o clock in the morning the prisoners would gather on the parade ground (Springhill Car Park) for work parade.
As soon as we had confirmed the numbers available for work the officers would lead them off to various places of employment.

For the remainder of the shift, I had to ensure that the prisoners stayed within the Farms and Gardens compound.

The task could only be described as soul destroying, which is exactly what it did to me. The Grendon Chief Officer must have realised in less than a week I would be literally climbing the walls to get back into Grendon. I consumed so much coffee; I was in danger of a caffeine overdose and I only lasted three days before I had applied to return to therapy. It felt like I was turning into a bigger cabbage than those that grew in the Springhill Gardens.

Fortunately for me there was a new project being developed by Principal Officer Ian Booth. It was the re-opening of the Grendon Assessment Unit which was to be located on F Wing.

Ian had contacted me and suggested it might be a good move. I would be meeting prisoners as they arrived from other prisons and he wanted staff that had experience of working in therapy. It was an ideal opportunity, and I almost bit his hand off when it was finally offered. By this time, I had spent less than three months in Springhill but it felt more like three years.

The new Assessment Unit would give me an opportunity to review my approach to the job and to look towards further developing my therapeutic knowledge. I began to read the work of Freud, Jung and Maslow in an effort to gain more theoretical understanding, but, more importantly, to consolidate this learning with my practical skills.

One of my colleagues called me a "Therapeuton" because I was constantly analysing everything that happened. "Even if I fart" he remarked "you will find something deep and meaningful behind it."

I was back, working face to face, with very difficult and demanding prisoners who were arriving into Grendon, and they were very defensive and quite paranoid at times.
I soon realised that the experience of the past nine years was beginning to pay off.

I used the same method that I'd used on G wing. Trying to ensure that no stone was left unturned, getting to know each prisoner that arrived, and assessing their suitability for therapy. The process would take an average of six to eight weeks but one of the benefits of working on the Assessment Unit was that I got to know every prisoner in the jail eventually.

There wasn't time to get to know their families as well as I'd wanted, so a chance to sit on visits was valuable.

When men arrived in the prison Reception their reaction to the welcome they got was quite amusing at times. They would have been held under difficult conditions in a prison Segregation Block a few hours before, and then suddenly, they are being greeted by a smiling prison officer who offers to shake their hand.

"Hi, my name's Joe. Welcome to Grendon, what do people call you?" I would ask politely followed by "as soon as you've settled in, I'll make you a cup of coffee and we'll have a chat." You can imagine the possible response you might get from a prisoner who, previously, has been only used to being greeted with "Stand on the white line, give me your number, name and address me as sir."

It's easy to see why some prisoners think that there is some kind of ulterior motive for our friendliness. However, the only motive was to get them to relax as soon as possible, but perhaps, on some occasions, it had the reverse effect.
It was whilst working on the AU there was an incident that really tested my vulnerability and caused me to examine my method of communication with prisoners.

A new prisoner called Ian D had arrived for Assessment. His crime was particularly unusual and horrific. He was serving eight years for the kidnapping of a Policeman, who he had forced at knife point to drive from the south of England to Scotland.

On the journey, he had also forced the officer to stop the car on several occasions whilst he raped him. Ian was very openly homosexual and I was assigned as his Personal Officer.

We had several one to one interviews, during which he had revealed some disturbing aspects of his childhood and he was able to offer a reason, as opposed to a justification, for his offence against the policeman. I felt that he was motivated towards therapy and we were communicating very positively.

I arrived at work one evening and found Ian alone in the TV room. He was crying and clearly very distressed so I suggested we go into the office and talk.

Ian told me that he had become very attracted to somebody on the Wing and had started to develop fantasies about what he would like to do to him. So, I asked "Does the other man know how you feel about him and if not do you think you are able to share the feelings you have?" I advised him that there could be no confidentiality at Grendon and at some stage he would have to talk about the issues on the group or even in the larger community meeting. I told him "It's really positive that you are able to recognise these feelings at a point when no harm has been done. I can fully support you in your disclosure."

We talked about the content of his fantasies for about half an hour. The details he gave were very vivid. Ian became distraught and said, "I feel like I am losing control, but I don't want to hurt him" I reassured him that the other person would be protected and supported by the community. Then I enquired "Are you able to tell me the person's name?"

Ian was shaking and said it was impossible to let me know. " It would totally ruin everything" but I persisted for another ten minutes before he finally said "OK, OK, the person is YOU"

For a few seconds, I was stunned into silence, and then I replied, rather nervously "That's fine. No problem," trying to reassure myself as much as him and continued "I'm going to help you work through this in the group and community. But you know I will have to inform the rest of the staff first?" Ian wasn't happy at all, fearing that the staff might want to get rid of him, but I managed to convince him that this would not happen.

Over the next twenty-four hours I struggled to convince myself and the other officers that everything was under control.

I felt it was positive that Ian could talk openly about his feelings. Equally, I knew that I would need to stay on my guard, knowing the details of his fantasies.

He found the strength to reveal what he was feeling to a group of twenty plus prisoners, who seemed more concerned about my feelings than his. By the end of the meeting Ian had revealed everything and said he was relieved to have spoken. The other prisoners praised his honesty and said that they thought he would do well in therapy. It seemed a positive result, but the rest of the staff remained concerned about my safety, and even though I had convinced them I could cope, deep down I still felt very anxious.

As the days went by my fears grew. It became obvious to Ian that the other prisoners weren't happy for me to be alone with him. Wherever I went, I had one or two minders. Even I started to get tired with it all and began to voice that opinion.

I began to relax as the unofficial protection squads made more space and Ian appeared to respond well to the trust, until one memorable evening.

I had gone upstairs to the storeroom to collect some cleaning material and most of the prisoners were in the TV room watching a film. The light wasn't working in the store but I could see what I wanted, which was on the top shelf. As I climbed onto a box, I was aware of a figure standing close behind me and when I turned Ian was standing in the doorway. I turned and faced him fully.

"What do you want" I asked, only realising later what a leading question that was but he just smiled broadly, so I asked again, "What is it"

There was no reply just the same fixed smile. Then another prisoner called me from the corridor and I shouted, "I'm in here," trying my best to sound calm. At that, Ian simply turned and walked out?

The next day I informed the staff group of last night's incident and they all felt that the situation was getting too risky. I reluctantly had to agree that I was also feeling uncomfortable.

Ian was "ghosted out" after lock up, which means he was transferred without notice, which sometimes happens for the protection of staff or other prisoners.

Usually there will be one or two prisoners who argue about this process, but in this case nobody did. This spoke volumes for me. Even so, believe it or not, I was disappointed that he didn't get the chance to work on his problems at Grendon. Some people are just too dangerous.

Maybe sensing I needed to review my ability to physically protect myself physically, I applied to do some extra training as a Control and Restraints Instructor.

The courses were held at the naval base in Weymouth. The training was enjoyable and quite a physical release. By now I had worked on the Assessment Unit for just over a year. It was a very rewarding and satisfying experience but I felt once again that I would like to return to one of the Therapeutic Communities.

Before I left the Assessment Unit, I was given the task of escorting a prisoner to visit his common-law wife in Cookham Wood prison which is near the town of Chatham in Kent. It was not customary practice for inmates to be allowed visits to girlfriends, but this man had convinced our new Governor that she was a special person in his life and was also a co-defendant in his offence.

Following the untimely death of the Medical Superintendent Ray Jillett, the prison had its first non-medical prison governor. Michael Selby was an extreme extrovert who many considered to be a buffoon, but for me he was a breath of fresh air in what had become a very stale regime. I liked him as a manager and a person.

He allowed the inter-prison escort, and it gave me the opportunity for a day out of the jail on a very sunny day. Also, the prisoner was categorised as C which meant I could escort him alone in those days.

Bernie M was serving a six-year sentence for armed robbery, a crime which he and his girlfriend had committed together. He had not seen her since the pair had been sentenced two years previously so he was naturally excited by the prospect.

I got on with him very well and on the journey down to Kent we talked about the plans he had for the future. We called in at a service area on the M25 for a coffee, after travelling for an hour. The other nice touch for me was that I didn't have to drive, as we had the use of a private taxi.

As we left the service area the taxi driver announced that he would be stopping in Chatham town centre to pick something up.

Bernie and I waited in the taxi as he disappeared into the shopping area. On his return he was carrying a cardboard box and reaching into it asked "What do you think of this little beauty then" He produced from the box a large handgun and pointed it towards Bernie.

For a second or two I froze. Had the guy suddenly flipped his lid and decided to dispense is own brand of justice. The colour seemed to drain from Bernie's face, then it reappeared again as the driver added "of course, it's only a replica of the .357 Magnum. I fancy myself as a bit of a Dirty Harry" he laughed (referring to the character played by film actor Clint Eastwood, in the film of the same name)

"You'll be a fucking dead Dirty Harry, if you point that at me again" Bernie warned.

Bernie had suffered a complete sense of humour failure, but I was more concerned about the wider implications of our driver's stupidity. "I've got it to frighten off any attackers on the light night taxi runs. Quite a few bus and taxi drivers have done the same."

I advised him to keep the gun well out of sight and fortunately when we arrived at Cookham Wood prison we weren't expected to drive the taxi through the prison gates, so I left the driver in the car park during our visit.

As soon as we entered the prison Bernie became Cookham's responsibility. He was searched thoroughly and taken into the visitors centre.

The female officer in charge of the visits said I could look around the place while I was there, so this was an ideal opportunity to view my first women's prison.

I was immediately impressed by the generally relaxed and friendly atmosphere and the relationship between prisoners and staff was quite good. I felt comfortable apart from the occasional squeal or wolf whistle.

It was quite a boost to my ego until the young officer that was giving the guided tour brought me swiftly down to earth. "Don't get too cocky, it happens to anything in a pair of trousers male or female. "

During the tour, we stopped briefly by the entrance to the prison laundry room and I was introduced to a small group of prisoners. One of the women took more interest than others. "Where are you from then" she asked in a very soft voice that I could hardly hear.

"I'm from Grendon prison. "I replied and told her a little bit about the way therapy worked.

"I've read about it before, it sounds like the sort of place I could make use of." She smiled and joked "Do you think anybody would notice if you took me back with you?"

I told her "I would like nothing better, but I'm sure somebody would notice you were missing eventually." The officer told me it was time to move on, so I said "Nice to have met you, good look for the future. Perhaps you could petition the Home Office to open a Grendon type prison for women."

"I don't think I could influence anybody with my track record." she laughed as I left the group and set off along the corridor.

"What did you think of our Superstar then?" the young officer asked.

I was puzzled and said, "Why is she your Superstar?" The officer was surprised that I did not recognise the woman. "You're joking, aren't you? That was the infamous Myra Hindley you were flirting with."

Of course, I was aware that she was being held at Cookham Wood and was sure that I would instantly recognise her if I saw her.

The tabloid picture of a peroxide blond with dark cold staring eyes was instantly recognisable to most people, but the woman I had just met was a complete contrast and in some ways quite attractive.

I thought she might have been larger, perhaps taller and scarred by the many beatings she was supposed to have had over the years. In fact, she was slim, about 5ft 4 ins with medium length auburn hair and a clear complexion. No obvious scars, other than a slightly crooked nose and as for her eyes- I considered them to be the most attractive feature; they were a sparkly grey/blue.

She seemed well educated, softly spoken and had lost the northern accent to a large extent.

Little did I know at this point but this wasn't to be our last contact, but that is an entirely different story for later.

After about two hours I picked Bernie up from the visitors centre and we were soon on our way back to Grendon. He never stopped talking all the way back and said that the visit had gone really well. His neck was covered in love bites as a reminder of the day. "I've also got something else to remind me." He laughed and began to open the front of his trousers.

"I don't think I want to see this. "I protested, but he continued "Don't worry the stiffy has gone away" and he revealed that he was wearing a pair of white lace knickers. "We did a swap half way through the visit and she's wearing mine. "he laughed.

Apparently, there was only one toilet in use, so they managed to leave each other's underwear behind after they'd been. I reminded him that he would face a strip search when he got back to Grendon but he felt the embarrassment would be well worth the trophy.

A further book could be written about the trials and tribulations of prison officers on escorts and perhaps that's one for the future. But for now, I will continue with my Grendon experience.

When I finally decided to move out of the Assessment Unit, I needed to find a staff group that could cope with the way I operated, as Grendon was undergoing a rapid change.

The experienced, long term, officers were leaving to be replaced by many new officers, who would not receive the same support from management that I had enjoyed in the past. The prison rules were being constantly revised and the therapeutic regimes were slowly being adversely affected by what I and others considered to be inflexible operational requirements.

The prison continued to succeed as a therapeutic regime and I was finding a large element of personal success and job satisfaction.

Although I had developed the reputation as a "Maverick", which was true to a large extent, the prison management accepted that the work I did was useful and productive, so maybe that is why I was allowed to become involved in more than most others might.

I was encouraged to do some public speaking to promote the work of the Therapeutic Communities and travelled out to local schools and colleges.

B Wing was short of officers and I already knew all of the prisoners. So on September 15th 1988 I transferred onto a wing that would provide me with the most rewarding experience of my career so far.

The therapists had become extremely concerned about Grendon's future.

In a report to the Home Secretary at that time they wrote "We are concerned that we the therapists are being used to give spurious credibility to a regime, which in fact, falls far short of therapy. It is important that we are able to demonstrate, that what we do in the name of therapy, is in fact therapy and not a form of control."

Now and again Grendon would hit crisis point and this was nothing new. However, this time there was a reality that the work of Grendon was only being supported by a minority group of staff.

I was delighted to be included in that group and continued to get support for my work outside of prison.

In May 1988 Governor Mike Selby approved in writing an application that I made to attend an inmates wedding in Stoke on Trent. He wrote "Yes you may attend - As a friend, not as a prison officer."

This small but very important gesture added weight to my own belief that what I was doing was right. Good working and social relationships with prisoners are the essence of Grendon's unique therapy regime.

My arrival on B wing was welcomed by two officers who I held in high regard.

Officer Jim Edwards was a man who didn't totally agree with the therapeutic process, but he was honest and fair in his dealings with prisoners and staff. You knew where you stood with Jim and he would not stand in the way of any effort to improve the regime, as long as security was not breached. The other important consideration for me was that he had a keen sense of humour, which was always important following stressful situations.

In short, Jim responded well even under fire. We could have our differences but there would be compromises made by each of us.

The other good man was Hospital Officer John Keen, who I had known since I arrived in Grendon. He would effectively be my direct boss (Supervising Officer) and that was fine by me. Again, he was honest and firm, but fair to all.

However, his main strengths were his caring and compassion for prisoners and their families and his belief in the Grendon ethos. He had many years of experience and I had gained a great deal from his advice over the years.

John was prepared to let his voice be heard and would not just sit back and accept change simply for the sake of change. Prior to my arrival on B wing he had written to the Governor echoing the thoughts of many uniformed staff, about concerns for the direction the prison was heading.

He wrote - "Could it be possibly true that because of Grendon's approach it is the reason why we have had only one escape in its history? That assaults on staff are too infrequent to readily call to mind. That our drug abuse record is good in comparison to other prisons? Inmates assaulting each other are not an everyday occurrence?

He added "There is always room for change and not to change is depictive of an organisation succumbing to apathy. But please let us ensure that any alteration of policy is enhancive and not detracting from what should be seen as a commendable track record."

For his efforts, John had been invited onto the next prison Policy Committee meeting and various plans were made to remedy some of his concerns. Such was the value placed on the views of a prison officer, who was respected for the knowledge he had gained from working with prisoners daily. None of this knowledge can be gained from text books.

John's main focus at this stage was the survival of the B Wing community and he welcomed my input. I got into the group work immediately and it was as if I had never been away.

Due to staff shortages, I took the therapy group on my own initially, which allowed me to inject elements of my individual style. I introduced myself to the six prisoners "You all know who I am and where I worked before coming to B wing. But I thought I would let you know a bit about my personal background, if that's OK?"

I gave the men a very short life history, warts and all, including areas of my life where I have messed up badly and then said" I know you will see me as a staff member. I wear this fancy dress (Prison Officers Uniform) and can't avoid that, but I am also part of this group as you all are. I am accountable as you all are and if you cut me you will find that I bleed just the same, but obviously, I'd rather you didn't". I hope you will come to know me as an advisor but more importantly as a friend eventually."

It seemed that my introduction was well accepted by the group members, although one of the men (Sean L) told the community meeting that I had actually used part of the group session. There was stunned silence as this was, apparently, the first time that a prison officer had given such detailed information about himself on a therapy group, certainly on B wing.

One of the less experienced staff felt that it was wrong for me to do this. He feared that they would expect him to do the same. I reassured him" I know it's not the norm but it's something that I have always done. Believe me none of the other prisoners will expect you to do what I do. They view me as being a bit mad and certainly untraditional. The fact that we are all allowed to behave as individuals takes us away from the stereotypical image that prison officers sometimes promote in other jails. i.e. - we all think the same, act the same and say the same. It' creates less "them and us."

I glanced at Jim who gave me a knowing wink. This would be just the first of many reactions to my "Modus Operandi" Jim would never dream of doing it, but he was happy for me to reveal everything. Most professionals would argue that a therapist/counsellor should be something of a blank canvas to clients and of course the treatment is for them and not me, but I found that prisoners would relate to me better and trust me more if I was less of a closed book and able to offer advice on occasions based on individual experiences.

I went straight into phase two and made sure that I spent at least two hours with every prisoner on the group. This was done during the evening or else at the weekend, when there was less happening around the jail. I made it clear to all of the prisoners that I would dig as deep as I could for information and welcomed the opportunity to meet their friends and relatives in the future. Not simply to extend my knowledge, but also to give their families and friends an opportunity to get to know me and to assure them that they could speak to me at any time, with an element of confidentiality but hopefully they trusted me to deal with any concerns professionally and safely.

As I stated previously, there can be no confidentiality at Grendon but people need to be encouraged to reveal sometimes difficult information safely and that includes prisoners.

I also made it clear that I expected everybody in the group to consider a "Family Group Meeting" at some stage during their time in therapy.
This was important, as it gave each prisoner an opportunity to "meet the family" and a chance for the family to ask questions of everybody, about anything at all.

Another bonus to working on B Wing was that Principal Psychologist Roland Woodward was the wing therapist. He was a colorful character and I liked his style. He worked very hard developing a regime that was well structured and had the flexibility to experience other "alternative" therapies.

During my time on B wing he managed to make the pages of the now extinct newspaper "News of the World," when he introduced a dance group. The paper reported that "roughy-toughy" prisoners dancing with each other, all leotards, muscles and tattoos."

There were many prisoners that I got on with and several chapters could be filled with individual experiences. I have very fond memories of that four-year period. It was undoubtedly the best time for me, in my career.

One prisoner was to haunt me for many years to come and working with him produced my greatest challenge to date.

Mark Leech arrived quietly towards the end of 1988 and later on in his own book "A Product of the System" he praised the Grendon regime for assisting with his rehabilitation. I have always felt that it was more due to his own motivation and effort (rather than a structured therapeutic process) that he eventually did succeed.
However, there is no doubt that Grendon laid the foundation stone.

Mark was a difficult guy to get to know initially. There appeared to be many facets to his character. On the one hand, he appeared to be quite cold, isolated and manipulative whilst on the other hand caring, empathic and the life and soul of the party.

When he arrived on the wing it was clear to me that he was not out to score points. He was prepared to give and take criticism in equal measure.

He mixed his serious therapy with a sprinkling of comedy. On one memorable occasion, he was cast for the role of one half of the comedy duo "Hinge and Bracket" in a short sketch that was done at an F Wing Social evening.

He may have appeared limp wristed and weak to some, but his strength lay in his ability to argue for justice and to confront inconsistencies, not just in the therapeutic regime but also in the staff's standards of reporting.

One thing was certain to me (as Marks personal officer), he would question my judgement, if it was not entirely borne out of fact. Nothing could be assumed and everything I wrote had to be cross referenced and well evidenced for him.

It was a challenge working with Mark because of his close attention to detail. Even a spelling mistake or misuse of a word could result in a discussion lasting for the best part of an hour. But he was also a pleasure to work with. He engaged in therapy from the beginning, even though he wasn't sure in which direction it might take him. He made some classic mistakes at a very early stage, attempting to deceive other prisoners was a mistake that many make. Mark was a past master in the art of deception but here he was attempting be open and honest in everything he did.

Almost immediately there were members of staff who didn't trust his sincerity but few could give a valid reason why? He carried himself confidently but I suspected that under the surface he was as vulnerable as any of us.
One thing that I was aware of from past records was that he could be a formidable opponent in conflict and his power of argument was very strong.

As time went by, we chatted a lot socially and I formed an early opinion that he would be a survivor no matter what the future threw at him. As it happened, to date, his future has been extremely successful and in 2017 we remain in contact.

Over the next twelve months the regime on B Wing improved vastly. Fresh staff arrived and we managed to retain an atmosphere that was conducive to good therapy. The prisoner population was stable which gave us the opportunity to build a solid caring community. We had been through the mill a bit, having had two officers sacked for corrupt practices. One had been bringing drink and drugs in for several prisoners and the other had been stealing cash from prisoners' mail. It is difficult to rebuild credibility when this happens, particularly in a therapeutic community, but we managed it thanks to the effort of new staff and a prison population who were able to reason things out.

The most important part of an individual's progress towards success comes when he is finally released onto the streets. No matter how good the therapy has been, how much advice has been offered or how deep the relationships becomes with other prisoners and staff, the experience that a man gets immediately after release can make or break him.

If a man has the support of family and friends and is returning to a familiar area, the opportunity for success can be twenty to thirty percent greater than somebody who moves to a new area for a fresh start. This of course also affects the individual's confidence or ability to communicate and make new friends.

There are dangers for both types of ex prisoner; the latter may feel lonely, isolated and worthless, eventually being drawn towards the criminal lifestyle once again. And the former may find that family and friends have not moved on, they may still be involved in crime and he will be tempted to return to learned behaviour.

Success can be very difficult, if he is returning to an area with a high crime rate, to deprived conditions, where violence is a way of life. The diagnosis for most prisoners who volunteer to come to Grendon was that they were suffering from severe personality disorders or some neurotic disorders such as anxiety and depression, which are not easily treated and problems are ongoing long after release.

It's very arrogant for professionals to believe that any period of therapy has been enough and the expectation or assumption is made that they are now able to make satisfactory progress. Quite often such professionals have no idea at all of the kind of lifestyles that ex-prisoners return to. It has been considered that Personality Disorders, as outlined by the Ninth review of the International Classification of Disease, are untreatable. So, what does this suggest about the value of a prison such as Grendon?

Many former prisoners who have succeeded since the prison was opened in 1962, state that their success was due to the strong relationships that they formed with prison staff, but more importantly they continued to feel welcome and supported for a considerable time after moving on or being released.

What hope could there be for Grendon, if the post release/transfer work ended? Ex Grendon prisoners cannot be simply "handed over" to another system or be released into society with nothing more than a current therapeutic MOT, it is not realistic.

The criterion for prisoners was quite clear. It was expected that men would be intellectually capable of understanding the method of treatment and to be "psychologically minded". Obviously, many slipped through the net, beginning their time in therapy very disadvantaged.

These men and others, who needed support and encouragement when they finished the therapy, were the ones that I would personally stick with for as long as I was needed.

I was giving the most positive input to the regime than I had since I arrived at Grendon in 1977 and my relationships with the prisoners, other staff and management were all positive. For the first time in ages I felt I had reached several personal goals and had a high level of job satisfaction. My annual staff report reflected these achievements.

Such satisfaction arrived at a time when Grendon prison was about to face the biggest test in its entire history.

On 20th December 1989, I received a bizarre telephone call at home and the voice on the other end was entirely unexpected, it was Mark Leech.

"Hi Joe, I just wanted to thank you for all you have done for me at Grendon and I hope we will meet up again at some point in the future." Mark sounded very depressed as he added "They've closed the prison down, and I'm being moved out to Winchester Prison. The rest are going somewhere else but I'll let John Keen tell you the rest, take care mate."

My brain tried to work out the implications of what Mark was saying. It definitely wasn't April 1st so perhaps he'd had a drop of the hard stuff, maybe he was on drugs or perhaps he had suffered a mental breakdown! I'm sure he said the prison was closing down?

Then John Keen's voice came on the line. "I can't stay long mate but Grendon is being closed because of an electrical fault. When you start back to work on Monday you've got to report to The Mount Prison near Hemel Hempstead."

"Alright, give me the fucking punch line" I laughed, but John remained deadly serious. "I wish it was a joke mate but it's not. We're all working at The Mount from next week, give me a call later and I'll tell you what's been happening."

Later, John explained that there was a major electrical fault in the prison which meant it had to be rewired. Everybody was being moved out to different jails. The plan was to come back together later.

They were moving most staff and prisoners to The Mount, near Hemel Hempstead but the Young Prisoners had gone to Feltham and Aylesbury prisons. The Acute Psychiatric Unit had moved to Parkhurst on the Isle of Wight and 29 prisoners (including Mark Leech) were sent to Winchester.

For those of you who have never worked in a prison it will be hard to imagine the scale of this operation, moving more than 220 prisoners all over the country over a twenty-four-hour period.

The Governor, Michael Selby, was the most unpopular man on the planet to some prison officers, who would be separated from their families over the entire Christmas period. For most Grendon's prisoners the festive period would be difficult but bearable in the temporary homes.

However, those who had gone to Winchester needed special consideration as they had been placed into a normal prison regime. Having been used to the very relaxed atmosphere in Grendon their arrival at Winchester presented an unusual challenge to the staff there!

Chapter 9

The Prison Officers who had to receive them at Winchester were as anxious as the prisoners and they decided they could take no chances. The men had to be absorbed into the hectic atmosphere and uncertainty of a busy local prison. They couldn't provide the level of support that they'd been given at Grendon.

Initially they had their Mufti teams (Riot Squad) standing by, but soon realised there would be no trouble. Mark Leach describes the experience in his autobiography "A product of the System" and Graham W also gave me his view of the move. He describes leaving Grendon at 16.30 hrs on December 21st, 1989.

"When we went through Grendon's gate there was a heavy police escort waiting to take us to Winchester" Graham was puzzled" "I thought it was a bit over the top. We were not being moved because we had caused any trouble" but due to a fault in the prison". Mike Selby wanted to keep everybody together as much as possible so he had hired a 48-seater coach.

Normally they would have been moved separately by taxi, requiring between 2 - 4 officers for each man. This way was considered more humane but was of course less secure, hence the heavy police presence on the journey. Graham recalls. "There was a lot of angry confused feelings about why had this particular 29 prisoners been picked to move together? Why weren't we going with the rest?

And he said "We were worried because we didn't know what would be waiting for us back in the normal prison system ". The men were right to be worried. Winchester Governor Mike Hughes said, "The feeling amongst prisoners in the normal system is that those who are in custody at Grendon are either "nonces" (Sex Offenders) or "nutters". And it was this type of prejudice that created problems for them when they first arrived."

The new arrivals were being intimidated and threatened within 48 hours and staff feared that it might escalate out of control.

The Grendon prisoners had been split up. "We were told before we left, we should be kept together but this wasn't the case." Graham said "There were 10 on B wing, 10 on D and 9 on A wing. We had been well and truly shafted. Barriers came up fast and the name of the game was survival in a dog eat dog environment of a normal jail."

One of the reasons for Grendon's success is that the whole prison works towards therapy. The majority are prepared to give it a chance but in a traditional jail "nick culture" prevails. Prisoners have to fight to survive. It's like the taming of wild animals. If you return them back into the wilds they will struggle to survive. The authorities failed to understand the destruction that would begin following this decision.

Graham continued "We spoke to Governor Jagger who asked us how it could be made easier for his staff and us. We said put us on a landing (Cell Block) together. He did, but put signs up over our doors saying that we were all Rule 43 (that means like sex offenders held under protection) so we ripped the signs down."

The Governor was apparently worried by their actions as he had put all of the Grendon men on A wing which was used entirely for the housing of sex offenders.

"We were called into the Governor's office again and he said he was concerned for the safety of the sex offenders. We told him that they were safe from us, including the men who weren't sex offenders" The Governor laughed. "This was the first time as a prison Governor I had negotiated with 29 prisoners from the comfort of my office."

But Graham said things began to get worse. "Staff didn't answer our cell bells to let us use the loo. Some of the officers who tried to help were stopped by bully boys who told them to lock us up and forget about us. They were keeping us locked up for 23 hours a day. Men were getting angry and there was going to be big trouble."

On December 28th, the prisoners were told once again that they would be getting a couple of officers from Grendon to look after them. But the men weren't impressed.

"We'd been told this before so we took it with a pinch of salt" Graham remembers "When the Grendon officers did arrive on January 3rd we were surprised but there was only two and the poor bastards were in for a very angry reception from many prisoners!"

I was approached by the Governor on December 28th and he said that they wanted officers to go and work at Winchester Prison for about 9 weeks until Grendon re-opened or they could re-unite them with the others elsewhere. He continued "You were a first choice. It has to be somebody who they will respect and who can communicate with them well. There have been a lot of problems so it won't be easy. We have sent Dr Cruickshank to care for them but he can't deal with all of the prison stuff. He's desperate for help."

I was asked to determine who I could work well with if I was given the choice and without hesitation I replied, "Derek Francis would be the ideal man for the job".

Officer Derek Francis worked on C wing and he was very well respected by the prisoners and staff alike. I felt we would work very well together. He had a great sense of humour, was calm under pressure and what was more important he cared about the welfare of the prisoners.

I didn't confirm that I would go until I had spoken to my wife Wendy. I wanted it to be her choice, but Wendy knew how much the job meant to me. She had visited the prison to meet the prisoners and had also spent some time in the company of ex-prisoners and their families. She had some understanding of my work and recognised that the prisoners' welfare was something that I was passionate about.

I would be home at the weekends and it was even close enough to travel home mid-week.

Derek had already confirmed that he was prepared to work with me, so we set about organising somewhere to stay. At this stage I don't think either of us knew what we were letting ourselves in for.

Winchester prison was an old Victorian style jail, a very busy local prison which we imagined would be a totally different atmosphere to what we had become used to. I think we both wondered how we would be accepted by the Winchester officers.

On the journey, there was plenty to chat about. How would we approach the task, what jobs could be shared, who would have overall seniority? I can honestly say, in my 14 years' experience, I had never faced such an enormous challenge in terms of having to cope with the fears and anxieties of so many individuals in what we imagined would be a very hostile environment. We knew that the prisoners were feeling isolated and very angry. Initially we had to face them with very little information of any use and could offer no immediate consolation.

We were also aware that being subject to the Winchester regime, the prisoners would have found conditions extremely difficult to tolerate. Derek and I knew our task wouldn't be easy and we were totally unprepared for the actual volume of emotional pressure we had to face.

The Winchester staff team was very welcoming particularly those on A wing, where the Grendon men were located. They immediately labelled us "The Care Bears" and gave us our very own office which we immediately took over and made ourselves comfortable. It did appear that somebody else already occupied the office but the Winchester officers assured us that it was nobody of importance.

The Governor set the boundaries within which we could operate and stressed that they would be as flexible as was humanly possible but we could not disrupt the normal day-to-day routine. We decided that we would share the workload equally and if we worked one evening each during the week it would allow us to give the prisoners "Open Association" on Tuesday and Thursday evenings, from 5.45pm to 8 pm. Our next task was to open each cell in turn, explain to the inmates that we had been sent to help them and answer any questions we could. We also asked them to give us any welfare problems that they had so that we could attempt to address them, particularly those that required immediate attention. Derek took one side of the cell block and I took the other. This whole operation would take us three hours to complete.

I opened the first cell door. The smell was almost unbearable, and I took a deep breath as I entered trying not to be too sickened by it. Unfortunately, I couldn't control myself. "Jesus Christ, has somebody died in here" I gasped "and if so how many fucking days ago?"

I gazed into the darkened room, searching for signs of life and then a familiar face appeared from beneath a heavy prison blanket. I recognised Malcolm M from C wing. He looked totally depressed, unclean, unshaven and wearing prison clothes that were about 10 sizes too big. Here was a man who in Grendon, had always been immaculately turned out and very proud of his personal hygiene.

I apologised for my introduction "Sorry Malc, I'm not even going to ask how you are it speaks for itself. I and Derek Francis are here to stay, so we need to know what problems should take priority. Apart from a good bath and change of clothes, how else can we help?"

Malcolm was barely audible as he said "You can start by finding out why I've been isolated from Grendon. What have I done wrong? I've opened myself up wide in therapy then within 24 hours I'm in this god forsaken hole, locked up 23 hours a day and ignored by the screws?"

I had no answers for him straight away but assured him I would find out what had happened and be back before lunch. I then gave him the opportunity to get rid of the slop bucket which was almost full of excrement and to get some fresh air into the cell.

Terry B his cellmate stayed under his covers, deciding not to respond to me at all. I locked them both up and moved on to the next cell.

The attitude towards us ranged from feelings of relief that at least there were two familiar faces, to anger because we represented a prison that had let them down badly, even "betrayed them". Each one wanted to know why they had been chosen for Winchester and more importantly what the future held in store. Many were afraid that their offences would be exposed in the Winchester system and they risked violence.

Several prisoners had only recently arrived at Grendon so they were not so committed to therapy. The others feared that these men might suddenly revert to the conventional rules of the system, especially those who weren't in for sexual offences. Some of the men were already getting verbal abuse.

By lunchtime on or first day we felt physically and mentally drained by the sheer volume of emotional outpourings from these men who believed they were Grendon rejects. We both felt that maybe we had bitten off more than we could chew. At this stage we did have thoughts of returning to Grendon, but we decided to stay, as we both held the firm belief that none of the men deserved to be in this situation.

We also considered the feelings of Dr. Roger Cruickshank who had been here alone until now. Whatever happened from here on, we knew that we would have to work to provide as much of the Grendon regime as we could.

Our next step was to gather the inmates together and hold a community meeting. Fortunately, the prison chaplain allowed us to use the chapel for this purpose, which wasn't an ideal venue but it was the only area available within the main prison. During this meeting, Mark Leech was elected as chairman and spokesman for the Grendon Community. He possessed good verbal skills and was well motivated to help us to boost morale.

The Winchester officers were asked to approach Mark first if any problems arose in our absence.

The idea of allowing a prisoner to play the role of "trouble-shooter" amused some of the Winchester officers but I warned them "If you fail to do this, you may find yourselves to be the subject of our next meeting and your attitude will be questioned". Many officers decided to risk it.

We were initially seen as something of a novelty. One officer described us as "a Mickey Mouse community" but slowly we began to prove that the Grendon method worked. Several officers quietly voiced the opinion that we had "got it right" when it came to "controlling prisoners behaviour."

We were quick to point out that the men controlled themselves because they genuinely wanted to change the pattern of their behaviour. One of the Winchester officers came to visit the Grendon prisoner's whenever he was on duty. He was affectionately known as "Mudguard" due to his bald head. When I asked why, a colleague said, "Because like a mudguard, he is shiny on top but full of shit underneath!"

In fact, Mudguard had nothing but praise for our work. "We just lock our prisoners behind cell doors where they continue to plot new crimes and disruption for our system, whereas you get them out and challenge their behaviour, which is what prison should do."

We held a community meeting once a week and I instructed the Winchester officers not to intervene if there was a disturbance of any kind. We can control violent situations without the use of C & R. Most of the control came from the prisoners themselves.

About the rest of the day, we asked to take on the roles of Probation Officer, Censor, Education Liaison and Psychologist, to install continuity. By the end of the second week we had constructed a stable regime. The men were unlocked as often as possible, for outdoor exercise, table tennis or TV. After six weeks Derek had to leave to take his summer holidays but he was ably replaced by Officer Sean Lanfear for the remaining period.

Just as feelings were beginning to improve we had to inform the men that Grendon was now being moved to HMP Wellingboro in Northamptonshire. Unfortunately, because Wellingboro was less secure some of the 29 men could not be transferred to rejoin the other Grendon men.

Sean and I began the task of selecting the men who could move and tried to recatagorise those who could be held in less secure conditions.

Fears and anxiety arose again. Some of the men were very angry that they were being judged on their security status again, rather than on their need for therapy. Derek, Shaun and I had been desperate to return as many as we could to the therapeutic regime.

We found ourselves to be in a peculiar position. Our routine was vastly different from the rest of the jail and we were sometimes in conflict with the Winchester officers.

We kept the tradition of talking to our prisoners using first name terms and we made ourselves available for interviews whenever we could during the working day.

Concern was expressed about the fact that we unlocked 29 prisoners alone and sat for extended periods conducting interviews in cells. Also, we soaked up a great deal of verbal abuse. However, the whole experience had been a resounding success.

By the time, we left to return to Grendon on February 8th, 1990, myself, Derek Francis and Sean Lanfear had proven that it was possible to operate a Grendon type regime within a normal prison setting albeit with limited resources. This was the first time such work had been achieved on this scale. It was an idea that was later to be repeated in HMP Gartree.

The return coach was booked, this time without a heavy police escort. And we were soon reunited with the rest of Grendon at HMP Wellingborough. I was also delighted to be back home permanently with Wendy and our daughter Sophie. Having considered the long-term future, we decided to get married on July 21st 1990.

The reasonably short period that Grendon was located in Wellingborough went very smoothly. The prisoners and staff had settled in well to the new surroundings and to some extent this location was better than the original one, with plenty of wide open spaces and amenities for staff very close to hand.

In order to be able to relocate the prisoners a full security audit had been carried out and all of those housed in what was effectively a lower security category 'C' prison were deemed to be not liable to attempt escape. However, significantly, during this time many prisoners were received who could not have been considered without risk.

Wellingborough prison was designed to hold category 'C' prisoners. These are prisoners for whom escape must be made difficult, who would not arouse too much public interest if they were to escape and did not require the standard elevated level of security afforded to category 'B' prisoners.

Grendon Prison was traditionally designated a category 'B' prison and certainly the prisoners it held were deemed to be some of the most violent and disturbed men in the system. An escape by any inmate would undoubtedly cause an outcry in the media. Therefore, security at Wellingborough was upgraded before our arrival.

In true Grendon style there were very few incidents of violence, no incidents of escape and although the local community had initially protested, particularly over the arrival of a high percentage of sex offenders, they soon welcomed the chance to meet the prisoners and staff.

We had arranged to do the Christmas pantomime entitled "The Other Dick Whittington". It was written by Mark Leech and featured a cast of inmates and staff who worked in harmony to produce an event that was "an overwhelming success". Ironically one of the prisoners referred to the pantomime as "a riot of fun".

Chapter 10

However, whilst Grendon prison was rehearsing its pantomime, Strangeway's prison in Manchester was preparing for its own riot which was to be far from funny!

I was continuing in my role of Control and Restraints Instructor and in between facilitating therapy groups and rehearsing the pantomime, I instructed the staff in self-defence and riot control. Therefore, when the prison riots kicked off in April 1990 we found ourselves travelling in a coach to assist with the troubles at Dartmoor prison.

The call to attend the riot came at the end of a 12-hour shift, as I and a few other officers were looking forward to our supper. We had no time to waste and all I could do was phone my wife to let her know where we were going.

There would be no more contact with her for two days! You can imagine how the families worried as they watched scenes from the riot on national TV. Communication between the prison and the families had been particularly poor, which served to heighten anxiety.

The worries were justified, as any riot can be unpredictable but the Grendon officers dealt with a difficult situation in true Grendon fashion. We sang songs and cracked jokes as our coach rolled across the Devon border.

There was a thick mist rolling over the moors as we approached Dartmoor and in the distance, we could see the prison buildings, with flames leaping into the sky. As we drew nearer we saw the blue flashing lights of the emergency vehicles and could hear the screams of protest from prisoners on the rooftops. It was almost 3 am and the riot raged on. "Let's party" one of our staff shouted as we got off the coach.

We had to wait until dawn before it was our turn to enter the prison. Many units had been battling all night to bring order and were emerging fairly exhausted. None of the Grendon unit had slept, and soon, dressed in full riot gear, we were told to make our way to the prison kitchen to provide cover for the kitchen staff whilst they prepared breakfast for the rest of the prison.

As soon as the rioters saw the lights in the kitchen come on they began to bombard the glass roof with slates and lumps of concrete. We used our riot shields as a temporary roof over the cookers.

Officer Jim Edwards was not one to miss the chance of a free meal "any chance of a free sausage sandwich?" he enquired as a huge lump of concrete came crashing onto a nearby work-surface. "Yeah, no problem mate" the cook replied "but you can make your own. I won't be hanging around here for long I can assure you!"

Within minutes we were at work, cooking sausages, frying eggs, making toast and even frying chicken pieces. Jim's request for a quick snack had turned into the preparation of huge breakfast. Riot or no riot we were not prepared to go hungry.

As I tucked into my fourth piece of chicken, stopping only to wipe some pieces of slate from the grill, the cook returned with the kitchen orderly, a prisoner who was well known to me. It was Mick M, and he had been denied the opportunity to move to Wellingborough, from Winchester, along with others, on the basis of his being a serious threat to security.

Obviously Dartmoor had considered him to be safe enough to continue working in the prison kitchen during a full-scale riot, with free access to carving knives and meat cleavers. "Surely this will improve his security status?" I thought. Imagine his surprise when I approached him dressed in full riot gear?

"Fuck me." Mick exclaimed as he recognised who I was. "Not while there are dogs in the street." I replied with a smirk.

"I only wrote a letter to you last week and I was waiting for your reply" Mick laughed "at least this will save you the cost of a stamp."

As the riot continued to rage furiously outside we continued our discussion about the possibility of his return to Grendon. He asked how my family was keeping and he asked about the progress other prisoners were making at Grendon. Our cozy chat was occasionally punctuated with the shattering of glass as another slate hit its target.

This was a surreal moment, a prisoner and his Personal Officer/Counsellor (wearing combat gear) having a therapeutic discussion in the middle of a full-scale prison disturbance. Such was the reality and value of relationships between prisoners and staff in Grendon.

For many prison officers at Grendon the therapeutic experience led to a much greater insight into the psychology of violent/disturbed men and even in the worst situations we could deal with prisoners in a humane, dignified manner. I had learned that the simple use of a man's Christian name in a violet situation could begin to calm him down so that I was able to communicate positively.

As Mick left the kitchen area, he said" I think it goes without saying, the sooner I can get out of this shit-hole the better." and he added "have a word with the governor for me when you get back please?"

"I promise to give it my best shot on my return to Grendon." I replied.

After we had finished our breakfast in the war zone we had twenty or thirty pieces of chicken left over, which was fortunate as we received a radio message from the Section Commander asking us to try and attract the attention of the prisoners on the roof, so that several other units could move further into the main prison and I suddenly had a great idea!

The rioting prisoners had not eaten anything for over 48 hours so they would be feeling very hungry by now. The main reason that they had focused their attack on the kitchen earlier had been to deprive the other prisoners of food, now it was my turn to deprive them!

I took a full tray of chicken and behind the cover of a riot shield called to a group of prisoners on the roof.

"Oi you lot, anybody fancy fried chicken." I yelled, attracting the attention of two men who were collecting more slates from the roof. They called to the other rioters and I soon had the attention of the whole group. I then threw the whole tray of chicken onto the floor and rubbed them in the dirt with my feet.

"Oh dear how sad" I shouted, "I bet you would have enjoyed these lads!"

The result was better than I could have expected. I was showered with roofing slates from all directions as I beat a hasty retreat into the prison kitchen. For about ten minutes they continued to bombard the kitchen roof until they ran out of slates but that was enough time for the other units to move their position forward, unconventional perhaps, but a good result.

Throughout the day, we moved in and out of the kitchen attracting more missiles from the rooftop protesters.

I may give the impression that the whole event was rather jolly, but in fact we treated it with the utmost seriousness. Staff could be hurt or even killed and we knew that a prisoner had died overnight in a cell fire. There were several occasions when our bottle went, even behind the cover of our shields which would protect us from a shotgun blast at close range. Danger and personal injury were never far away.

Officer Mike Smith devised a little game to while away the hours towards early evening. He produced two large score cards which would be held up, according to how accurate the rioters were.

If they hit our shields with slates or concrete they would score 9.5, if they missed it would be 5.9.

Several of the rioters got into the spirit of the event and were delighted each time they scored. Yet again this drew their attention away from the more serious work of the units below them. The remainder of our time was spent gathering information from prisoners who were trapped in their cells.

Every now and then a prisoner would drop a note from his cell window or hang out a sheet on which was written things such as:

"I am prisoner CX5492 Clarke, Cell 295, am not taking part in this riot, and I will come peacefully."

The commander would gather all intelligence that might bring the real culprits to justice. In all riot situations, there is a minority group of violent prisoners who lead the disturbance. Many prisoners are forced to go along with things or risk being beaten up or even killed. It is not unusual for inmates to barricade themselves into a cell during a riot, simply to protect themselves from other prisoners, particularly if they are sex offenders.

Before the riot had ended at Dartmoor one prisoner had been burned to death when his cell was torched by rioters who suspected he was a "Nonce" (sex offender). Ironically, several of the men who led the disturbance had a history of sexually offending but they had convinced other prisoners they were "Blaggers" (armed robbers).

In my mind and certainly in my experience armed robbers are no better than men who abuse women and children. In the twisted minds of some criminals they are falsely held in high esteem. Grendon officers have suffered ridicule from prisoners and staff in other jails for their apparent "softly softly" approach to dealing with convicts and yet on a daily basis we challenge nick culture and stereotypical images of villains.

Prisoners, who decide to take a stroll down "Felony Lane" at Grendon, soon find themselves challenged if they try to glorify their crimes.

Grendon officers have proved that they can use force when necessary but in their day-to-day dealings with prisoners they learned to calm a situation by talking to the prisoner who was contemplating violence. I was asked at the time if I felt a conflict of interest between the role of a counsellor/therapist, and the role of C & R Instructor?

There was some prison Medical Officers who were against the use of what they believed to be "excessive force" against a prisoner perpetrated by a "gang of prison officers". I would argue that in many incidents the force used was minimal and the officers worked as a skilled team. In any event, it was my task to ensure that there was fair play and reasonable behaviour.

Francis Crook, Director of the Howard League for Penal Reform, wrote a scathing article condemning the use of C & R. I responded by strongly defending its use as a protection against any further harm being done to prisoners or staff. Once again, this is a prime example of an academic interfering with a situation that she had not experienced first-hand and indeed many of the people who choose to write articles about the ups and downs of prison life have seldom had hands on experience.

Struggling physically with a prisoner during a heavy group meeting in HMP Grendon has long since disappeared.

The opportunity for a member of staff or even another prisoner to be charged with assault is a very real prospect. The risk of legal action being taken against a prison officer prompted me to make a statement about physical contact during therapy meetings. "In most group therapy situations, the prisoners themselves provide the control. They are here to learn to exercise that control in confrontations, thereby not resorting to acts of violence".

The "No violence" rule continued to be the "Golden Rule" in therapy and this remained the case particularly in the unfamiliar surroundings at Wellingborough. "If the situation has developed outside of an officer's control or the control of a therapy meeting, the alarm bell must be used to summon further assistance. The days when an officer would place himself between two inmates have gone. In the event of yourself or any inmates being injured during confrontations the correct Control and Restraint procedures must have been adhered to."

Effectively this meant that eventually a valuable piece of Grendon's work would disappear. That is its ability to "take people over the edge" so that they and the group can examine the feelings that are there at the point of "no control".

To experience somebody's anger boiling over, particularly if they have previously killed is a very frightening situation. However, it was one that was commonplace in the early days. When working in the Acute Psychiatric Unit staff faced the possibility of physical violence daily.

In Wellingborough deeply disturbed and violent prisoners were held alongside others who were classed as medium risk and most of the trouble that occurred came from the latter. This was totally because they were not in therapy and retained their "nick culture."

The prisoners who arrived whilst we were based at Wellingborough had to be assessed by the individual wings.

There have always been arguments about whether it is important to assess men for therapy. Why can't they simply be placed into the communities, after all they are assessed every three months anyway? Controversially I don't think you need a separate unit and I can point to many good examples. One man who arrived at Wellingboro as a direct entrant to therapy became perhaps one of Grendon's greatest success stories.

I will refer to him as John and he was serving a life sentence for the manslaughter of a little girl. He had spent fourteen years as a category A prisoner and had hardly spoken to anybody during this time.

His probation officer had convinced him that it would be good for him to come into therapy but he arrived very suspicious about the system and not at all comfortable about talking about his offence in front of a group of prisoners. However, his story eventually unfolded.

John lived in a small village in Northamptonshire. He was the eldest child in a family of seven and they lived in a cramped terraced house. He described his father, who deserted the family when he was very young, as a drunkard.

He often witnessed him being violent towards his mother. He spoke in detail about the many "men friends" that his mother had and how other kids "tried to take the piss out of him" at school, calling his mother a "prostitute."

He played truant from school and wandered away from home on many occasions but even when he attended school he would have temper tantrums and fight with other kids.

At the age of 10 he was placed in a care home because his mother could not control him. It was obvious to me that John had no satisfactory male influence in his life and perhaps he had shown signs of a psychological problem from a very early age. In fact, a doctor had recommended a period in a psychiatric unit at the age of 12. This was ignored and the local authorities believed his disturbed behaviour simply stemmed from a "lack of discipline" at home.

John unsurprisingly continued to get into trouble until he left school at the age of 14. Before his fifteenth birthday he was in an approved school. He described this as the happiest period of his life having "30 brothers and 4 House-Parents". He was there for two years until 1968 when he was released without any support.

I recall that it was significant to me that he left approved school at the same time that I left secondary school to go to College. We are almost the same age and yet worlds apart in our life experiences. I had stability, love and understanding, which he could not relate to and he was well on the path to destruction. At this stage in his life, none of his problems could be related to drink or drugs. However, drink and drugs often play a role in the perpetration of some of the more horrific offences and are used by defence barristers as mitigating evidence, as was the case for John.

I was immediately impressed by his refusal to blame Alcohol or drugs and by his eagerness to look at social and psychological factors. He chose in a sober state to become a "skinhead" in the same way as I chose to follow the "Hippy Culture".

He chose to engage in gang violence and I chose to promote Peace and Love. John chose to use cannabis, amphetamines, LSD and alcohol, as I chose moderate social drinking. And yet, we recognised that at the same time in our lives we were searching for the same thing, social acceptance, marriage and a regular income.

When I began studies at engineering college in 1969, John was sent to a detention centre. I was learning to fix machinery as he was learning to hate authority, fight hard and reject all responsibility.

In 1971, he was married to a girl who was already pregnant but the marriage broke up after two years due to his ill treatment of his wife. They divorced in 1975. By this time, he was living with another woman but continued to be irritable and depressed.

John told me that he felt better after a game of rugby but would soon return to drugs, drink and violence. His personal relationship was a disaster and in 1976 she asked him to leave. He returned to live with his mother thereby making his "cycle of destruction" complete.

Coincidentally 1976 was the date that I decided to make a fresh start and join the prison service. As I prepared my application John set out on a path to destruction that would bring us both into contact 14 years later.

The details of his crimes are difficult to understand and there was no apparent motive.

On Saturday afternoon, a young girl was walking to a friend's house nearby, to attend a birthday party, which included a trip to the theatre. As John walked towards her, she smiled. His actions within the next ten minutes would devastate a family, horrify a nation and cut short the life of another innocent child.

I will spare you some of the details of this little girl's death but must say that she was killed in a frenzy of sexual violence and mutilation which defies belief or understanding. Her body was set alight and she had a deep bite mark on her stomach. Another horrifying aspect of this case was that during a search for the missing girl it was her mother who eventually discovered her in a derelict garage.

The following day he attacked and tortured a 55-year-old man by throwing him into a sewage tank and pelting him with stones and lumps of concrete. Within 48 hours he had been arrested and charged with the attack on the man and the killing of the little girl. At the time of his arrest he declared "she started laughing, I was a bit pissed anyhow" and he added "I just flipped, I do it a lot".

He said he had attacked the man who had previously been his scoutmaster because he tried to "touch him up". He felt he deserved it because he was a Queer. At the time of his trial the authorities said he displayed a self-centered and arrogant attitude towards his victims and he was eventually found guilty of "Manslaughter on the grounds of diminished responsibility" and was sentenced to "Life Imprisonment."

The police felt that although he denied some aspects of the offence and stated he could not remember the events, he did in fact remember "but simply did not want to say".

As I stated earlier, John had been encouraged by his probation officer to come to Grendon for therapy and he had arrived in 1990 prepared to tell everything.
However, his progress in therapy was distracted by the news that his son had been killed in a road accident.

His son's death was difficult for him to handle but it also became the catalyst for some very powerful soul searching and therapeutic work.

At this point I must stress that working with some of the country's most notorious criminals in the way I chose to do did not make me popular. However, I believe that there is a great deal for society to learn from very tragic circumstances and the only way to encourage offenders to look at their faults and weaknesses, to examine their crimes, is through the development of good positive relationships.

To this end I will be prepared to go that extra mile for men and women who ask for help and advice. Through this approach, I have made lasting friendships with prisoners and ex-prisoners, with many that society might permanently reject, or in the past would have executed.

You will recall that one of my anxieties when I first became a prison officer was that I might have to work with men who had committed sex offences or killed children. My views were very strong, and I thought I could never change that opinion!

Grendon had not only given me the opportunity to examine that prejudice but it also helped me to change it. Don't get me wrong; I was still able to feel the horror and revulsion towards these crimes but not so easily towards the men and women who committed them. The more I understood some of the reasons the more I felt I could help.

I had the ability to detach myself from the emotional involvement, to examine the facts and come to fairly accurate conclusions. I had developed a method of testing a person's commitment or motivation to change through various personal yardsticks. Using therapeutic theories and psychological testing was fine, to some extent, but there had to be other methods of encouraging change and judging progress.

I had tried to communicate with John during the first couple of days but he was very withdrawn and isolated. It looked like he was not going to survive in the therapeutic environment. However, the break came under very tragic circumstances.

He had been informed that he would not be welcome at his son's funeral but arrangements were made to escort him in handcuffs to the graveside. I would be the officer who was cuffed to him.

On the day of John's escort, it rained very heavily and when we reached the graveyard it was dull and gloomy overhead. Perhaps the weather added to the feelings that were aroused as we stood together over his son's grave but I suddenly felt a wave of emotions sweep over me. He was shaking and I felt I wanted to leave him alone to grieve, but of course the shackles prevented this happening.

I recall thinking that he was experiencing what it felt like to lose a child, perhaps he can now understand what his victim's family felt like. They have had to live with those feelings and are serving a life sentence of their own.

But I also felt there was something else happening. A non-verbal communication was going on which said, "This is a bad as it gets, the only way is up, it's time to put things right, no more victims". The words kept going around in my head.

Later on, He said, "I knew at my sons graveside, therapy was what I needed and that you and other prisoners were there for me."

Our professional and personal relationship started as soon as we returned from the escort.

John fed back to the community how he had felt and received their support, which gave him the ability to begin to open up further.

I mentioned some of my rather controversial methods earlier but I was now beginning to follow a definite pattern, particularly with the more "high-risk" offenders.

My experience with John showed me that there is always a possibility that somebody will open up, given the right encouragement and more importantly I should trust my intuition more than I had in the past. Such experience was a valuable resource.

Roland Woodward, Principal Psychologist later wrote - "Mr Chapman has an impressive ability to accept people for who they are and extends this beyond the confines of the prison setting. He clearly believes that the people he works with should not be regarded as work time only concerns, and is willing to accept responsibility for community contact when this is appropriate. "He adds "He is sensitive to the needs of others and the possibilities of development. He is however very practical and understands the world our clients return to".

Although Roland and other staff recognised the very diverse backgrounds of the prisoners, referred to as "clients", on occasions, the policies of the regime were administered without any flexibility whatsoever.

When the Grendon community was reunited on the Buckinghamshire site, the policies were reviewed again and certain prisoners that had been in Winchester were penalised for their behaviour whilst away from Grendon. Given the circumstances of their separation from the rest of the communities, it was hardly surprising to me that some men chose to return briefly to the behaviour that they had before they volunteered for therapy.

For instance, Mark Leech openly admitted that he had used Cannabis during the early days in Winchester as did many others. However, the staff group decided to invoke the "No drugs" rule and transferred him out even though the rest of the prisoners felt he deserved a chance. I expressed the view that this was a very unfair situation but unfortunately the staff vote was 16 to 1.

There were conflicts within the staff group on B wing which could not easily be resolved.

Fortunately, within a few months of our return, the majority of the group was replaced with new staff and I was given promotion to Temporary Senior Officer, working alongside John Keen and another Senior Officer Roy Moore who was flexible enough to try new ideas.

Roland Woodward left the wing to open a new Assessment Unit on A wing, so we were left without a wing doctor or psychologist. This gave John Keen and me the opportunity to restructure the treatment programme to suit the needs of the new group of staff and prisoners.

1990 and 1991 proved to be very positive years. My time on B wing had been very positive professionally and it was just over three years before I looked to move on.

I had decided to do another period in the Assessment Unit whilst I considered what to do next. A new and very capable therapist had joined B wing, Dr Ayesha Mutheveloe, and before I left she presented me with a piece of paper that would eventually lead me in an entirely new and different direction.

Ayesha had nominated me for The Butler Trust Award which was annually presented to prison staff that had exceptionally contributed to the work of the prison service.

The nomination came in July 1992. Ayesha wrote "I have observed for myself the skills and professional qualities that make him a very special officer - an asset to the prison service but more importantly of great benefit to the therapeutic work of Grendon", she added

It felt very rewarding that Dr Roger Cruickshank and Ayesha had recognised the effort I was making and she added "My predecessor Dr Cruickshank recommended him for the award some years ago based on the Therapeutic Community he helped to set up and run for Grendon inmates in Winchester. Even if I didn't receive the actual award their recognition meant a great deal to me.

A couple of weeks after being nominated one of the female governors, Lynne Davies, met me in the corridor. "Joe, how would you like to go to Holloway prison?"

She explained "We're researching the possibility of opening F Wing for women prisoners and we are putting together a visit to Holloway to discuss the issues. Are you up for it?" F wing had originally been intended for women prisoners when the prison was built, so this seemed like the ideal opportunity to be involved in a new project. I accepted the offer without any hesitation.

On October 8th, 1992 a team from Grendon went to Holloway to give information about the therapeutic regime and to ask the question "Do women prisoners need therapeutic treatment? If so, how can it best be facilitated"?

We arrived punctually at 10.30 am and were taken to the Training Centre which is situated outside of Holloway Gate Lodge. The team was led by Lynne Davies and included myself, Dr. Peter Lewis (Consultant Psychotherapist), Officer Liz Bibby, Lynne Garnett (from Grendon Education Department) and two prisoners who both were serving life sentences, Ron W and John from B wing.

These prisoners were chosen because of their commitment to therapy and of course it gave me another opportunity to observe John in the outside environment without any physical restrictions to his liberty.

It was disappointing that Holloway had not managed to include representations from the uniformed officers, Governors or Medical Officers but there were two female prisoners to represent the views of the women in Holloway. Several people represented various outside agencies and this was my first meeting with a woman called Chris Tchaikovsky who was the director of a charity called "Women in Prison".

The day proved to be very rewarding for everybody. There was a fairly heavy exchange of views and ideas concerning the feasibility of women coming to Grendon.

However, no conclusion could be made and it was decided that Holloway would form a committee to make a return visit to Grendon at some point in the future.

John proved to be excellent ambassador for Grendon and I was particularly impressed with his ability to communicate at all levels.   His skills had increased one hundred percent since his arrival at Wellingborough two and a half years before. I left Holloway with the realisation that women prisoners seem to get little or no opportunity to work through their offending behaviour in depth and perhaps Grendon was a viable option?

The seed was planted firmly in the back of my mind.

In December of that year I was interviewed in London as part of the process to determine if I would receive the Butler Trust Award. On the interviewing panel was a former prison Governor from Maidstone prison, the Rev. Peter Timms, He questioned me rigorously about the Grendon regime. I wasn't familiar with who he was at the time but our paths were destined to cross as some point in the future.

Before the end of the year I received notification that I had been successful and would be invited to attend a ceremony in the New Year. The award was to be presented by Her Royal Highness the Princess Anne at Holyrood Palace in Edinburgh.

The confirmation of the award was a positive note to end the year with as it marked a period of fifteen years working with prisoners and their families.

In March 1993, my wife and I flew to Scotland for the award ceremony. It was a grand affair, mixing with Lords and Ladies prior to the actual presentation at the Palace and being able to stay in the Edinburgh Thistle Hotel.

Forty-four staff had been honoured for outstanding work in Scottish and British jails, but for the first time I began to wonder if I really deserved it.

I had carried out my work without any consideration of the effect that it might have on those close to me. Half of the sacrifice and effort that had been made was during my days off. I still couldn't disclose the number of rules that needed bending in order to achieve the end result. If somebody should be honoured it was my wife Wendy.

She had tirelessly followed me around while I continued to build on the experiences with ex-offenders and there were odd occasions when she would remark "It would have been easier if I had married a plumber." or "Can we arrange a night out with somebody who hasn't raped or murdered anybody?" But believe it or not, the only concern she had right now was the prospect of having to meet Princess Anne, which she thought she had got away with until a lady standing nearby said, "Have you met Her Royal Highness yet?"

Before Wendy could offer any excuse, a meeting had been arranged. She needn't have worried. The Princess was very natural and friendly, "How do you cope with him as he's so dedicated to his work? And "It must be difficult managing the family around his work"? Of Course, Wendy was going through experiences that most wives could never imagine?

The Butler Trust was a registered charity and its Chairman was the Right Honourable Lord Justice Woolf. Two of its Trustees were the Rev Peter Timms who I met earlier and the Right Honourable David Astor. Both who were present at the ceremony.

It would be a couple of years later I would meet them again in very unusual circumstances, but for now with the small metal badge pinned proudly to my chest, Wendy and I returned home.

Chapter 11

Back in August 1991, Grendon held a special conference in response to a report by Lord Woolf following the riot in Strangeways, Manchester. The aim was to bring together a large group of professionals and more importantly prisoners, to explore ways to introduce the changes recommended by the Woolf report, within a reasonable time scale and in a cost-effective manner.

The Home Secretary, Mr Kenneth Baker, attended the conference on August 21st and asked for a report on the debate to be on his desk by September 2nd. In the same month, he presented a paper on the Criminal Justice Bill to the House of Commons and at the end of his speech announced "There is to be a second Grendon."

Sadly, a great deal of the Grendon debate was ignored.

The great and the good, together with a handful of bleeding hearts, took the ideas away and filed them under "too costly" or "politically suicidal", where they would gather dust until another career builder came along and reinvented the original idea. Egotistical politicians all too often crushed many of the truly constructive ideas from Grendon prisons conferences.

And so, almost two years later, with the recommendations of the Woolf report struggling to be endorsed and the report from the "Power Sharing" conference gathering dust in Grendon's archives, something exciting was to be offered. Governor Michael Selby had retired to sit on the Parole Board, and new Governor, Tim Newell, replaced him. Tim had been the Governor at Winchester during the time that Grendon had been there and it had alerted him to the prisons potential. He was seen by many to be a very nice man "too nice to be a prison governor".

He was forward thinking and prepared to forge ahead with new ideas. One idea that was spoken of at the 1991 conference was that Grendon should have its own purpose built Pre-Release Unit to be run by Pre Release Officers.

This was an opportunity to put all of my experience into the role of a Pre-Release Officer and to be able to put my money (or should I say the Prison Service's money) where my mouth was!

The recommendation to the Home Secretary was "A halfway house or hostel with a regime somewhere between the closed conditions of a prison and open society with hostel placements to become an implicit part of every sentence." (Remember the earlier comment about a file marked too costly or politically suicidal?)

The hostel should be an integral part of and thus funded by the individual, specific prison and in some cases the hostel will be sited within the prison boundaries.

Delegates had argued that "the last third of their sentence should be served in hostel accommodation. It was thought that such a system would substantially increase the number of prisoners successfully rehabilitated whilst at the same time provide a more cost-effective system for the taxpayer. "

The transition from prison to freedom was recognised to be a most challenging time and "the current practice of discharging prisoners at the end of their sentence with just a few pounds and a wave goodbye must stop. Such practice often negates, in days, the good work achieved over years."

The main task of the Pre-Release Officer was to limit the negative social input the prison sentence will have had on the inmate, and so I applied for the post of Grendon's first full time Pre-Release Officer. Using the conference report as a blue print I set about developing the PRU (Pre-Release Unit) which would later become known as the IDU (Inmate Development Unit).

One thing that the Prison Service are extremely good at is developing units but I was determined this would be more than just a unit; it would be a Centre of Excellence.

As most of the Grendon Hospital Wing was now closed, it was decided the new unit could be developed at the end of this wing with the provision of five cells above it; these would be used by prisoners who were awaiting transfer to other prisons, rather than release into society.

Whilst waiting for the building work to be completed in the downstairs area of the prison hospital, I obtained the governors permission to move two prisoners into the upper level so that they could help me to refurbish what would eventually be the new pre-transfer unit.

It was decided that only two staff would run this facility, under the supervision of a Governor and Hospital Principal Officer with the provision of a full-time Probation Officer.

Eventually I would work with Hospital Senior Officer John Gilbey and Probation Officer Debbie Patterson. This "pack of three" experienced Grendon staff would work like "Criminal Justice Condoms" hopefully preventing society from being shafted by prisoners who had conned their way through therapy, protecting the public from "unwanted acts of theft, violence, rape and murder" by ensuring that ex-prisoners received adequate and effective support on release, but more about that later.

In the initial foundation stage, it would be just two prisoners and I who would prepare the unit for occupation, cleaning, painting and furnishing as the budget would allow.

My choice of men was not going to be difficult as I had already identified two who I knew could be trusted to work without supervision, but more importantly they had to get along with each other socially. In the initial stages I would be away from the building for long periods and the prisoners would be left unlocked, entirely to their own devices.

John was my first obvious choice. I had been his personal officer and group facilitator on B wing and we had developed a very strong working relationship.
The added bonus for me was that I had grown to like him and felt that he was strongly motivated to succeed on his eventual release. He was just a little younger than me and shared a similar sense of humour, as well as a passion for good therapy.

I felt he had travelled a long way in his two and a half years in therapy and was certainly not the personality who had killed an innocent little girl almost sixteen years ago. I sensed real remorse and he had said on many occasions "I wish I could turn the clock back and return the child to her loving family". He was realistic that it would be difficult for most people to forgive him for what he had done. "How can they, if I can't forgive myself?" he would say.

His crime had been committed under the influence of drink and drugs, although he never sought to use these as a justification for his actions. They had helped to unleash the demons that had become part of his personality at that time. The little girl was in the right place but at the wrong time. She came to represent everything that was wrong with his life and everybody that he hated.

Having been found guilty of Manslaughter on the grounds of diminished responsibility he was given a Discretionary Life sentence.

He had served his tariff, which was the minimum amount of time he was expected to stay in prison and was awaiting a review by a Discretionary Lifer Panel headed by a high court judge which might mean a possible move to less secure open prison conditions.

He had worked extremely well in his therapy and had earned the privileged position of Education Red Band which also meant that he could travel around the prison unescorted.

My second choice of inmate was a man called Derek O. He was also from B wing and knew John well. They had both developed a prominent level of trust within the jail and were hard working and reliable.

Derek was also preparing to move out of Grendon soon. He was a mandatory lifer, which meant that he would have to move to a less secure C category prison and then an open prison before the Parole board could consider him for release.

The different between a Discretionary Life Sentence and a Mandatory Life sentence depends on the circumstances of the crime.

John had killed a child under the influence of drink and drugs when the balance of his mind had therefore been impaired. The court had ruled that he was guilty of Manslaughter rather than Murder, on the grounds of diminished responsibility. He was given a Discretionary Life sentence.

On the other hand, Derek had killed his wife and mother in law without the influence of drink or drugs, in a pre-meditated and calculated act of violence. The court ruled that this was clearly a crime of Murder which carried an automatic Mandatory Life sentence. Derek had murdered his wife and mother-in-law, and his two children had witnessed their deaths. There is no doubt in my mind that he carried real guilt and remorse for his crimes which had a devastating effect on his children.

Through the therapeutic process, he had examined the reasons for his actions and had gone to great lengths to rebuild his relationship with the kids.

Potentially John could have served the shorter sentence, although this need not have been the case, as each man is given a Tariff which is set by the judge at the time of trial. The tariff is the minimum period that a lifer must serve before being considered for release. It is at times, a complicated, confusing process with many variables and the end result for most lifers will depend on their behaviour during sentence.

Given Derek's positive progress over a brief time, it was quite possible he would serve a shorter period than John overall.

I had not been Derek's personal officer but we had spent a lot of time together socially. When he arrived on B wing I was surprised to find so many similarities between his personality and my own. We had a shared sense of humour and a very positive relationship. I knew that he could carry out any task given to him to a high standard. He was also able to "acquire" useful items, tools, furniture, paint etc which was very valuable during the empire building stage.

When he first arrived at Grendon he completed a Psychometric Test and I was amazed to discover that he had answered 80% of the questions the same as I had done. Over the next two years I realised that our personalities were remarkably similar and I could predict fairly accurately how he would react in given situations.

This may sound very odd but a bond had begun to form between the three of us during the period on B Wing and I knew that this would make the process of development much more enjoyable and rewarding.

The governor provided a £10,000 budget towards furnishing and fittings and we were also able to collect items of furniture, household utensils, electrical goods, carpets and curtains from staff, friends and family. In the initial stages, almost six months, there would only be myself and the two prisoners in a large empty building and we were destined to spend many hours in each other's company. It was inevitable that strong lasting friendships would develop.

The situation I found myself to be working in is unique to Grendon and even unique for a uniformed prison officer.

I spent many hours in the company of John and Derek, sharing concerns, anxieties and ideas for the new unit. We also shared personal aspects of our lives and not surprisingly good friendships developed. I was not being conditioned any more than they were and it proved to be a recipe for future success.

Aside from the psychological work that was in progress there was an enormous amount of physical effort required.

We set about the task of painting and decorating the upstairs cellblock, preparing the communal areas and furnishing my new office. During this "nest building" period we roamed around the main prison looking for any items that might come in useful for the new unit.

Derek proved to be very resourceful as he managed to charm curtains, carpets, furniture and electrical items from the hospital and Education department. In fact, everything that wasn't screwed down and didn't appear to belong to anybody would be lifted and brought into the unit. We referred to this as "redistribution of wealth".

The usual day would begin by my unlocking John first and he would immediately put the kettle on and make some toast with jam or marmalade. We would both have breakfast while we waited for Derek to emerge from his cell. We began to guess what sort of mood he would be in by the music that was playing on his stereo. Handel's water music or a Strauss waltz would signify a good mood but if we heard the Ride of the Valkrey or the 1812 Overture, John and I knew something was bothering him.

One morning it was the Dance of the Sugarplum Fairy so I decided to cash in on his good mood. "We need a large coffee table for the meeting room in front of my office, I know where I can get one, but you'll have to give me a lift Derek".

"Don't forget my medical restriction". He warned "I might have to sue you if I pull a muscle."

Of course, I ignore him. "The table I've got my eyes on isn't too heavy but it's in an awkward place. We will need to move it when nobody is looking. Lunchtime would be the ideal moment. Are you up for it?"

The table had been standing inside the main entrance to the prison for the past twenty years. It was just an ordinary Formica top table with tubular steel legs nothing spectacular but with plenty of history. It would be good to have the table as a centre-piece for the new unit as it signified the merging of the old regime with a new era.

"You realize that you could put my sentence plan back about five years if I'm caught helping you to nick this table" Derek moaned as I opened the double doors onto the prison centre.

"Stop whining and grab the table while I hold the doors open" I ordered.

Within seconds it had been lifted from where it had stood for almost a quarter of a decade and was on its way to a new home in the pre-transfer unit. As we placed the table in the centre of the large Axminster carpet which had once graced the floor of B Wings community room there was only one slight problem!

"It's too high for a coffee table." Derek exclaimed!

"Say no more" I declared, and reaching into my briefcase I produced a large hacksaw. "I'll soon sort this slight problem out." I chuckled. And I began to saw a length of about two feet from one of the legs. Within less than twenty minutes the table had been cut down to a more reasonable height of ten inches.

We made some coffee and sat around the new acquisition as we decided what we would need to get next.

"A nice fish tank would look good" said John, "perhaps one of the staff might want to donate one to us?"

We examined the possibilities as the phone rang in my office. It was the Security Principal Officer and he didn't sound too pleased. "You were seen nicking the table from the centre area so I want you to return it to its rightful place and no more questions will be asked. If you don't get it back there within the next ten minutes" he raged, "you'll have me to answer to"

"But" I tried to interrupt. "No buts just do it," he stormed and the line went dead.

"Oh shit Derek you've gone too far this time," I shouted, "best you return the table where it came from." There was no reply. And as I came out of the office I saw Derek and John disappearing down the stairs. So much for the loyalty we had pledged to each other when we first moved into the unit.

It was quite a struggle to get the table back to the centre on my own but I managed it just as the Security PO appeared at the prison entrance.

"Fucking hell what have you done?" he screamed, staring wide eyed at the shorter version of the original table. "We can't use that now. Take it away and get out of my sight before I do something I might regret," he stormed.

In hindsight, the funniest thing about this incident was that he was more interested in the damage I had done to the table rather than to question how I had managed to cut through the metal legs. After all, a hacksaw is not something you see every day in a high security jail?

The brand-new Pre-release and Pre-transfer unit was completed over a three-month period. Towards the rear of the Hospital wing the works department had converted a single cell and two hospital dormitories into self-contained flats.

There was a single bed-sit and two double bedroom flats with a shared fitted kitchen.

Each accommodation area had ordinary doors which might be found in any block of flats outside of prison. All fixtures and fittings were the general household type and every utensil was the same as that which could be found in houses in the community. There were steel knives, forks and spoons, carving knives, full power bleach, spray aerosols and garden tools for the use of all residents in the Pre-Release flats.

The only thing that differed from similar accommodation outside was the high tensile bars at the windows and the outer security gates.

The prisoners who lived in the flats had keys to their own doors and could go in and out of each other's flats, on invitation of course at any time of the day or night.

The residents were classed as low security "D category" prisoners, living in a non-secure environment within a higher security "B Category" prison. As the new Unit consisted of both a Pre-Release regime and a Pre-Transfer we soon decided to change its title to the Inmate Development Unite (IDU).

It's difficult to describe how the Unit worked but the concept was to provide living areas for two types of prisoner who had completed their period of Therapy. Upstairs, were five prison cells for inmates who were moving out of Grendon, progressively to other prisons, who were deemed to have successfully completed their Therapy. Downstairs, were five self-contained, furnished flats for prisoners facing release but both groups mixed socially. Once the unit was finished John and Derek would live in the Pre-Transfer cells above the Pre-Release self-contained flats.

Towards the end of the initial building programme John and Derek felt disappointed that they could not live in the relative luxury of the Pre-Release area, even though they had been responsible for decorating, furnishing and cleaning prior to the arrival of the first resident.

Instead, they had to live upstairs in the Pre-Transfer Unit cells because they were not deemed suitable for lower security conditions. even though I trusted them more than some of the residents we had downstairs. They still had to be locked in their cells at eight thirty every night.

When the IDU was opened, we began the task of working with prisoners as they finished their therapy during the transition from prison to freedom or from Grendon to another prison.

At the 1991 conference, it was felt that prisoners might spend one third of their sentence in less secure conditions, but in the IDU we decided that they would spend a period of three months getting used to moving out or moving on.

We felt it was our task to examine the needs of each individual and ensure that they had the necessary skills and support to survive on release into the community or when they arrived at their next prison. To some extent it would be a stage of testing them following the "successful" completion of therapy.

I was personally looking forward to using the experience that I had gained over the past ten years working with prisoners individually, in small groups and socially outside of prison. It was also another ideal opportunity to involve their families at the most important stage of their sentence, particularly those who were coming towards release.

Once again, the conclusion to the 1991 conference was that "Grendon is not a place where the inmate is either oppressed or vulnerable. Such an atmosphere is conducive to self-analysis and group therapy. It is under such conditions that some attempt is made to analyse our own criminal behavioural patterns, in an effort to understand as opposed to defending or excusing the inexcusable."

Socrates said in BC420 "The unexamined life is not worth living".

It would only become relevant to me ten years later how much the statements made at the Power Sharing conference would form the blue print for other prison reforms. However, for the time being we started putting the inmates through the IDU experience and I was not surprised to find that some of our findings would begin to highlight many areas of deficiency in the therapeutic regime and show how ill prepared some prisoners were for release. Some were considered to be extremely dangerous, even after two or three years in therapy?

Grendon targets men towards the later stages of their sentence ideally and about 35% were serving life sentences in 1994.

There has always been a debate on Grendon's effectiveness and the traditional view remained that the development of personal insight and re-integration of personality are sufficient targets for the prison. What happens to men after they have left prison is obviously beyond the control or influence of the establishment, because so many factors come into play it is impossible to predict.

Grendon had lost sight of much of the extra work that it did after a prisoner's release.
Continued communication with the ex-prisoner and his friends and family was a vital part of successful rehabilitation.

In the Inmate Development Unit, we tried to retain ties with all of the men who passed through and therefore learned a great deal about the effectiveness of therapy and "what works" for successful integration in society. Unfortunately, it soon became clear that the inmate development unit would ultimately fail in its purpose.

Most men were leaving Grendon either because they had fallen foul of one of the rules forbidding drink, drugs, sex or violence or because they are transferred (either by choice or as part of a sentence plan) to other prisons. Only about eight percent of the prisons population would leave Grendon on release.

The prison had developed a white elephant which would not survive as a viable resource in the long run.

In the aftermath of the Strangeways riot (April 1990) the Woolf Report recommended changes to take place in the prison system. The report highlighted overcrowding, poor conditions and negative staff/inmate relationships in most jails. It also examined the rehabilitative process in the management of Sex Offenders.

At the end of a period of research by the Home Office it was clear that there were enough medium to long term female prisoners who could benefit from a therapeutic regime. Eighty percent of the women interviewed expressed a desire to be helped but it had already been decided that Grendon would not house females.

As part of my Butler Trust Award, I had been granted money to visit all of the female prisons in the UK to examine the possibility of a therapeutic prison for women and through this piece of work my thoughts were focussed on the plight of women prisoners with children.

Theirs was a difficult experience from women who had no dependents... Suffering imprisonment was one thing but having to endure the separation from their offspring was a pain that persisted everyday of their sentence.

During a trip to Holloway prison I shared some time on the train with an elderly lady who was visiting her daughter in prison. She was travelling from Leeds on a fortnightly run which could take up to 5 hours each way. The lady was in her mid-60's and was struggling to care for three young children between the ages of eighteen months and six years. She would ensure that the mother could see all of the children each visiting day.

This was a mammoth task. The plight of her daughter was not a unique case and I would meet many women in an analogous situation over the next three years. She had been imprisoned for defrauding the DHSS to the tune of £1500 and was given a three-month custodial sentence, which she began to serve in HMP Risley.

The prison experience had affected her badly. Having made two serious attempts to kill herself, the authorities decided to transfer her to the psychiatric wing in Holloway. She now had less than a month to serve but was still at risk of self-harm.

She was not a violent person, more of a danger to herself than others. Her sentence had already cost the taxpayer an estimated £8,000 and she would undoubtedly be a further burden to the state on her eventual release.

It occurred to me that this was not just a terrible waste of money but also a pointless exercise in punishment. There had to be a realistic alternative.

Over the next couple of months, I began to develop an idea for any alternative to custody for women with dependent children which could operate in accordance with probation service policies. I had also visited several mother and baby units which further convinced me that there had to be a better alternative.

I had also been granted the unique opportunity to work as a private counsellor, with women prisoners in HM Prison Cookham Wood and in Holloway prison, whilst still working as a uniformed officer at HM prison Grendon. This proved to be a difficult balancing act.

It wasn't easy having the role of Prison Officer and also a counsellor in other prisons and there were bound to be conflicts. As I continued the work with women prisoners I was often treated with suspicion.

One of the main concerns was always that of professional boundaries and I firmly believe that with sufficient guidance a person will soon identify a comfortable limit to the level of personal contact that he or she is able to have with a prisoner and to what extent self-disclosure is acceptable.

Under the code of discipline for prison officers, the boundaries are made quite clear. However, recent experience had shown me that the level of contact between officers and inmates varies between establishments.

Officers who have worked in local prisons often have less anxiety about the amount of information that prisoners have on them, mainly due to the fact that they often live together within the locality.

There is obviously the security angle to be considered in terms of a prisoner knowing exactly where a member of staff lives but contact outside of the prison cannot easily be avoided and should not always indicate the need for any panic.

In 1980, I lived in an area shared by five ex-offenders and their respected families, and there was never any hint of trouble. In fact, the good relationship that existed between us was a source of comfort in many ways.
Believe it or not my biggest problem came from an ex-inmate from miles away Brighton, during a period when he was on the run from the police. He used an ingenious method to locate my home address, then after pestering my wife he was finally arrested in the kitchen of our home.

At no point in my career have I been compromised by anyone or have I laid myself open to corruption. Obviously, there are times when I will not be above suspicion but I remain accountable for my actions and ensure that my activities are well documented.

At this point you may be wondering why there is a role conflict as I clearly appear to understand what my role is, and more importantly what can be achieved by demonstrating a little humanity and understanding towards those in our care.

The problem lies within the code of discipline for prison officers, which lays down clear guidelines between that which is acceptable and that which is not. In my own perception of boundaries which often stretch much further than those of my colleagues, the conflict is therefore, how can you determine that which is professional conduct and that which is not.

On the one hand I am extremely grateful for the support that has been given by the Prison Department which has allowed me to work outside of the traditional boundaries, but on the other hand I was continuously frustrated by some manager's inability to accept my approach, even though I had a proven track record.

I was still reminded that first and foremost I am a prison officer and that I should not be so familiar with prisoners. In this case, I would argue that being a prison officer should not rob me of my right to be an individual.

I had learned from working in Cookham prison that my personal boundaries must be more clearly defined and that perhaps I would not be able to have the same level of involvement with the female inmates. However, after only a short time I realised that I could in fact work in the same mode and that the women welcomed this approach.

I remained constantly aware of the dangers of transference and therefore maintain a sense of perspective as regards personal involvement. Transference is a counselling term, which basically means being aware of the influence that a counsellor can have on an inmate and to ensure that anything other than a working relationship does not develop.

I have found that it is still possible to work closely with relatives and friends in order to achieve results. In fact, I felt quite comfortable in the present role and I was told that the women respect my position and welcome the level of care and support that is offered.

So once again, I am in a situation whereby I feel a sense of achievement but also, I have to face further criticism due to the fact that my method of working does not fit into the theoretical role of counsellor or the traditional role of prison officer.

In the Cookham regime I was not working as a prison officer but the staff team was aware that this was my main employment. Therefore, they were not readily able to accept the work that I did or indeed the way that I did it.

The main problem is communication and I feel that it is important that management should first of all recognise that staff are working at different levels but more importantly that this should be communicated to the rest of the staff group.

Problems obviously ensue since there is lack of understanding within the staff group.

At Grendon prison no confidentiality existed but in the women's prison confidentiality is the most crucial factor. The contrast between the two principles is obviously quite startling but I managed to separate the two regimes quite effectively.

At Grendon I wore a uniform but as a counsellor I did not. The latter enabled me to be seen as more of an individual and removed the air of authority and discipline. I still carried a set of keys but the women can ignore the fact that I was an officer (screw) in my daily role. However, I could never ignore this and stayed aware of the obligations that I had concerning security within the prison.

I insisted that the women may tell me anything that they wish in complete confidence but I stated clearly that I would have a duty to act on information that had implications for security. I could therefore not be compromised.

As you can well imagine there were many other areas of difficulty when considering the difference that exists between the role of counsellor and prison officer but safe containment alone will not guarantee public safety in the long terms.

Although rehabilitation had become somewhat of a dirty word, the truth is that unless people are encouraged to change their ways then there will always be victims in the future.

The project that I began to develop considered the problems experienced by the Prison and Probation Services and served to bridge the gap that existed between the release of women with dependent children and the point at which they could be successfully be reunited with them.

At the beginning of 1995 a young writer was given a placement in Grendon to study the work of our Inmate Development Unit and it was decided she would shadow me for a brief period. Her name was Lucy Astor and I was surprised to find out that she was David Astor's daughter.

Initially Lucy appeared to be very timid and quite overawed by the regime in Grendon. She was not at ease in her discussions with the prisoners and totally unsure of her capabilities in this unusual environment.

Mixing socially with men who had robbed, murdered and raped was not a concept she had dreamed of six months previously   Offering her a seat in the communal dining room seemed to affect her in the same way it might had it been an electric chair.

Lucy had been brought up to believe that she was very fortunate through no efforts of her own. Derek instilled a sense of social responsibility through his example rather than dictation.

The Astor family fortune came from property development on Manhattan Island in the 19th century and Lucy had been given an amount of money to set up a charitable trust. She had developed the idea of "The Encore Awards" for best second novels. More recently David and Lucy had sponsored a Lady called Mary Dines to set up Asylum Aid for those in need of it.

As she followed me in my duties we talked about the ethos of Grendon and how I would like to have developed a therapeutic community for women prisoners. And I mentioned my idea for an alternative to prison for women and children. This was of great interest to her and I arranged for her to visit Cookham Prison.

On her return to Grendon, Lucy asked if I had considered developing the project further "Would you consider leaving the prison service if you had the funding to enable this." She inquired.

The suggestion that I might want to leave the prison service had come at a time when I was feeling particularly disheartened with my work as I felt the Inmate Development Unit was not working well and I was beginning to discover that the quality of the therapy had deteriorated drastically.

More and more men arrived in the unit ill prepared for release into society or transfer to another prison. Many had managed to con their way through the programme and were displaying offending behaviour with no time left to correct it. I had a feeling that I would see many familiar faces returning to prison soon.

Another contributing factor was the fact that security and containment was beginning to take precedence over the building of trust and confidence within staff/prisoner relationships.

The old Grendon regime was being forced to give way to a newer more structured - less flexible process. There were small pockets of good practice but on the whole an atmosphere of oppression.

I responded to Lucy's suggestion within forty-eight hours and we started to determine how my dream might best be achieved.

On July 10th, 1995 I handed in my resignation to the Governor of Grendon.

In a three-page memo, I wrote: "I am leaving Grendon on July 24th after eighteen years of devotion to its ethos and early policies. As I leave I know I will feel saddened, not because I am leaving some dear friends and colleagues but because I genuinely fear for the future of an establishment that could once take pride in being a unique place in which to work, a place where inmates and staff showed caring and concern for each other.

Over the past six months I have examined why I am finding it so easy to walk away from a career that I thought would last for a lifetime. I have become "gate happy" for so many reasons but the main areas of concern as I leave are as follows:

The gap that exists between the therapeutic communities and the security department has never been wider than it is today. Over the years, it has been traditional for staff who have no interest in therapy or rehabilitation to elect to work in the security and operations group but now they are joined by many disillusioned officers who might have survived in the therapeutic community if they had been supported and encouraged when it mattered.

The security/ops group is infested with cynical, bitter and twisted individuals who can see no further than "the Woodcock report".

These people feel threatened by the concept of dynamic security and are turned on by the power that they exercise over prisoners and their families.

The tighter the security and control becomes then the greater will be the feeling of inmates and certain staff that their democracy is under threat. No one needs reminding that Grendon is a prison but many need to be reminded that it began its life as a unique therapeutic community.

      The past three years have seen a constant parade of visitors through the establishment. There has been good and bad publicity in the media and almost monthly there has been some form of public relations exercise designed to impress on other prisons and outside agencies that Grendon's therapy is alive and well.

Most visitors are impressed by the prison's friendly atmosphere and by the welcome response that they get from most of the inmates but it is a fact that those who look below the glossy exterior are surprised by the lack of experience and expertise within the staff teams, not to mention the absence of substantial training and support and the diverse and destructive methods employed by the therapeutic communities.

Prison officers that show dedication and concern for their roles in the therapeutic community are constantly frustrated by management decisions that are made without full staff consultation and the introduction of policies that erode the therapeutic regimes.

These policies are introduced from outside Grendon and are designed to increase security and containment. They conflict with the ethos of a therapeutic community and yet they are embraced by Senor Management and the 'anti therapy brigade.'

In my years of service, I have developed effective communication with prisoners and their families at grass roots level and they all report that they are increasingly being made to feel degraded and criminalized by the prisons 'over the top' security measures.

The prison's response to their feelings is to construct a Portakabin where visitors can be humiliated in private. At lease the comfortable visits centre restores their faith until the next visit when they face the ritual yet again.

Recently a theological student stated that it appeared to him that "Grendon existed for the staff and not the inmates" he added that "it feels like too much time and effort is being spent on trying to impress outsiders but only a minority of staff spend time listening to and caring for the welfare of the prisoners." I feel Grendon should stop the PR (public relations) and concentrate on the TR (therapeutic regime).

On a more personal note I feel disgusted that the Inmate Development Unit has been allowed to degenerate into a "one man show".

The initial burst of enthusiasm, the promise of better resources and a productive future for this unit have materialised as empty gestures designed once again to impress those who were listening at the time.

This unit was borne out of the 1992 conference during which inmates' views were sought as to the usefulness of such a regime. All inmates greeted it with enthusiasm and praise and two years later they still do.

However, sadly it was never really owned by much of our staff and it now faces the prospect of closure unless more life is pumped into it. It has been well and truly shafted by the Home Secretary's Office and almost beaten into submission by the prison department's risk assessment policies, not to mention the wonderful "Sex Offenders Treatment Programme."

Our own security department have raised objections at every turn and yet it lives on for the time being, full and still trying to help inmates with their transition into other prisons or into society.

I have been forced to work alone over the past four months as one officer on a two man shift pattern. There is no continuity of staffing, little or no security and certainly little or no concern for my welfare or that of inmates in my sole charge.

I sincerely hope that this unit is not allowed to close through lack of interest and that it will continue for many years but unfortunately, I fear that it has already outstayed its welcome.

I extend my best wishes to all of those who care about the rehabilitation of prisoners and hope that you will be encouraged and not condemned for caring.

I left Grendon prison to run a charity for ex-prisoners called "The Replay Trust" mainly for high risk female prisoners, but also offering accommodation and floating support for males.

Unfortunately, this venture, although successful, could not sustain me as a director and nearly four years later, having been forced to take voluntary redundancy, I was once again looking for a new career.

Chapter 12

Towards the middle of 1996 several life sentenced prisoners were living in the central Oxford area who had spent part of their sentence at Grendon Prison. Two of them, who were well known to me, and had befriended a third man who would ultimately attract adverse media attention yet again.

Gary Watkins had been at Grendon for a two-year period just before I had resigned in 1995. He had supposedly completed his therapy successfully and was released from Leyhill prison near Bristol. He was offered the hospitality of other ex-offenders and was deemed by the authorities to be safe to manage by the Probation Service in the community.

Towards the end of November that same year, a young college student was walking towards her home on a cold, dark and foggy evening "I had just left my violin class and was walking home thinking about doing some revision for my music exam. It was about four in the afternoon." She recalls.

"I remember this man walking towards me. He looked very ordinary, like someone's dad. He had eyes that reminded me of the comedian Steve Martin. I thought he was going to ask me the time or for directions to somewhere."

But Gary Watkins was no comedian. He pulled a knife and held it to her face, and then he took her to his car and forced her into the passenger foot well, covering her with a blanket. He drove for forty minutes until they were in the countryside and pulled into a lay-by near to the village of Tiddington, Oxfordshire, where she was subjected to a brutal three-hour sex assault.

The spot where the offence was committed is only three miles from my home. It's sickening to think that while I relaxed in front of my TV in the comfort of my lounge a young girl feared for her life at the hands of somebody I knew.

Even though I have worked with some of the worst criminals in the UK, occasionally I am personally connected to the horrors of certain reconvictions.

His victim was referred to in the press as "Sabrina". She was an Asian girl who had never had a boyfriend. He was a man who had been released on licence after serving sixteen years of a life sentence for three serious sex attacks.

He had convinced many at Grendon, including myself, that he was no longer a danger.

Sabrina will never be able to forget the events. "I was cold and shaking. He tied my hands behind my back and held the knife in his mouth. He threatened to mutilate me with the knife and I shouted Oh my god. He told me, God isn't going to help you now." She was subjected to a horrific, degrading sexual assault.

His victim was left with one question that haunted her. "Who decided that a monster like Gary Watkins should be released?" She had been told that the correct procedures had been followed, that the prison service had acted correctly and the police did all they could. But for her none of it was enough.

She added" Before I can get on with my life, I need to know why Watkins was allowed out of prison. How did he convince the Psychologists he was safe to wander the streets and attack me?"

She was understandably angry "This case proves once again that sex offenders, indeed any offenders, can con the experts, con the system and get out and offend again. If Gary Watkins can do it, others can too."

This is the million-dollar question, when faced with repeat offences and it is one that few professionals can adequately answer. Much of the theory does not stand up to scrutiny in such cases and of course no risk assessment can be an exact science. I wanted to know why he had chosen to re-offended and if any new lessons could be learned?

I was personally angry with him for two reasons, the first that there had been yet another innocent victim and the second that he had placed a spotlight onto the local hostel once more and abused the trust of those who had welcomed him on release. I had no way of finding out where he had been taken so I made a decision to contact him through the very media that I had often criticised.

I wrote an open letter to the Editor of the Oxford Mail and Times which I hoped might come to Watkins's attention in prison.

I wrote: Dear Sir, having read the article by Becky Gaunt in the Oxford Mail on March 12th (Sex Fiends Term) and having spoken to Becky, I feel compelled to share my views with your readers regarding Judge Harold Wilson's comments and those of the Home Office.

I am a former prison officer and worked as a counsellor for eighteen years with serious male and female offenders. I have been personally involved in the resettlement of lifers into the nationwide community, retaining contact with several men and women. It is something that I encourage and one man has become a very close friend.

Gary Watkins who has recently received his second life sentence was known to me and to some of the other men I refer to. He chose to live in Oxford since he had formed relationships with people who offered full support to him on release. He had more than most men have on release, which is why he could never consider himself to be isolated, lonely or rejected. (These are sometimes reasons that ex-prisoners give for their re-offending)

Prior to being released from Leyhill Prison in Gloucestershire, he spent a lengthy period in therapy at Grendon Prison in Buckinghamshire. During this period, he was given every opportunity to talk about his past history and offending behaviour. He was encouraged to change and was finally considered to have successfully completed his therapy. He was granted a transfer to less secure conditions to begin a release plan.

There were those who doubted his commitment and expressed that he was not as dangerous as he would want them to believe (They were wrong) I felt he was a predictable coward, hence his attack on defenceless women. He was a Mr Angry who found criticism difficult to take. At Leyhill he followed a similar pattern and was gradually granted periods of temporary release to work in the community. He was pictured by the "News of the World" at the end of last year waiting for a bus to take him to work.

Temporary release is a very necessary aspect of a good release plan. Once again Watkins cannot give the excuse that he was ill prepared for the outside world. Judge Wilson's comments echo my own feelings and those of other lifers who knew him
(Or thought they knew him).

The strong feelings are that he should remain in prison for the rest of his life. He has proven to those who doubted him at Grendon that he is a very dangerous man. The word is that this is exactly what he set out to do, and given his past history it is a very strong indication that it would be impossible to trust him again.

I have no doubt that he will feel sorry for himself and that he will feel guilty. Not for the terror he produced in his young victim but for the fact he let others down. I am always prepared to offer support to those who I feel genuinely want to give something back to society. The ease with which Gary Watkins convinced the staff (including myself) of his safety should not reflect badly on those who tried their hardest to understand and help him. Instead, it should mean that it would be impossible for anybody to be convinced of his safety in the future.

In normal circumstances a tariff of ten years is considered high but experience has shown me that Gary presented unusual circumstances. He seriously abused his chances and doing so deserves to remain safely behind bars. If he is ever released, his only form of transport should be a Zimmer frame. Sincerely, Joe Chapman

A couple of months later I received a response from Watkins which I have included in its entire form.

Dear Mr Chapman, I read your comments in one of the national newspapers a while back and felt then that I ought to write to you. Having repeatedly thought about it, I have gotten around to it at last.

Let me state immediately that if it hadn't been for the work done at Grendon the consequences for my victim would have been far worse - resulting in her death. Whether an explanation of this is required I don't know, you may have already been informed of what happened. But for the sake of understanding how Grendon did have a lifesaving effect let me say how it was.

For many years prior to Grendon I harboured and nurtured a sadistic sexual fantasy, one that kept raising its head in previous offences. The origins of this and my general disposition towards others had its roots in a very hostile upbringing. Grendon sorted all this out with me except that I never relinquished this fantasy - it had become ingrained and was very comforting!

So, going into Grendon there was nothing incongruous with my demeanor or outlook on life and this fantasy.

It wasn't until I began working out from Leyhill did the contradictory thoughts strike me. There I was getting along with folk in a way I had never dreamt possible, it felt great and there was this fantasy, years old by now.

I knew that the chances of me re-offending was high but in my fantasy, I got away with the crime. This "getting away with it "clause kept the fantasy alive, the expected sexual satisfaction was to be out of this world and yet in reality- I no longer felt hostile to the world or towards women.

This became obvious as soon as I had my victim in my car.

What I should have felt according to my fantasy I didn't - what I felt was sorrow? I thought that once the sexual elements were started my feelings would change and that the fantasy would "begin". Again, after I undressed the poor girl, all I felt was guilt and shame and a lot of feelings for my victim. I simply could not carry out my fantasy. I had to let her go.

In making this decision I knew I had forfeited my life in the "normal" world.

Pre Grendon selfishness would have prevailed, post Grendon, and as out of place as it sounds, compassion prevailed. I could have still killed her and attempted to get away with it but I couldn't, and despite knowing where I would end up, where I am now, I don't regret not doing this.

I regret the harm I have done to my victim, her family and mine; I regret the loss of a future. But the most frustrating thing of all and yet the most relieving, is that after years of fantasising and having finally put myself able to fulfil it - I didn't. It wasn't pleasurable, any part of it.

Grendon enabled me to recognise and live with my true nature and I thank you for this. If my victim knew the part Grendon played in the making of one decision, "my life her hers?" she would thank you also.

The point of this letter is to acknowledge the work that Grendon does, what it did for me, and what it will do for others. As you said Mr Chapman, you cannot help a person who consciously holds things back. Perhaps I can be a lesson to those who might be so inclined themselves. I know that if I had spoken of this fantasy it would have dissolved the same as other problems did - the question as to why I didn't will be with me until I die.

Sorry, I know why I didn't, it was so "comforting" - The question is why was it so comforting that I couldn't let go of it?

The person who "brailed "prevails, and will endeavour to lead as positive a life as possible, within the confines of prison walls. Yours sincerely, Gary Watkins

PTO- Why I felt the need to write was because it may have been put to you that I simply reoffended. As far as my victim and her family are concerned I did, and what I did would have been terrible to them, this cannot be minimalised in any way.

The fact that I stopped the offence before anything physical happened, before it was too late and, despite knowing that in letting my victim go I would spend the rest of my life in prison, "I" stopped - thanks to Grendon.

The advice he gives to other prisoners about the retention of fantasies justifies my reasoning that good therapy must be about forming a close, supportive and eventually completely trusting relationship with offenders. To reveal the most disturbing, violent, sexual fantasies, there must be a mutual trust and understanding between therapist and client, but furthermore, I believe that there cannot be any boundaries in that relationship.

Ultimately, I have proven to myself more than anybody else that my approach has worked with remarkable results and the people that I have chosen to befriend over many years are those with whom I developed a relationship that has gone much further than that of a "normal" prisoner/prison officer relationship or therapist/client.

It cuts through all that I learned in my professional training and has not been damaging to me, my client or my close family.

Unfortunately, the Prison Service is drawn towards the continued use of modular offending behaviour courses, which foster a "classroom mentality". The expectation of many psychologists is that prisoners will safely reveal all, within very rigid boundaries and often without any relationship at all with the "facilitator".

However, this can simply become an even easier game for offenders to play during their process of apparent change.

Anything that is revealed must be worked with effectively. Support must be sustained for as long as it takes to ensure there will be no more victims and quite often for a prolonged period after their release from prison.

Watkins's behaviour brought back the memory of a man that I worked with in 1980. Unfortunately, He was reconvicted and jailed for life following the murder of a young boy.

His offence occurred a few weeks after he had been invited into my family home for tea with my wife and son.

The incident had a profound effect on me and I decided to examine the way that I worked with offenders. Although my colleagues tried to reassure me that nobody could have predicted the murder, there were warning signs that I had ignored. I failed to report certain circumstances to his probation officer, potential warning signs that his behaviour was deteriorating, but more importantly I made an excuse not to see him seven days before the killing.

I went through my own therapy shortly after and although I no longer seek to blame myself, the memories still exist as a reminder that whatever happens, I must ensure that I have no doubts whatsoever if I am involved in the recommendation of a prisoner's release.

As my wife and children have shared some social time with ex-prisoners, I would ensure that they were never in a position whereby I could not protect them or where I could not trust the person they were meeting. But complete trust is a difficult position to reach because it is so easy to be deceived.

Some might say that any possibility of deception must surely make it not worth risking.

Gary Watkins followed the same course as many others in the past and the process was well defined.

All prisoners go through Grendon Prison's Assessment Unit, where they are subjected to Educational Tests and Psychometric Tests. They live in a regime that operates immediately as a therapeutic community, on first name terms with other prisoners and staff.

They must attend all the small therapy group meetings and the larger community meetings (consisting of up to forty prisoners and staff)

If a prisoner appears to be open and honest about his previous offending behaviour and if the prison authorities believe he has the motivation to change his ways, he will be transferred into the other therapeutic communities to begin treatment.

At the assessment stage, there is no pressure on a prisoner to reveal the complete details of his offence to others on his group. However, the staff have a responsibility to ensure that his attitude towards the offence is well recorded.

Gary Watkins had shown remorse and guilt towards his victims and it was hoped that more victim awareness would develop as time went by.

The assessment process can be inconsistent, especially when there are staff shortages or if the assessment period is cut short to fill bed spaces in the rest of the prison.

Prison officers should do the bulk of the report writing, which is then presented to a multi-disciplinary team, consisting of a doctor, psychologist, teacher and probation officer.

Sometimes prison officer's lack the interest or the ability to write accurate reports. They are trained briefly in report writing skills and to observe behaviour but many attempt psychoanalyses without any real understanding of the process. I certainly did and only learned more through dogged determination.

A prisoner's assessment may be quite comprehensive when he arrives in therapy.

He can spend well over two years in group therapy and in this time, would be asked to go through a complete life history in detail and through previous offences.

His intellect might enable him to go through this process with no difficulty at all. Even if he is challenged on his behaviour, he might still have the strength of character to survive. The problem sometimes arises when, even if a man's assessment record is very comprehensive, details can be missed, because the prison file is not read completely or some of it is blatantly ignored.

His progress would depend on how good his relationship with the group is and how well he gets on with his personal officer. The personal officer is very important to the process, because if the officer does not spend enough time with the prisoner, reports have no depth.

Without some knowledge of the psychology of offending behaviour by the report writer, some important aspects of his personality might be missed.

I know that when Gary Watkins moved to Leyhill his reports were glowing, but other ex-prisoners claim that they had concerns about his behaviour and that he had learned to use "Grendonspeak" (a term used to describe the ability to cover up problems by intellectualising) and I felt he was very good at this.

Often groups were run without a member of staff on them and the feedback given by prisoners was not very precise. It was my opinion that he was allowed to become too comfortable. His angry outbursts were not sufficiently challenged.

The very real danger is that men like Watkins can hold on to their fantasies and nobody can predict when they might materialise. Despite the uncertainty of working with such an unpredictable client group, I still felt that my approach was the right one, even though it proved at times to be quite exhausting.

Chapter 13

To counter the periods of exhaustion, I tried to foster a decent work/life balance and family time was important now more than any other time.

Wendy and I would take the kids to a seaside resort, cutting the cost of our holidays by using the £9.50 bargain breaks as advertised in The Sun and Daily Mail newspapers.

Some prisoners and ex-prisoners would complain to me "What the fuck are you doing subscribing to the gutter press, they are the same bastards that delight in giving us a tough time?"

I managed to convince most of them to bury their pride for a brief time and use these deals for their own cheap breaks "After the tabloids have given you a hard time, what can be more satisfying than having a good time under the very noses of your critics?"

On one holiday in Weymouth, we arranged to meet up with a couple of close friends who happened to be in the same area at the time.

It was always enjoyable to be in their company and our children, Sophie and Reece enjoyed the extra attention they got whenever they were around. John and Elizabeth had a lot of stress in their lives and needed to get out and about as much as possible. Having the kids around was a source of pleasure to John and I must admit he could communicate with them in a way that I often envied, even though he wasn't used to having children around him regularly.

On this occasion, as we all sat on the beach enjoying brilliant sunshine, John splashed around in the sea with the kids. They were having sand fights and he would chase the kids into the waves. Every now and then Sophie would be caught and she would scream with delight as he threw her head first into the water.

This was an ideallyic picture of happy families enjoying typical sea-side fun to most uninformed onlookers.

I paused for a while to reflect on my thoughts as I watched the children enjoying themselves in the safe company of our friends

I had to once again remind myself that this was no ordinary situation, because all of us knew the extraordinary circumstances surrounding our friendship.

John was the man I referred to earlier, who was serving a life sentence for the brutal rape and murder of the little girl in Northampton. At the age of eleven, she had been not much younger than my daughter Sophie, when her life came to such a tragic end.

Sophie's screams of joy today echoed around my head, mingled with thoughts of how his victim might have screamed on that fateful evening in 1976. For a few moments, I considered the reality of this situation.

We knew our children were in safe hands, but how many people, I pondered, on this very crowded beach could accept that the man who was playing so happily with the kids was a convicted child killer. Only a few months ago he had been hunted by the newspaper that now provided our holiday. It was a surreal moment, but to Wendy and me it had been a regular occurrence.

We had learned to trust him one hundred percent and he had never abused that trust. He had earned our respect through his own demanding work towards a successful rehabilitation, and his very real remorse towards his victim's family.

We had spent many hours in his company over the past two years since his release.

Shortly after I left the prison service, John had been released from Leyhill prison, nineteen years into a life sentence. Following a period in a probation and bail hostel he had acquired his own independent flat. I met with him socially, and then gradually, with the approval of the probation service, I introduced him to Wendy and the children.

In fact, Wendy had met him on several occasions whilst he was still in jail. During his time at Grendon he had helped me to raise funds for a local charity.

I had elected to do a 24-hour non-stop drumming marathon in the prison visits centre.

The rest of the jail had been locked up at 8.30 pm as usual, but John could stay out of his cell overnight. He remained by my side providing food and drink into the early hours, and a total of £450 was raised through our combined efforts.

In some ways, John was fortunate to have missed the introduction of the SOTP (Sex Offenders Treatment Programme) which might have delayed his release. However, he was less fortunate because his release plan was ill conceived.

There were insufficient contingency plans in the event of a crisis, which he was soon to face.

Whilst residing in a hostel he was approached by a journalist who declared that he knew who he was and was going to produce a story about his release. John felt that he had no choice other than to give the man the full story of his rehabilitation. He was proud of his achievements and this guy had said he was "sensitive to his position" and he thought the article could be positive.

He had been through the therapeutic process at Grendon which requires total honesty, and prisoners are told that honesty is the best policy.

I told him later that I had spent the last two years in Grendon telling prisoners who were about to be released, particularly sex-offenders, that they could not afford to be so open and honest with everybody they meet. There are people who would still condemn them regardless of the amount of therapy they had done. Some people could not be trusted with personal information and most journalists are at the top of that list. Success stories that involve notorious offenders do not sell newspapers. They will often cover another angle which further vilifies the ex-prisoner.

Sure enough, a few days later, sensational banner headlines appeared and John's brief period of resettlement was over. For the next few weeks, on a tidal wave of bad press, he was shunted from pillar to post to find a safe house. Even the seclusion of a Buddhist monastery failed to provide a safe retreat. The pressure from media attention was too much to bear.

The authorities suggested it might be best to return him to jail until the dust settles.

At this point I suggested to the Probation Service that there was a way to resolve the situation using private funding. I felt that I could obtain sufficient funds to remove him from the benefits system for a while and together with a name change and a secret address he would be out of the spotlight.

Of course, the probation service would have to trust my judgement when deciding where he could reasonably be housed and agree that we could produce fake references for him in the interim period.

It was clear that the authorities were desperate for a solution and they readily agreed.

Fortunately, John had met The Hon David Astor during his brief visit to Grendon and David had been particularly impressed with his personal progress. I asked David if he might be able to provide funds for his re-housing in a new area and he immediately agreed, trusting my judgement in this matter.

The only problem initially, was the transferring of money from David's charity "The Avenue Trust" to John's personal bank account. The charity was not able to give cash to individuals but it could fund the probation service and in turn they would move the money through a housing association into his bank account.

The probation service felt that Brighton would be a good area to relocate to. There was an abundance of social housing and many private agencies to choose from, who would house people on benefits.

John and I travelled to Brighton to view selected areas before we could narrow down the search to specific properties. We were eventually looking for a bedsit or one bedroom flat.

As he was a Schedule One offender (a person who had committed an offence against a young person under the age of 17 years) our choices were limited.

He could not be housed near to schools, amusement arcades, youth clubs etc, anywhere that children were likely to congregate on a regular basis. Also, he could not occupy an area in a building that was also occupied by a family. The final choice of location would of course have to be approved by Brighton Probation Service.

It took us several days to find suitable accommodation but eventually we decided to rent a basement bedsit on the seafront. It was literally underground (below street level) and therefore not overlooked. It was dark and depressing but at least it was a place to hide away from the media pressure. John decided to take a 12-month lease.

Before we approached the letting agent we had to make sure that our story would be plausible enough to convince them and more importantly hope that they had not paid too much attention to recent tabloid photographs.

I had suggested that I could be introduced as his current employer, and our story would be that he was working as a landscape gardener. He was moving to Brighton to be close to his mother who was ill. I would say I was reluctant to lose him, but was supporting him under the difficult circumstances. I told the estate agent that he was an excellent employee and hoped that he would soon find work in the new area.

The agent appeared suspicious at first and asked why he hadn't found employment before moving? John said that he had savings and I confirmed that I would help him financially in the first twelve months. The agent was impressed and said, "There are not many employers these days who would offer such support." It felt terrible lying to the man but in these situations, there is no option.

We had to provide references from his current landlord and a reference from somebody else who could confirm he was of good character.

Wendy supplied the character reference and another family member supplied a bogus reference as his landlord. By this time his name change had been completed and the new name appeared on all official documents. The only hiccup came on the day that we moved him in. There was a slight delay in the transfer of the money for the lease and a little more suspicion when I refused to allow the agent to chase it up.

He had also offered me the use of his office phone so that I could speak to them myself and I had to think fast. I told him I was anxious to get back to the van which was parked on a double yellow line (another lie) and I managed to contact the probation service from my mobile phone, and asked them to chase up the funding, before returning to the office.

The money came through within the next 20 minutes or so and we both breathed a sigh of relief as soon as we had the keys to the property in our sweaty palms.

I felt a smug sense of achievement because I had managed to succeed where the authorities hadn't, but this was only our first hurdle.

Wendy and I visited him as often as we could with the children but each time we returned home it was clear that he was lonely and very unhappy.

During our first visit to Brighton he had asked "How can a man like me hope to find happiness in a relationship? What sort of woman could seriously consider living with a guy who had an history like mine and how can I possibly be honest about my crimes?"

I agreed that it would be difficult to form close relationships with strangers. It is a difficulty that many ex-prisoners face, especially those who have committed the less socially acceptable crimes. In the past I have known men and women who have declared that they have been in prison but have changed their offence category.

For instance, a rapist might claim that he was convicted of burglary or theft.

In the case of a life sentenced prisoner there is no way that they can hold a secret for long in a close relationship. They are on a life licence and are controlled by the probation service until the day they die. The probation service must be informed of any significant changes in an ex-offender's life.

"Perhaps the type of woman you eventually meet will come from one of the caring professions, a social worker, probation worker or even a nurse. I am sure you will find somebody to love one day and somebody who will love you." I assured him.

Little did I know at this stage that there was a woman waiting to walk into his life, a professional woman who was able to fully understand his unique situation.

Within a couple of months, he had embarked on a relationship that would again change his life for the better. She became the reason for another fresh start in a new area and he could start putting the past behind him. However, this does not mean that he can ever forget the past, his regular contact with the probation officer will ensure this and he will always be looking over his shoulder.

Having met Elizabeth and having received clearance for their relationship to develop, the couple shared meals with us, attended birthday parties and joined in with festive celebrations.
We would meet up as often as possible, and when they once again found themselves in the media spotlight, we arranged for them to stay at our home for a few days until it was safe to return to their home.

We were happy to do this because they were accepted almost as part of our family and I felt that John had become a close and valuable friend.

In order that he could temporarily live with us, Wendy and I had to agree that we would place our children on the Social Services "At Risk" register and be scrutinised by the local social work team.

Such was our commitment to John and his partner Liz.

Sadly, our friendship was not to last. I entertained quite a bit of negative media coverage due to my work and relationship with Moors Murderess Myra Hindley and after making several revelations in the national press, John and Liz decided it was safer to cut ties with me and my family. I assured both that I was not about to betray their confidentiality in the press at that time.

Of course, Wendy and I were saddened by that decision, particularly as we had personally invested so much effort into helping them, but we respected their decision to move on.

Liz had been particularly scathing about the challenges I had made to Myra Hindley in the press as had a few others, including David Astor, but I had my reasons and have no regrets many years later, although I often wonder what happened to them both.

The sad thing is that the kids had been left wondering why they had suddenly disappeared from their lives and we have since been able to share the truth with them. They both understand why I become involved with ex-prisoners but struggle to understand how John and Liz could simply walk away with no further contact since.

My simple explanation is that their personal survival outweighed any friendship that we might have had and I am far more relaxed these days about ex-prisoners who move on after benefiting from the initial support I offer.

In many ways moving on marks the gaining of independence for them and let's face it, any future contact with me is bound to remind them of their prison years, such is life.

There is always a reminder for all life sentenced prisoners and building a life around people who have no knowledge of their past is a positive thing.

Chapter 14

I had spent a period of just under 4 years away from the Prison Service running a charity for ex-prisoners but due to a funding crisis I was forced into redundancy. I felt it was an obvious choice to consider returning to the Prison Service.

An ex officer I knew, Les Cleaves, had re-joined in 1998 and having spoken to him, I decided I would once again apply to become a prison officer, but this time my sights were set on working with juveniles.

The first main hurdle I had to jump was the new entrant's criteria that had been set for Prison Officers since I left.

Previously, in 1977 there were no formal qualifications required but now I was told that I had to have 5 GCSE's before I could be considered.

I had left school in 1968 having obtained 8 CSE's but these were now considered worthless (as was my previous eighteen years as a prison officer!!) Therefore, I decided to offer my engineering qualifications, which were 3 City and Guilds Certificates in Mechanical and Electrical Craft maintenance. These were confirmed as being equivalent to 3 GCSE's but this was obviously still not enough!

Just by chance I happened to mention to the Personnel Officer at nearby Aylesbury Prison, that I had passed the Prison Service Senior Officers Exam in 1993. She confirmed that this was equivalent to 2GCSE's. - Brilliant!!

New entrant officers were also sent to a Job Simulation Assessment Centre (JSAC). Here they have to perform several role plays which involve scenarios that might be faced during day to day work in a prison.

It was decided that perhaps I had role played enough over the last 22 years and I could be accepted without this test.
However, as I had been out of the service for a period of just over four years I would have to attend the training school again (in Wakefield) and be trained as a recruit.

My decision to work with Juvenile Offenders made sense to me, if I could be involved in their rehabilitation at an earlier age I felt I would be helping to prevent them from wasting many valuable years behind bars. I had been waiting for a vacancy at Aylesbury Young Offenders Institution but Grendon's governor, Tim Newell, informed me that a new regime was being developed at Huntercombe YOI near Henley on Thames.

The prison was being adapted to suit the requirements of Juvenile Offenders between the ages of fourteen to eighteen. It seemed an ideal place to start.

Having been interviewed by the Huntercombe Governor Paul Mainwaring and Principle Officer Paul Newton, a position on a wing called "Patterson House" seemed the ideal placement for me.
My decision to accept the job was coloured by my experiences with Young Offenders at Grendon and having viewed the work currently being done on Patterson House it looked like my Grendon experience would be valuable.

The Governor stated that he would use my skills to develop group work with the young offenders and I would be actively involved in a structured rehabilitation programme.

During a preliminary visit, I realized that Huntercombe was going through a very difficult change. The officer's morale was very low. However, many of the original staff group were being gradually replaced and I was assured that there would be much more stability when I returned from the Wakefield training school at the end of September 1999.

And so, I found myself boarding a train bound for the Prison Officers Training School (twenty-two years after I had first joined) but this time I was determined to buckle down to some hard work. I wasn't returning to the Aberford Road college where I had previously been. Instead, I would be trained at The Love Lane College which is adjacent to Wakefield Prison.

At the ripe old age of 47, I wondered if I was the oldest person on the course.

After 48 hours of scanning the faces of other recruits for signs of wrinkles and blemishes, I was informed by the Governor to stop looking. He said "I can officially confirm that you are an old bastard and you are expected to be a role model to these youngsters. God help us all."

Governor George Ridley had previously worked at Grendon Prison as a Principal Officer, so any thoughts I had of keeping my past misdemeanors a secret were blown right out of the window.

As it turned out, this course was to be a very enjoyable and rewarding experience. I stayed away from the dreaded night life and heavy drinking sessions and was pleased with my personal achievements. More importantly, I was to meet many new friends in the next eight weeks and I was impressed by the good calibre of the men and women who were joining the modern prison service.

It was a very strange feeling to be wearing the prison officer's uniform again but I was pleased that I had made the decision. There were some friends who had doubted my judgement but on the whole I felt supported, even by a group of ex-prisoners who had heard the news.

During the first week in training I received a letter from the lifer (Derek O) who was still in Littlehey Prison awaiting a move to less secure conditions.

David wrote, Dear Joe, by my calculations you'll be polishing up your C&R Techniques and knowledge of the Security Manual round about now, in preparation for re-entering that erstwhile profession - and I use the term loosely - of Prison Officer.

I shall be thinking of you in the next few weeks of course, especially while you strut your stuff at the training college once again and thereafter begin rolling around the landings with YP's.

Each to their own I suppose. I feel quite sad for you really, that it's all come to this after earning your parole and making a bid for freedom - I never thought you'd get a re-call! Still we must work with what skills we've got and market them accordingly.

It takes courage to do what you are doing, though frankly my dear I think you're absolutely barking to even contemplate such a career move. But then I try never to retrace my footsteps, preferring to strive for new and challenging experiences.

I think you have more chance of changing the status quo by working outside the criminal justice system than within it, but also would have been highly effective working alongside rather than taking it on at times.

I guess the past four years have been an adventure, nevertheless, time to rise to a new challenge now, with a little more security.

I heard news of an ex lifer Principal Officer here who retired and is now down south as an OSG (Operational Support Grade) in one of the nicks down there. It gives him something to do and a little bit of pocket money to top up his pension whilst at the same time having no real responsibilities."

His letter continued to let me know how well he was doing and I was pleased to have played a part in his rehabilitation. However, Derek's comments echoed some of my own anxieties. I was concerned that I might struggle with some of the changes that had taken place since I left but I was determined to succeed.

Sadly, for all concerned, Derek had less success than me and after being released, on licence for 2 murders, he went on to kill his new partner and himself. This is a stark reminder to me and the Grendon regime that there are those who can con the system in the most tragic way.

With these thoughts in mind, I concentrated on the expectations of a new and quite demanding training course.

The new selection process had been criticised by older experienced staff as being inconsistent, unfair and unrealistic. One of their arguments being that the modern prison service is forfeiting new recruits with dynamic personalities and good interpersonal skills, in favour of young academics with very little life experience.

A letter penned by a Principle Officer with 28 years' experience, in the Prison Officers Magazine "Gatelodge" (When dinosaurs ruled ... June 2000) suggests that these "youngens" can't talk to (or listen to) staff or prisoners without issuing orders. The writer asks the question "If life experience is so valuable, how come the prison service disregards it so vehemently?"

He's got a point I suppose, as it is quite clear that the current criteria of 5 GCSE's will undoubtedly stop candidates with excellent life skills from joining the service. And it was a policy that the Police force were forced to abandon eventually, in a drive to increase recruitment. I guessed that the service might have to do the same at some point in the future but for now the new criteria stood.

Having said that, I would argue that the young people coming into the service are more than capable of doing a decent job, given the right training and guidance.

On that note, I discovered that the atmosphere on this course was much more refreshing and vibrant than I recall it being in the late 70's. The mixing of male and female officers in all aspects of training (apart from the sleeping quarters!!) was a welcome change and in balance with the well-established tradition of cross sex postings.

Previously we had only been permitted to mix socially and the work of the female officer was shrouded in mystery. This time around I found our daily interactions much more rewarding and much more educational. In general, Prison Officers are now more aware of their own interpersonal skills than they used to be.

I firmly believe, the discipline required by prison staff today is vastly different to the kind of discipline that I was subjected to years ago, even to suggest that it is in fact greater! Personal boundaries are more easily defined and prejudice or discrimination, thankfully, is more effectively targeted. But the first major change I noted was on the first evenings briefing by Governor Ridley (George)

Twenty-two years ago, new officers were not given a uniform until they reached their first postings and the briefing was very informal. Then, all the domestic aspects of the course (living and working) in the college were explained. We were given poorly produced handouts but more importantly free tickets to the local nightspots, with advice on where to go for cheap drinks and an enjoyable time.

Places such as Heppy's Fish and Strip and the "Grab a Granny" nights at Tiffany's were legendry.

Now, in the year 2000, these are replaced by "Mustang Sally's, The Sports Bar and The Buzbar" where many fantasies can become a reality. It's the same scene, but different furnishings.

I found myself standing to attention with 99 other officers "in uniform" and listening to a list of rules and regulations that must be obeyed, or we would find ourselves returning to our home establishments (referred to as "being back squaddied ") to be disciplined or in some cases dismissed from the service.

The Governor made it very plain to all "Get your heads out of beer glasses and sexual relationships. You're here to train as Prison Officers."

Passing weekly tests and two examinations became everyone's goal and getting through this required great discipline, given the temptations of the night life.

Still in evidence was the daily Orderly Officers duties which had to be performed by every POINT (Prison Officer In Training) with the ritual raising of the college flag each morning (woe betide anybody who raised it upside down).

 Also, still included was the Radio Procedure, with much rehearsing of the phonetic alphabet. This time around we used more sophisticated equipment. A single transmitter and receiver, (rather than a handset with a receiver that often got left behind in the locker room and a separate transmitter, with an arial that shot up your nose when you switched it on.)

The morning parade was still a tiresome duty. It attempted to create a finely tuned marching mass of men and women, out of a group of people who could hardly walk straight on the best of days and could never remember where they stood the day before!

This exercise was a constant wind up for the ex-armed forces personnel, who were in a minority group this time. But just imagine how they would have felt in the 70's when they would be marching, not in uniform but in blue flared trousers, with perhaps a paisley patterned shirt and multi coloured kipper tie.

At least the wearing of a smart uniform gave the illusion that we were all united!

Gone (and good riddance) were the JUDO sessions, where we were taught how to throw prisoners to the floor in two dozen easy lessons, using dried peas (aimed at the face) as an initial distraction, followed by forcing our assailant against the cell wall using a large pillow.

Back in the 70's the prisoner would be finally pinned to the floor by as many Prison Officers that you could cram into a cell.

This dangerous and sometimes suicidal practice has long since been replaced by the highly effective and disciplined "Control and Restraints" technique, which occupied 24 sessions of the new course.

This provided an enjoyable but sometimes too painful change from the classroom sessions.
If one thing could be changed, I would advocate that the instructors should always take the role of the prisoner in mock incidents. It isn't necessary for officers to know exactly how painful the wrist and arm lock are (fully) in order to be satisfied that they can apply locks securely and with confidence.

I speak with eight years' experience as a C&R Instructor.

There were many silly injuries on the course and I myself suffered at the hands of an overzealous young officer, who decided to pull my legs from under me during a mock fight. I suffered a split lip and two cracked ribs during the last two weeks of the course.

If I had been back squaddied it would have been disastrous. I still suffer lower back problems to this day, but no claim was made.

Fortunately, every officer (including the "wet behind the ears" academics) passed this module with few problems.

The physical fitness sessions differed slightly between Aberford Road and Love Lane, due to the shortages of facilities in the latter. However, I felt that the amount of PE was adequate for me and more than sufficient to bring staff to a reasonable standard of fitness.

Again, I would suggest that sustained physical fitness is higher on the agenda than it was when I first joined in 1977.

The morning runs and circuits were little different from previous years and now there is less emphasis on team control and sporting prowess. Knowing the rules for non - stop Cricket, Captain Headball and Crab Football are no longer a priority, which we should all be thankful for.

There were more practical sessions on team building, which is an improvement on the 70's training. The imaginary shipwreck on a desert island or throwing your colleagues out of a falling Hot Air balloon is replaced by the Electrical Spiders Web.

In this, the team has to pass each member through a web made of rope (without touching the strands) you have to imagine that each strand of rope carries a 10,000-volt electrical charge. If you touch them you are fried!

Fortunately, I completed the eight-week course without getting "pickled" or fried and I achieved just above average marks in the tests and examinations. My instructor's comments reflected my previous experience.

"He is confident and has a self-assured attitude, without being over confident or arrogant. It is to his credit that he quickly realised that even with his previous service, he still had a lot to learn. He is confident and outgoing, a good team player who gets on with his colleagues and he has proved to be popular with the rest of the section."

Along with a glowing report I received a certificate of competence that certified I had "Demonstrated competence in the skills required of a new Prison Officer". Furthermore, I was expected to complete an NVQ course in Prison Skills which would be further proof of my ability.

Clutching my final reports and polishing my cap badge, I headed for a fresh start at Huntercombe Young Offenders Institution.

Chapter 15

I only wore the standard black and white prison officers uniform at Huntercombe for a week, until I was issued with a blue polo shirt.

I had to purchase my own blue tracksuit bottoms and a pair of trainers (as there were none available in the stores). This was the new uniform worn only by officers in Patterson House and it was treated as something of a joke by other officers. However, it was much more comfortable to wear when working with young energetic prisoners for reasons that I would soon discover.

The first morning on Patterson came as a complete culture shock to me.

As I walked through the main gate towards the staff office I could hear iron gates crashing and screaming and shouting on the landings.

Fearing an early morning riot, I started to run towards the noise and then stopped in my tracks as I realised it was a single adult voice. 'Wake up you little bastards, if I'm awake you all are - wakey, wakey, hands off cocks and on with socks'.

As I reached the corner of the first corridor I was greeted by a short stocky officer carrying a chair leg, which he had been rattling against the iron gates at the end of each cellblock.

The officer introduced himself and explained why he was making so much noise. 'The lads have to be ready for a cell inspection before they can come down for breakfast. The first officer on duty in the morning must wake them all up. If you don't do it the little fuckers will say they've overslept'.

I soon learned how to rattle the cell doors and scream as loud as I could before I settled down to make tea and coffee for the staff team.

There were twenty-three young boys in the cells who would have previously been kept in local authority care homes.

The prison service had accepted responsibility and the Youth Justice Board were eager to fill all the cells they could. However, Patterson House had managed to keep thirty empty.

The reasoning behind this was not simply to save space. If the numbers of young prisoners were kept to a minimum on each unit, the staff to prisoner ratio would allow for some very valuable rehabilitation work to be done.

These young offenders were classed as Section 53 juveniles, 'the worst of the worst'. They were long-termers, serving sentences of up to six years for crimes ranging from manslaughter to street robbery. As adult prisoners, their sentences would be equivalent to a 12 - 15-year stretch.

'The social services want us to refer to them as children' Officer H explained, 'but these are not typical children, they're not even built like children. Some stand at five foot nine and weigh in at fourteen stones. Don't be fooled, they can do some severe damage and will use any weapon they can find'.

The early morning routine was that two officers would inspect each boy's cell. The beds had to be made, floors and work surfaces cleaned and rubbish bins emptied before they were allowed breakfast. They were each scored on their efforts - A was acceptable, B - barely acceptable and F - failure. Any boy found to be still in bed when the cell was unlocked or who failed the inspection, would lose one evening's association period.

Three consecutive B's also meant a loss of association with other prisoners (commonly referred to as 'loss of soash').
This 'loss of soash' meant that some boys would be locked away from teatime (1730) one day, until 0730 the next. This was a total of 14.5 hours, behind a cell door.

They would all be expected to attend the dining area for breakfast between 0730 am and 8 am, then be locked in their cells again until 8.30 or 9 am depending on what had been organised for them. In fact, they were locked away whenever there was nothing constructive happening, or whenever they misbehaved.

Initially there would be between 6 - 8 staff on duty, which included a senior supervising officer and the boys would be split into four manageable groups (A-D). Ideally two officers would supervise each group.

In the early days of my time at Huntercombe this would be a group of 5 - 6 boys.

When group A was having their education period, group B would be using the gymnasium. The programmes were developed so that each group (in theory) should participate in structured activities. This might also include an Offending Behaviour course, motor maintenance workshop (Kwik-fit) and music or crafts.

This could have worked well had it not been for the severe lack of resources and staff shortages. In the end, it became a logistical nightmare. Patterson officers were often seconded to other areas of the prison, thereby reducing the staff team to just four.

These so called 'children' were the most disturbed, disruptive and violent offenders I had ever come across in my life (in one group). The majority had no interest at all in education or offending behaviour courses. They would fight anywhere and at any time given the opportunity. There were alarm bells calling officers to serious incidents every day of the week. On numerous occasions, young boys would receive injuries which required hospitalisation. Staff attempted to encourage boys to seek court action against their abusers but none did because they feared reprisals or else they would be classed as a grass (informer).

Most fights developed because one had insulted the others mother or sister, or called someone a 'batty boy' (homosexual). The phrase 'suck your fucking mum' was guaranteed to start a fight.

Boys would be threatening each other through their cell windows all night long and as soon as the cell doors were opened in the morning, they would attack each other with razor blades molded into toothbrushes, batteries in socks (favourite) or chair legs. In fact, anything that was sharp or heavy was useful.

All of the officers that worked on Patterson House believed as an 'enhanced regime ', we would only have to work with a maximum of 35 offenders (called trainees). When the average numbers of staff on duty was reduced to just a senior officer and three other staff, this made any constructive programme almost impossible to run.

Very soon the unit was being asked to take even more short-term offenders which further increased the pressure.

On many occasions a group of offenders would be forced into a classroom (whether they wanted to be taught or not) and the special needs tutor would have to do the best that he or she could under very difficult and dangerous circumstances.

The potential for serious violence was never far away and yet there were times when we were instructed to lock the classroom door to 'stop them wandering out'.

Governors told the officers (who locked these so-called children back in their cells when they wandered) that this was unacceptable. The regulations were that they had to spend at least 12 hours a day out of their cells, even if this meant somebody would get seriously hurt.
The atmosphere in this 'kid's jail' was as far removed from the peace and tranquility of Grendon than you could imagine.

In January 2000, I was asked to develop plans to incorporate the Grendon ethos into Patterson House and I produced a document for staff discussion.

Principal Officer Newton encouraged me to forge ahead with the ideas that would increase the flexibility of the programme.

However, it would also conflict with Huntercombe's traditional working practices. He knew that some officers would resist the ideas but assured me 'The ones who don't want to work with the boys are leaving anyway and as new officers arrive they will have not known anything different. The culture will change gradually'.

I explained that my methods were already unpopular with some staff. I had been accused of 'doing my own thing and not working as a team player'. PO Newton assured me that he would deal with any problems if I kept him informed. I tried to remain optimistic - but it wasn't easy.

The young prisoners (sarcastically referred to as 'baby burglars') would resist any effort to examine their offending behaviour, particularly if it was stuffed down their throats in a classroom setting. My first move would be to attempt to develop better relationships with them, so I attempted to introduce the idea of using first name terms.

Many prison officers strongly disagree with the use of first names for prisoners, claiming that it breeds over familiarity and increases the potential for being conditioned. This has never been my experience, in fact quite the reverse.

However, it remains a myth that continues to be cultivated by some members of the POA (Prison Officers Association) and there were still enough at Huntercombe to render my first task virtually impossible. To the extent that one young officer refused to speak to me for a period of seven weeks.

I felt like a square peg in a round hole and my personal stress levels rose to an all-time high. I took some comfort from the fact that the staff turnover was high and hoped that any inexperienced staff would be a little more responsive.

During April and May I started to attempt group discussions with trainees.

I attended a 'Protective Behaviors Course' which was to be wholly adopted by Huntercombe prison and the concept of 'caring' for the young men held in custody would (I believed) fit neatly into the plans for the new regime. Once again, its success would be dependent on the acceptance of a culture change by the majority of staff. More importantly, by staff resources being increased to a much more acceptable level.

Sadly, by the end of May, it was clear that staff morale was falling fast due to several factors, the first being 'cross deployment' to other units.

As one bright new female officer complained 'I was interviewed and accepted on the strength of my past teaching experience and social work qualifications, to work closely with these vulnerable young men.

How can I develop good relationships with them when I don't know where I shall be working from one day to the next'? This was a common complaint and the inexperienced staff felt let down, to the extent that many considered leaving the job within the first three months.

One of the most experienced officers on Patterson House was a lady called Cherry Myerhoff. Cherry could balance her role as a caring, empathic listener with the more disciplined role of custodian. She had worked successfully with young offenders for over ten years and had a very positive approach to her task. Even on some of the worst days she would manage a smile and had a calming influence on new officers and trainees.

Cherry and other long-term staff feared that officers were in danger of losing control of the units and she wasn't afraid to air these views with anybody who cared to listen.

Because we were attempting to build good relationships with our boys, none of the staff liked to be re-deployed to other units.
On a strange unit, we would face the dangers of working with an unknown quantity.

It is very important to know who the trouble causers were and to be able to isolate them from the rest of the regime.

The offending behaviour programmes were failing and basic skills education also suffered due to an increase in uncontrollable young men. I was starting to wonder if I had made a big mistake by not returning to Grendon prison when I had the opportunity.

I made a comparison with the provisions in local council run facilities. In local authority, Secure, Units there would be a dozen or so staff to supervise and care for perhaps 8 - 10 trainees. These custody officers, also classed as 'key workers', benefited from one to one relationship with trainees.

This level of achievement was far superior to Huntercombe and matters would soon become worse.

Prison Service Headquarters confirmed in June 2000 that Patterson House would be required to house up to sixty trainees. Therefore, this meant that the regime changes could not take place and the level of staff recruitment had fallen.

On average, the ratio of staff to prisoner was often 1 to 20. The stress levels rose to unimaginable levels and officers risked severe injury. Some began to fear the working day.

As I arrived at work one morning I noticed one of the female staff sitting in her car in the staff car park. At first it appeared that she was reading a book, but as I got closer it became obvious she was crying. I tapped on the window which she slowly opened 'What's the matter, can I help you'? I enquired. She was totally distraught and could hardly speak.

'I don't feel able to go into work, I haven't slept all night. I can't cope with the job, but I feel guilty if I let my colleagues down. They already think I'm not up to it. It's hopeless' she sobbed.

I didn't know this officer well but I was aware that she was regularly working on a unit that could only be compared, on a good day, to a Beirut war zone. The young prisoners were some of the most dangerous and disruptive in the system. This officer had been in the job for less than 3 months.

I advised her to go home and speak to her GP. It was clear that this woman was heading for a major breakdown and although she felt a sense of guilt that she might be 'letting the side down' her own health and well-being was far more important.

As she drove out of the car park I was filled with intense anger. Any system that can affect a person in such a dramatic way is a liability to all its employees. I also realised that this prison could not bring the job satisfaction that I hoped for and I was missing the work that I had previously done with prisoners at Grendon.

There were many aspects of the regime that I struggled to cope with, such as cross- deployment to other units.

As I mentioned earlier, this reduced consistency of staffing in all units. This was coupled with an increase in violent and disruptive behaviour, which brought about an increase in assaults on staff and other trainees. We were unable to move problem trainees and restore safety. What was worse, to cope with their own stress some officers developed an over punitive attitude towards the trainees and were intolerant towards other colleagues.

It felt as if my personality and everything that I had previously stood for was being sucked out of me and I began to display the same kind of attitude that I disliked so much in others. At home I was not sleeping and I became very distant and was clearly unhappy.

On August 13th, 2000, as I got dressed to go to work, my attention was drawn towards the emblem on my sweatshirt. It read, "HMYOI Huntercombe, Officer J Chapman, Patterson House, Access to Opportunity."

I felt I could no longer stand to wear the uniform that symbolised a liberal caring and forward-thinking service.

To highlight how I felt, I removed the Patterson Unit sportswear and changed into the traditional prison officers black and white uniform. On my way in to work, I handed a memo to the Governor which expressed my despair and that same day I reluctantly requested a transfer back to Grendon prison.

The Governor and Principal Officer were not amused and it was made clear that if I chose not to wear the Patterson uniform I would be cross-deployed to 'Rich House' (the Beirut war zone). I chose to refuse!
It was at the end of this day of change I received my first assault.

The atmosphere on Rich House was as bad as it could get and a young trainee was refusing to go back to his cell having been let out to have a shower.

He had to be restrained and during re-location he kicked me between the legs and spat into my mouth. The assault resulted in police proceedings against the boy and I was encouraged to take 3 or 4 days of work to recover.

The Governor interviewed me on my return and although he agreed with the comments in my memo (concerning the deterioration of the prison regime) there was nothing he could do to change the circumstances. However, what he offered in return surprised me.

I was offered a period of temporary promotion to Senior Officer, to oversee referrals, admissions and discharges from Patterson. I would also be allowed to oversee the Offending Behaviour Programme.
The Governor also stated 'If by May 2001, you have received the job satisfaction you are looking for, I want you to reconsider your transfer to Grendon'.

I accepted the deal, feeling that maybe the temporary promotion could provide the inspiration I needed.

Perhaps I could achieve more at this level. I would have the flexibility in my personal duties to build more meaningful relationships with the trainees and I could be pro-active in the task of rebuilding Patterson's programme. Hopefully staff resources would increase eventually.

I had my appointment confirmed on August 25th, 2000 and I anticipated it would be for at least 6 months (due to the priorities for extra staffing elsewhere in the prison). I had renewed optimism.

The rehabilitation of juveniles is a key area of work and Huntercombe was still hoping to lead the field.

Having received the encouragement from senior managers to play a key role in the development of the rehabilitation programme, my hopes and aspirations were very high. However, on the one hand I was being asked to participate in the building of a more humane, understanding and eventually therapeutic regime, whilst on the other, it became clear that the prisons priorities were changing.

Containment and control began to take top priority.

The Governor was being forced to fill as many bed spaces as he possibly could. In fact, prisoners would arrive from courts as late as 10 O'clock at night with no opportunity for staff to assess their dangerousness or vulnerability before they were locked in their cells in the reception wing. In my opinion this was a recipe for disaster.

Patterson House had received a constant stream of violent and disruptive prisoners who were a serious threat to other inmates and staff. There was reluctance from other prisons to take on our problem cases and this meant that we could only remove them to the Segregation Block for a fleeting period before they would arrive on one of the other units to continue their bullying and intimidation.

Staff who had challenged the boy's behaviour would find themselves facing the prisoner again whilst working on another unit.

In one particular incident, a very violent young man was transferred from Patterson House across the corridor to Rich House, where he only stayed for a short while before being moved once again to Fry House. It was my opinion that he should have been moved from the prison entirely.

Cherry Myerhoff was on duty in Fry House when a fight developed on one of the landings. Cherry and another officer attended the incident as the alarm was raised. As a proportionately small number of staff arrived on the scene, the numbers of prisoners involved and the potential for further violence overwhelmed them.

In the panic the landing gates were locked off. Cherry and a male officer found themselves locked in with a group of angry prisoners.

To make matters worse, the prisoner who had days earlier been transferred from Patterson House, restrained Cherry and prevented her from leaving the landing. This situation should not have occurred and indeed would not have done if resources had been sufficient.

There was no doubt that Cherry feared for her life and was rendered helpless. The incident destroyed her confidence; self-esteem and trust in the prison management. As a consequence, Cherry was on long term sick leave and eventually medically retired from the service.

Following this incident and several others, I became driven by an enormous amount of nervous energy, which was soon to take its toll on my own mental health. I became sensitive to the pressures on the less experienced staff and the suffering of the more vulnerable young prisoners.

Everyday there was always a potential for serious violence, although I did not recognise it at the time. It would only require one more frustration to tip me over the edge.

The 'straw to break the camel's back' came at a point when my morale was at its lowest.

On Friday October 17th, 2000 I received a letter from pay section confirming my appointment as Temporary Senior Officer and my new salary scale. For the extra responsibilities, I would receive the princely sum of £20 per week.

On the very same day I also received a memo from my manager suggesting that I was going to be replaced. This was a complete bombshell, which shattered any illusions I might have had about making any further progress. In the next couple of weeks nobody explained why I was to be replaced and I received no thanks for the work that I had done so far.

However, I got support from other staff and several trainees. One young prisoner sent a letter to the Governor, which read: Dear Sir, I have heard a rumor that SO Joe Chapman is getting dropped from being a Senior Officer. I know this may not seem a lot to you, but Joe is one of the nicest blokes I've met since I got sentenced eleven months ago, I am doing a sentence of 3 years 9 months and Joe is the only person I've met that I feel I can sit down and talk to. He understands all inmates and does not think of them as something that falls of the bottom of a shoe. Joe is totally against bullies and is willing to do something about this.

I am not the only inmate who is against Joe Chapman getting dropped there are 60 inmates on my wing and if they had voted 60 inmates will tell you, Joe is the best person be an SO'. As I am doing a long-term sentence I think of Joe as a kind of father figure. This is all I must say, but I really do think Joe is your best man, as it goes - I think Joe should be a PO, Yours sincerely, Matthew.

Despite such support the situation was unchanged and my self-esteem was lower than it had ever been in my career.

I tried to hide my disappointment, pretending that I could cope, but I became emotionally drained and requested that my original request for a transfer should be actioned.

During the few weeks before I moved from Huntercombe I began to relish the idea of returning to Grendon prison, I had long forgotten the feelings I had before resigning in 1995 and hoped that my return would provide me with renewed job satisfaction.

Little did I know at this stage that Grendon's chaplain had resigned with grave concerns about the difficult working environment there, and more specifically its effect on the prison officers.

He said" there were issues around 'investigations, arguments or splits amongst staff groups, complaints of unsupportive and weak management and lack of trust and togetherness, which is spreading slowly through the ranks with no efforts to find a cure.

Staff sensitivity (support) meetings were losing credibility due to a supposed lack of trust amongst staff, or that generally, confidentiality is not being respected. Management is not stressing the importance of staff sensitivity meetings'.

He continued 'prison officers at Grendon are expected to be all things to all men, namely jailer, therapist and emotional blotting paper. Their role, as it stands, breaks the boundary of what in therapeutic terms constitutes safe containment with dubious ethics and practice. How can they claim to look after others if they can't look after themselves?'

Unfortunately, I would only become aware of these difficulties after I had returned to the jail that I still considered to have been a second home to me.

For the time being, I set out optimistically to return to Grendon. Prior to leaving Huntercombe I did receive a belated letter of thanks from Governor Peter Knapton.

He wrote, Dear Joe, throughout this period, your leadership, vision and sensitive management style was greatly appreciated. You have clearly demonstrated many of the qualities and competencies of the higher grade. If such an opportunity were to arise in the future I would have no hesitation in asking you to carry out the duties of the higher grade.

Thank you for your support and well done!

On that positive note, I drove away from the gates of Huntercombe thankful that this brief episode was now over. Two weeks later I made my way back to the jail that had given me so much job satisfaction for many years.

Chapter 16

The route to Grendon prison was very familiar and as I approached the entrance to the former Prison Officers housing estate, I could see a group of five or six inmates from Springhill open prison waiting to catch the early morning bus on their way to various jobs in the community.

When Grendon Prison was opened, there was an agreement made with the local villagers that prisoners from this higher security jail would not be allowed to transfer straight into the open prison next door as they were always considered to be more dangerous.

However, on occasions the Prison Department would manage to find a way around this by transferring Grendon men to another jail for a short period first.

Some of the men currently held in Springhill were finishing long sentences (sometimes life) for crimes such as Murder, Robbery and GBH (Grievous Bodily Harm). Therefore, the men waiting at the bus stop might have committed crimes as serious as those in Grendon, but they were now being tested in less secure conditions.

None were sex offenders but it would be no surprise to find that at some point in the future, plans would be drawn up to include them. With the amount of psychological and resettlement expertise in one area, to a considerable extent Springhill is purpose built for this category of offender.

This group mixed freely with schoolchildren and families from the estate.

The houses had once been rented entirely to prison staff but over the past fifteen years the majority had been sold off to the public. When the house sales first began, I had attended a full staff meeting expressing the opinion that at least twenty houses should be kept solely for the future use of new officers to Grendon.

There would always be those who could not afford to live in this high-priced area.

My opinion was dismissed with a declaration "Prison Officers salaries will continue to rise according to inflation and will be more than adequate to provide a reasonable standard of living in any area of the country."

As we entered the new Millennium, approximately 30 staff in Grendon had no permanent accommodation; in fact, one young man from Lancashire was renting a caravan in a local farmer's field (with only a herd of cows for company). The prison had the same problem as The Thames Valley Police Force, they could not recruit sufficient staff because the new workforce could not afford to live in the area!

The Home Office in its infinite wisdom also decided to sell off the staff hostel. By the end of 2002 it would be converted into private dwellings. However, money was found to build accommodation for a further two hundred or more prisoners in Springhill open jail.

Often the priority of care for prisoners and staff is out of balance and officers are quite rightly disgruntled by this.

Driving up the hill I approached the steel barrier that secures the entrance to Springhill prison.

The original barrier used to be controlled by a uniformed officer who would interact with visitors in a friendly manner but in a cost cutting exercise it is now under the control of Grendon's Gatekeeper via an intercom system. Visitors must approach a small metal box and press a button for service.

"Name and destination?" asked the little box. I immediately recognised the voice of my old pal Jim Rodick.

"It's Joe Chapman, you old bastard, returning to produce more chaos and mayhem." I replied cheerfully.

"Fuck off. How did you get back in the job?" was his not too polite response and the barrier was raised slowly. I stuck two fingers up to the CCTV camera as I passed beneath it.

Reaching Grendon's main gate, I rang the doorbell and entered through the old familiar "Wicket Gate" to begin my work as a "born again group therapist." Jim handed me a bunch of keys and told me to report to the Training Officer Pete Hill.

"Ah good," I pondered, "at least this is another name I can recall from the past. Pete was an officer of the old school who believed in the therapeutic process and was prepared to take the odd calculated risk here and there. It will be good to see him again." However, Pete had been forced to change his ways more recently.

Over a cup of coffee, he offered me a warning

"Grendon is nothing like it used to be Joe. You will have to be careful about what you say and do these days. There is a climate of investigation over the most trivial matters and a culture of blame, rather than the understanding and support we were both used to. Officers are afraid to make real relationships with the prisoners. They might face accusations of corruption or else it is implied that the prisoners may be conditioning them."

This was not quite the comforting introduction I had expected, but I thought surely nothing could be as bad as the experience I had at Huntercombe?

I had expected to start work on G wing, which was predominately used to house sex offenders and hoped that I might be able to work on the Sex Offenders Treatment Programme eventually.
However, the governor had decided that C Wing might benefit more from the input of an experienced officer.

Pete explained that this wing had gone through a lot of upheavals over the past eighteen months and needed to find some stability.

As it happened, C wing turned out to be an ideal placement and I soon settled down into the group therapy role again.

The difficulties that the wing faced were not unfamiliar to me but I did sense an atmosphere of mistrust and suspicion, not just between staff and prisoners but also within the staff team. C wing officers were the friendliest bunch of people I had met for a long time and it was a pleasure to work with them. However, they were exhausted by an extended period of staff shortages caused by long-term illnesses and the suspension of one female officer over alleged inappropriate behaviour.

Two very capable Senior Officers managed the staff group.

Chris Dowthwaite and Andy Pedley had contrasting styles of leadership but the most important thing was that they cared about the health and welfare of their staff as well as the prisoners, which is what Grendon was all about.

The Principal Officers were no longer situated in an office on each wing. Instead, they worked from a central office and were responsible for two wings each. Their role was now more administrative, rather than having daily hands on interaction with staff and prisoners. Some of the PO's were unhappy about this situation but there were one or two who relished the opportunity to build little empires.

As middle managers Chris and Andy were the "whipping boys" for the Residential Support Team. If anything went wrong on the wing they would ultimately carry the can. This responsibility, and the pressure that went with it, earned them about £16 a week more than I was earning as a basic grade officer, so there was not much of a financial incentive for me to seek promotion.

The C wing therapist, David Jones, believed Grendon was now a much more structured and professional place to work than it had been a few years ago.

He was partly right, but unfortunately Grendon's move towards accreditation as a recognised TC (Therapeutic Community) and its obsession with "professionalism" meant that much of the jails uniqueness might soon disappear. As I had stated before, the introduction of inflexible professional boundaries can only spell disaster for the incredibly flexible regime that made Grendon a much more exciting place to work.

It appeared to me that the prison had lost its direction and the introduction of managers who gave too much of a priority to security and operational procedures were responsible for this its demise. They had arrived without any concept or understanding of the balance between good therapy and a safe secure confinement.
Their sights were firmly set on promotion and there appeared to be no real ownership of the regime.

I soon discovered that many very dedicated and well-qualified staff felt they were being bullied into giving security far too much emphasis and the less experienced officers were frightened of being conditioned by the prisoners.

Unfortunately, the process of conditioning often contains many of the important qualities of a good therapeutic relationship, which (in the past) was what made Grendon different from other jails.

Apart from changes in the ethos, I also noticed many structural changes. Grendon's physical security was changing beyond belief. There were many more gates along the M1 and M2 corridors and internal fencing, which felt very claustrophobic, compared to my previous experience.

Tim Newell had retired as the jails governor during my first year back there but he had stated during a conference in July 2000 "how important open space was to therapeutic communities." Grendon took pride in its "open door" policy and there were some areas where prisoners and staff could forget they were in a jail. The flower borders, lawns, trees and an ornate fishpond were the central focus to everyone who entered through the main gates.

This view was now destroyed by an ugly green security fence which provided a "sterile area" for incoming vehicles. The only aspect that might improve the situation would be the removal of the cold grey prison boundary walls in preference for fencing, which had been the experience at Wellingboro.

Today a more politically correct Grendon is attempting to produce perfect specimens of society (inspired by very middle-class values) with little comprehension of the lifestyles that the prisoners (specimen) will eventually have to return to.

The blanket approach towards physical security throughout our prison system undoubtedly affects many other regimes, but here it has a negative effect on the quality of therapy.

Grendon had only one successful escape attempt in its forty-year history and surprisingly the prisoner who had accomplished that had also returned to the jail at the same time as me.

Bob B had returned for his second attempt at therapy.

As I saw him sweeping the main corridor I joked "Back for another go Bob? Try to go through the gate this time mate."

Bob replied cheerfully "This is it for me Joe. I am here to change for real now; it's not going to be easy though. It's a lot different from when I was last here."

Some might argue that Bob had previously managed to escape because Grendon had been too relaxed and he confirms this in a way.

"I did exploit its weaknesses. To some extent staff had been conditioned to trust too much. You can have a relaxed atmosphere but you still need to check a few basic things out from time to time. The only trouble is, now it's gone too far the other way. Prisoners involved in therapy also need to feel that they can be trusted and that the prison staff really care about them. They need to see that change is worthwhile."

Of course, he's right. One of the most difficult aspects of running a prison TC is to balance the needs of good security with the special needs of an efficient therapeutic programme.

This has always been a problem for Grendon but the introduction of systems of work with rigidly defined boundaries (that remove the responsibility of staff, prisoners and communities of making their own democratic decisions) make the therapeutic process more difficult to sustain.

Sadly, daily handouts (Information bulletins to staff and prisoners) had become the preferred mode of communication between management and wing staff. This once democratic therapeutic community seemed a hierarchical structure to me.

When Grendon celebrated its 40th anniversary the theme of the conference had been "Life begins at 40". However, the truth is Grendon faced changes that would undoubtedly make it unrecognizable from the original model.

In 2001, Grendon's next crisis would seriously test its ability to survive in its current form.

At the rear of the prison is a large sports field and it had been the traditional opportunity
at weekends, for prisoners and staff to enjoy fresh air exercise. The almost uninterrupted views of the open countryside gave prisoners a large space in which to relax or wind down through sporting activities.

The use of this facility always carried an element of risk. The physical security was only a single fence with razor wire on top. However, it was always inspected on a daily basis and in the past, there had been external patrols in the country lanes in case there was an escape attempt.

Many officers would fight for this duty, as it gave you the chance to sit in your car for a couple of hours on a Sunday morning (reading a newspaper or listening to music).

I recall an incident at the beginning of 1980 when I had been sitting there for about an hour. I suddenly spotted a man dressed in prison sports clothes running along the main road towards me. In the distance, I could see the yellow prison escort van with its headlights flashing, also heading in my direction.

I had heard nothing on my UHF radio but assumed that somebody had escaped across the fields. This was my opportunity to foil an escape bid and although I was a bag of nerves, I wasn't going to let him get away. My car was parked well inside a gateway so I guessed the escapee hadn't spotted me yet.

As the prisoner drew closer I appeared from behind the hedge and ordered him to stop running.

"This is the end of the road for you mate, stay exactly where you are." I commanded with authority, but the man just kept running.

"I'm running boss, there's no problem," he replied breathlessly.

I grabbed his arm as he attempted to pass by me and the horn was sounded on the prison van as the runner tripped and fell (taking us both into a slimy ditch beneath the hedge). He tried to struggle out of the ditch but I held on to him firmly.

The van pulled up alongside us and the driver wound his window down.

"Let him go you fucking mad man. He's taking part in the Springhill (Open Prison) road race and. I've got a tenner on him to win."

I wasn't aware that the open prison had organised their cross-country event at the same time that Grendon was hosting their sports day. You can imagine my embarrassment and it took me several months to live that down.

Although this could have been a costly mistake (especially for the van driver) it did serve to highlight the value of this duty if there had ever been a real escape attempt!!

The reason I have offered this description of an incident that occurring some years earlier, is because in 2002 there was another successful escape attempt, which ended with three dangerous and potentially violent prisoners being on the run for a period of twenty-four hours.

Despite the daily ritual of a daily "fence check" the men escaped through a large hole in the reinforced steel fence and drove away in a stolen car. This was an operational blunder (combined with human error) that had been predicted for many years.

I and several other long-term colleagues had complained about the positioning of security boxes within the sports field and we had indicated a blind spot along one section of the fence, but this had been disregarded by a succession of security staff.

Immediately after the escape, several of the prisons anti therapy mob began to blame Grendon's regime for the disappearance of the three villains.

This major investigation (like many others) felt like nothing more than a witch hunt. I suspected it would be another excuse to lay blame on the doorstep of the therapeutic communities, rather than to admit to various operational failings and learn a big lesson from the incident. However, on the very day of the escape a new governor was taking up his post as a successor to Tim Newell.

William Payne was the man who I felt could strengthen the prisons battered ethos and unite the senior management group in a more positive way.

It would be interesting to see how he would deal with the aftermath of such a serious incident. What restrictions might he have to enforce within the regime?

William had arrived with an impressive track record of working within HQ (in the Director Generals office). He was appointed Governor of Feltham Young Offenders Institution in May 2000 but unfortunately fell ill and was forced to leave (taking up a post in the personnel directorate) before applying to become the Governor of Grendon in 2001.

Despite the short time he was at Feltham, it was felt that he had some very impressive personal qualities and I sensed that he cared about people, both staff and prisoners.

I knew him previously in his role as a local school governor and felt that his arrival at Grendon was a breath of fresh air.

When William revealed his initial plans, he said "Probably the biggest thing I have to learn most about Grendon is the therapy itself. Therapy is not something, which can be simply described, it is deep and complex. I profoundly respect the decision that you who live in Grendon (Prisoners) have made to enter therapy. It really is a tough choice because it involves confronting some very painful and difficult personal issues. He added "Essentially I see my role here as trying to put things in place (and keeping things in place) so that therapy can take place safely, and that is quite a complex job too.

He believed it was not right to offer excuses for anything that might be lacking.

"It's easy to say that resources are the cause of the problems Grendon faces, but in Grendon's case, resources truly are a big issue. Put simply, we do not have enough money. To address this, we have conducted a review of staffing requirements which will identify what type of staff and what levels of staffing we need to run Grendon as five therapeutic communities and an induction wing (F Wing)

Once the outcome of the staffing review has been considered and then agreed by the Area Manager and the Deputy Director General, we will I hope be given sufficient funds to run the establishment better."

It was clear to all concerned that he wanted to take ownership of the therapeutic regime and wanted to succeed in achieving the right balance between operational matters and those concerned with therapy.

He commenced a review to determine how some of the current prison service standards might affect the work of the therapeutic communities. I personally welcomed this as it would provide an opportunity to develop consistent standards between all the therapeutic communities.

Unfortunately, William was unable to finish what he had started as he only remained at Grendon for a few months before he became ill again. His leaving left the staff and prisoners bewildered, with many questions unanswered.

Later on, he explained "Becoming Governor of Grendon and Springhill was, as I said at the time, simply the best appointment I could have had. Both establishments stand, and have long stood, for all that is best in the prison service and all that the Prison Service itself needs to achieve.

That I am no longer Governor is therefore an immense disappointment to me and by leaving so soon I know I have let you down. The last thing Grendon and Springhill needed, after the longevity of Tim Newell's tenure as Governor, was a "here today and gone tomorrow" successor. Grendon and Springhill's staff and prisoners needed a better outcome than the one you got.

While I was Governor I felt well supported: I was new, with much to learn, and there was an extraordinary willingness to help me. My reasons for leaving therefore have nothing to do with lack of commitment or help I received from you.

The reasons essentially concern my inability to leave work at work, and a difficulty in investing my energy wisely: everything was important and too much demanded my personal attention.

These shortcomings played havoc with me for several months despite all that I did to do things differently. but this does not adequately explain my reasons - it is difficult to find the words I need to express meaningfully what I would like to say. However, I thought it important to try to find some words.

I am sorry I am no longer Governor, but it is I regret for the best. I shall never govern a prison again. I wish you every good fortune."

This must have been a very painful thing to say and although it didn't go far enough to explain matters fully, it did highlight the often-unseen pressures that a prison Governor must cope with.

Rumours had been rife prior to his statement, that he may have been forced into submission by the powerful influence of some managers who were determined to crush the regime.

In fact, the internal political wrangling was the main source of frustration for many staff (myself included) and situations like this didn't help.

It appeared to me that Tim Newell's departure marked the end of a lengthy line of Governors and Medical Superintendents that had fully endorsed the ethos of Grendon's regime and had managed to resist the ministerial pressure to fully conform to the normal standards for a B Category jail.

In my opinion, as Grendon had become "first and foremost a Category B prison" it can never hope to replicate much of the work that it did in the first 3 decades of its existence, but maybe that was what the desired outcome is, to produce the type of model for treatment that could be replicated elsewhere, run solely by psychologists, using accredited programmes for prisoners who no longer freely volunteer for treatment.

As William Payne left, the jail was left for a short while in the control of several managers who continued to push the need for extra vigilance and security.

I believed they paid only lip service to the concept of rehabilitation and they would be determined to undermine the wing therapists at any opportunity.

Eventually, at the end of September 2002 a new Governor arrived to take the helm.

Dr Peter Bennett arrived from HMP Wellingboro. He too arrived with an impressive track record and I understand he was quietly regarded as something of a trouble shooter.

Peter had been a student for a considerably long time (not getting into a job until the age of thirty) and he held a degree in Anthropology and History. He then did a PhD in Anthropology over a two-year period. He had declared his interest in rehabilitation, stating that he had been "interested in Grendon since he joined the Prison Service ". He said "I thought this was the ideal prison for me ".
I wondered why he had not applied to come here earlier. Had he done so, he would have discovered an entirely different regime to the one that existed. And he might have been as concerned as I was to find so much missing.

William Payne had arrived on the day of "The Great Escape" and now Peter Bennett arrived at the start of another incident that would go down in Grendon's history as "The Big Spin".

In prison slang, a "spin" is the name given to the searching of an inmate's cell or any other area of the jail.

A prisoner from C Wing returned from the Education Department carrying a small hand drill. He handed this tool to a prison officer and asked him to lock it into a secure cabinet in the wing office.

When the staff team changed duty, another officer saw the drill and was alarmed by its existence. More importantly he was alarmed that it had been given to the prisoner for unsupervised use in his cell.

One might feel that the existence of any drill in the possession of a prisoner must warrant a fair amount of alarm. However, this was not an item that had just been handed to a prisoner over the last few days. It had existed in the prison for twelve years or more!!

This serves as just one example of the policies that have been developed at Grendon over a prolonged period, which are suddenly deemed to be unacceptable in the current climate.

I and several other officers can recall the drill being handed to prisoners on a regular basis, sometimes to use overnight in their cell. Over the years, the item was considered by many of us to be insignificant in terms of a serious threat to security, but in the current climate perhaps it was the ideal excuse for security staff to flex a bit of muscle.

The fact that the Security Department was totally unaware of its existence (therefore questioning the effectiveness of its own audit system) was brushed under the carpet for a while.

It was announced that a power tool had been discovered on C Wing.

Most the uniformed staff were led to believe that it had been found hidden away, rather than simply being handed to staff by a prisoner for safe keeping. This served to cultivate a feeling that "the convicts were up to no good" and to create further alarm we were told that the drill could "cut through the metal bars like a knife through butter." Stating that the tool could penetrate the fabric of the jail this obviously meant that the priority for a full search had to be raised.

Previously this tool was used to create decorative (Faberge type) eggs and I had witnessed a prisoner some years earlier trying to drill into the shell of a goose egg (with little success). I imagined the prison fabric was built of much sterner stuff, surely?

If this drill could somehow breach the physical security - this must have serious implications for the whole prison?

So, having generated a reasonable amount of excitement and hysteria amongst some of the more "action starved" officers a complete search of the jail was organised without any consultation between the prison therapists or the prisoners.

You might think it rather odd that I should suggest consulting with prisoners prior to conducting a security check?

If this is the case, you have obviously missed the point of what the majority of my book is about. In a democratic therapeutic community, consultation must be one of the highest priorities. Once again, it is what made Grendon such a safe place in which to live and work for several decades.

Simply letting the communities know that such a drastic action is needed, gives prisoners the opportunity to combine with staff to make the process more consistent and in keeping with policies of a prison Therapeutic Community.

By keeping the prisoners in the dark about the reasons for a full search and keeping the guidelines for staff very broad, meant that chaos and mayhem would be the obvious result. The anticipated breakdown of relationships between prisoners and staff was given a further helping hand by the antics of a few anti-therapy staff that seized the opportunity to take control.

Prior to the search commencing a bullet-headed Principle Officer announced at a meeting in the gymnasium, "Let's show them this is our prison."

To be fair, Peter Bennett had only just arrived and it was a difficult call for any governor to make. He had no choice other than to trust in the capabilities of the other managers and their legionnaires.

Many uniformed staff, who conducted the very time consuming and difficult operation, with the utmost humanity. Unfortunately, there was a minority group who seemed to be overcome by the mass hysteria.

The instruction "to remove any unauthorised articles from cells and ensure that nothing exists on outside walls" (for some) translated as, "Do as much damage as you can."

Cells were discriminately torn apart. Prisoners personal possessions, correspondence and photographs were strewn across the floor, and cupboards, shelves, plaques and pictures that had been on the walls for the past ten years were ripped down. Several tons of rubbish were eventually removed from the jail.

Even though many staff resisted the bullyboy tactics of some of their colleagues, the damage was done, and it was going to take a long time to restore full trust and confidence within the communities. I feared that it might never completely return.

Our new Governor later described the dynamics of Grendon as "Fascinating. In some ways it's very open, and in others, it's just people hurting each other. And that's just the staff!"

He added "I've got to be careful that I don't influence things before I know enough about them." He saw his priorities to be "enhancing the regimes and making sure we've got a secure prison".

Many prisoners and some staff were traumatised by the big spin, as there didn't seem to be any rhyme or reason for the way it was conducted. Peter Bennett declared "I've done a lot of wondering what it was about as well."

Of course, it wasn't his idea. He took responsibility for the search but admitted that it was already going on when he arrived. Many staff and prisoners felt that the power drill was merely an excuse by some managers to shake things up, and Peter's reply to this accusation was as good as any Westminster politician's.

He said "It seemed to be totally legitimate and reasonable to have a search, if you find a tool within a prison. The system is that you report it straight away and it's normal in any prison to have a search.

Since this, I have been involved in debates about whether everybody knew it was there and everything else. It's quite normal to have a search."

But of course, experienced officers knew, what had occurred had been far from normal. I certainly felt that Peter Bennett had arrived at Grendon prison bringing nothing of value and would undoubtedly leave at some point having contributed little to the therapeutic regime.

Peter didn't anticipate the reaction by so many people. But this was the sort of thing that directly challenges the therapeutic work done at Grendon. He accepted "it can be very traumatic for prisoners, but also more so for staff." and he echoed the thoughts of the Rev Peter Stell a few years earlier. "The uniformed officer is expected to be a prison officer on the one hand, carrying out security measures etc.... You are working with people you get to like and support and everything else and it's very difficult to say you are also going to be searching that person."

The point that he seemed to miss, was that traditionally Grendon officers and prisoners have always understood this concept well and have worked with it. However, he did admit that "This search seemed to take on a life of its own. It became very destructive."

In an open forum, the views of prisoners varied.

Graham (A Wing) said "Personally my cell was OK, but around the wing they were heavy handed."

Nick (A Wing) said "I was extremely angry at the damage caused. They're not keen on correcting mistakes and are a law unto themselves. No thought went into it. 12 years ago, Grendon was run differently. There was more interaction between staff and inmates and there were more therapists. Security has a grip on this place and they don't know their arse from their elbows."

Jamie (B Wing Chairman) said "It was an exercise to get the staff back on the job because they were getting too comfortable - or uncomfortable rather at having to rub down or strip search inmates they've become friendly with.

It was a message - You've got a job to do. I understand it's hard for staff and there's a conflict between therapy and security. A lot of excellent work has been put back by this."

I was affected more than most officers and the incident seemed to be the catalyst for many other emotions. My experience felt like the ones I had at Huntercombe prison.

Whilst other officers angry and some shed tears behind closed doors, my disturbance went much deeper and I was very disturbed emotionally. I was consumed by intense anger.

On the second day of the searching I refused to get involved with any of it and had a heated argument with one female Principle Officer, who was urging the C Wing staff to repeat the same abusive process that had been so damaging the day before. I felt it was time to stop the process, to look at the damage that was being done, not just physically but emotionally to everyone. She seemed unable to see anything further than her next command.

I urged her to see sense "Can't you see the damage you are doing to the staff group and the communities?" but the only response she could find was to order me to "Shut it".

I continued to refuse to personally be involved in the search at all.

Significantly, in December 2002, I was involved in a further argument with the prisons Deputy Governor over my behaviour during an escort with a prisoner, to nearby Stoke Mandeville Hospital. During the escort, I had taken the man into a local newsagent and on the return journey had stopped to do some shopping at a Tesco supermarket.

In hindsight, I was on a collision course with people who I saw to be standing in the way of good therapeutic progress and was resistant to any policy that obstructed the therapeutic process. However, whilst I wore my heart on my sleeve, this also made me a very vulnerable target for some managers.

Each of the individual Therapeutic Communities were seeking accreditation and within this framework lay a disturbing classroom mentality. Although some therapists argued that the changes would lead to a more professional regime, the reality is that the uniqueness of Grendon would eventually disappear, but, for me, it had gone already.

I felt I was witnessing the prison that I respected so much, being dragged screaming and kicking into the more traditional prison systems and regulations.

The fact is there used to be a waiting list of at least 250 prisoners who wanted to come into therapy. Now that figure is seriously diminished and The Director General (Phil Wheatley) suggests that "This is because many other prisons have now developed courses that are like those found at Grendon."

Not only did his comment show a lack of real understanding about the nature of Grendon's therapy but it also endorsed my previous concern that some prison managers have no comprehension of a true therapeutic community. There was much of Grendon's regime that could not be accredited.

Some prisoners are rightly convinced that a move to Grendon would be a positive step forward, but they soon realise on arrival into the assessment unit that they may have made a big mistake. They might discover that there are prisoners in the therapeutic communities who have been accepted regardless of their lack of motivation to change and a failure to accept the wing policies.

I suspected at some point soon the policy would change so that prisoners would be told to come to Grendon as part of their sentence plan, rather than being able to volunteer, that would ensure adequate numbers were allocated and the TC would survive.

Also by housing more and more indeterminate sentenced prisoners, there would be less prisoners released from Grendon and its efficacy as a model for resettlement into the community would disappear.

At this stage, officers on the Assessment Unit openly declared men to be unsuited to therapy but were over-ruled by senior management, to keep the prison population to its highest CNA (Certified Normal Accommodation).

Once the objective was placed on their Sentence Plan they could not refuse to "volunteer" for therapy!

If you consider that Grendon prisoners had previously freely volunteered to come into therapy, we now have a prison system that will force them in, whether they like it or not!

Lifers have always been particularly vulnerable to being trapped. If they volunteer to undertake therapy and then ask to be transferred out, either at the assessment stage or later, the chances are that their decision will be recorded negatively.

Prisoners feel a real sense of powerlessness when faced with the prospect of a damaging "End of Therapy" report.

For those who do find the therapeutic experience rewarding and there are still many who do, several might experience a frustration at the end of therapy, because they must wait for a progressive move to less secure conditions or even an open prison.

They could still be waiting for nine months or more at least.

Another problem I encountered was connected to the style of therapy that was being endorsed by the accreditation process. Under such a rigid system of accreditation, the theory of "free association" (of thoughts and ideas, with informal discussion) has become less evident.

The regime that exists today relies on clear boundaries, less risk, less attention to written evidence and very often no contact at all with significant people in the prisoner's life.

It is my opinion that the use of a more rigid analytical psychotherapy model of treatment can lead to some essential information being missed. It is easier for men to hide aspects of their behaviour (particularly key facts leading to their offences). Many stones are left unturned and it is possible that some prisoners might move through the Grendon programme having not sufficiently addressed important aspects of their offending behaviour. This worries me.

I became very unhappy with my role at Grendon, but the worst thing of all was witnessing some of the injustices which were affecting several of my colleagues, as well as many prisoners. If you dig beneath the surface of this seemingly relaxed, sometimes very pleasant regime, there had always been things that were a source of frustration, but now I felt a daily atmosphere of suspicion and mistrust.

I despised the "block headed" managers who to me were nothing more than bully boys and I had to try to develop a method of relaxation that would distract me from the problems I was experiencing.

I chose to run a musical workshop for twelve to fifteen prisoners during my lunch breaks. I gave this session the name 'United Isolation' because it gave me a chance to unite with a group of musicians for a brief period. We were isolated from the strict policies of the therapeutic communities and the operational constraints that were being imposed on the wings.

I was grateful to Governor Derek Stewart for granting me the opportunity to move freely around the jail with a group of prisoners during 'patrol state' (the period when staffing levels are at the lowest) but unfortunately with this privilege came a variety of other (hidden) pressures. My main source of frustration was with the security department who seemed to delight in causing obstructions at every opportunity.

Following the big spin, it became obvious that the security managers had not audited for a whole load of equipment that was in the jail and to cover up their inadequacies they were going to extremes to retain control. I was even given responsibility to list each guitar string in the jail and to supply a detailed monthly inventory. It was an impossible task, and of course they knew it!

I wish I could have had the ability to treat my job as 'just a job'. Many officers view their role as being simply security and containment. They seem able to leave the problems at the gate, resisting any temptation to become too involved. However, those that choose to involve themselves with the rehabilitation of prisoners unwittingly open themselves up to a multitude of pressures that cannot easily be left behind at the end of the day.

So, having developed a reputation of going further than most, particularly with the more difficult and demanding prisoners, I had chosen to accept the stress that goes with the territory. However, at least, in the past, I had been supported in my 'extra mile' by a progressive management. They knew the problems involved and left it to my discretion to decide when and where to take risks.

At this point, I feel a need to mention Officer Paul Johnson who I was privileged to work with on C wing. Paul had the nickname 'Bizzy' because he was often rushing around the jail trying to achieve as much as he could for the prisoners, always busy working towards something positive. He was well thought of, and rightly so. The prisoners knew that he cared for their welfare and he therefore held their respect.

Paul had suffered through his efforts too, but had found a method of managing his daily workload and recognised his limitations; I admired this and felt comfortable when we worked together. However, we were different in our approach, and despite his warnings I carried on my journey towards personal destruction.

I felt that I could still calculate the risks based on my knowledge of individual prisoners and the strength of the relationships I had with them. I was heading for a big fall.

Gary B was one such prisoner and my relationship with him was to mark the approach to the most devastating experience of my career, in fact my life.

Gary was abusive, disruptive, threatening and deceitful. Described by other cons as 'a no-good smack head', by therapists as 'a psychopath' and more eloquently by prison officers who had come across him during this sentence, as 'a complete arsehole'.

He had been transferred from the assessment unit to C wing, despite the reservations of many staff and prisoners who doubted his motivation to change his offending behaviour. I became his personal officer and immediately set about the task of searching for his positive points. He was no different from many others that I had met in the past and I found his Achilles heel after only a few weeks.

He was from Liverpool (which doesn't make him a bad person), a 'scouser' with a wicked sense of humour, which appealed to me. It was through this avenue that I began to build a rapport.

He was also very quick tempered and would come to the boil without any warning, never mincing his words or stopping to check out who he was abusing. He made many enemies over a brief period of time amongst the staff and fellow prisoners.

Some might describe him as a 'scally' (likeable rogue) but there were others (myself included) who could appreciate how dangerous he might be, particularly when he felt vulnerable and his main area of vulnerability were his immediate family.

There was no doubt in my mind that he loved his mum and dad deeply. He had been a drug addict and thief for many years and his love for them alone would not stop him offending in the future. To succeed he would have to raise his self-esteem and build the confidence to move away from his life of crime, which would initially mean kicking the drug habit.

He was in the initial stages of his therapy and he viewed his own success through the eyes of his parents, particularly his dad. He wanted his dad to be proud of him.

Having brought heartache and shame to his family he wanted to put things right.

Gary was looking forward to a visit from his dad soon, to show him what he was doing. He said, 'My old man is great, he has always looked after the family and I want to prove to him that I can do well'.

A family visit had been arranged but sadly it was cancelled due to his father being unwell. His mum had assured him that it was nothing serious but Gary was unconvinced. I had spoken to her on several occasions and felt that his family might have been protecting him from the truth, which his dad's condition was in fact much worse.

Gary wanted to apply for accumulated visits at Walton jail in Liverpool (which would have allowed him to have visits with his parents over a period of 28 days). At least he could then assess his father's health for himself.

However, he was told that he couldn't take accumulated visits at such an early stage in his therapy. The break in therapy wouldn't be productive and it was felt that he might use the opportunity to return to his drug habit. The only other option available was to pull out of therapy altogether and eventually return to Walton where he could re-apply for a return to Grendon once he was satisfied dad was well.

The last option was not really an option he could take as he did not have sufficient time left to serve.

I explained to him that we might be able to arrange an escort to the family home, although he had to be in therapy for at least twelve months to qualify. This might be allowed on compassionate grounds and only if we could verify his father's medical condition by a letter from a GP.

He was in the process of obtaining this letter when the prison received a call from a Liverpool hospital to confirm that his father was terminally ill and not likely to live through the night.

The effect on Gary was devastating and he expressed a mixture of anger and sadness.

"I told this fucking jail that my old man was really ill but they didn't believe me. If he dies, I swear I will smash the fucking gaff up. None of you's will be safe," he threatened. Then almost in the same breath he said "What am I gonna do Joe man? My dad means everything to me. Please get me out there. I know I make threats but it's because I'm scared. I don't wanna lose him". He shed real tears and genuinely hated himself for the pain and grief he had caused his family over many years.

It was decided a full escort had to be arranged, to leave the prison early the next morning.

This proved to be a challenging task. There were very few prison officers who wanted to do the job for any one of three reasons. Firstly, they might have to agree to work on their rest day (as was the case for me) or agree that they would not return by the end of the usual shift.

Secondly, Gary was not a very popular prisoner and only a handful of staff could get along with him, never mind control him in a setting outside of the jail.

Thirdly, an escort to visit a dying relative is one of the most difficult and traumatic duties an officer can undertake. There is all manner of pressures placed on the escorting staff. The main problems are obvious but there are others that cannot easily be foreseen prior to the escort.

Gary had been locked in his cell from 2030 hours on the Thursday night until he was unlocked for the escort at 0530 the next day, so there was no way to assess his emotional state when I unlocked him but it was clear that he had not slept at all.

I was extremely grateful to the two prisoner officers who eventually volunteered for this difficult escort as both had never experienced this before.

Officer Nick Shepherd was new to the job, but I was impressed with his attitude to his work at Grendon. He was compassionate and understood the psychological implications of our task, a young man who was eager to do the best. He could perform the escort duties with dignity and humanity. He would be the one to drive the escort vehicle, but we had agreed to share this task due to the distance from the prison in Buckinghamshire to the hospital in Liverpool.

Lisa Copas was a young female officer who worked on C wing and knew what a difficult and demanding prisoner Gary could be, but she had also seen how he had been affected by his father's illness and gave up her social time to take him. As she was the most junior officer, Gary would be handcuffed to her for the entire escort.

It had been pre-determined that Gary would go 'double cuffed'.

In a double cuff situation, his hands are cuffed together at the front and then one arm was cuffed to Lisa. I was ordered to keep him double cuffed always throughout the escort. I had no discretion to remove a set of cuffs without authority.

The escort left the prison gates later than anticipated and we raced towards Liverpool, hoping that Gary's father had held on for him.

Gary was sandwiched between me and Lisa in the back of the car as we approached the outskirts of Liverpool. I checked the handcuffs at regular intervals to ensure they were secure but also that his blood flow was not being impaired.

It was clear that Gary was emotionally drained and he dreaded the thought of seeing his father so ill. I was secretly dreading the prospect that we might have to return to Grendon before his father had died and how might Gary cope when his father did eventually die?

As we neared the hospital, I rang to let the hospital know we would be arriving soon.

She thanked me for the call and then said 'I'm sorry to have to tell you that Mr B died half an hour ago. The family said that they will break the news to Gary when he arrives at the hospital'.

I made every effort to conceal my reaction to hearing this sad news and replied 'Thanks a lot, we'll be there soon'.

Gary stared at me as I ended the call and said 'Everything is still ok, hey Joe'

I turned to face him and found myself considering the eyes of a frightened child. The stone faced armed robber and drug addict was transformed into an emotional wreck. I was aware of Nick's concern as he glanced at the rear-view mirror and Lisa was scanning my face as I responded.

'What do you want me to say Gary'? (I couldn't lie to him). 'I'm sorry mate, but your dad passed away half an hour ago'.

'Oh, no man', he gasped 'What am I going to do'?

I started to prepare him for the meeting with his family at the hospital but more importantly the visit to his father's bedside which he dreaded the most.

It's difficult to adequately explain how it feels to oversee a man (or woman) who is suffering bereavement. The offering of words of comfort or a supportive arm around the shoulders would under normal circumstances suffice, but I am acutely aware of the heavy chains which add an extra burden to his already heavy load. It starts to feel abusive regardless of his status as a convicted arm robber.

In these circumstances, the man and woman in our charge take on the form of a vulnerable human being. Only a hard-faced bastard could ignore this.

Nick, Lisa and I could empathise with Gary's plight.

As we approached the main doors to the hospital, I was aware of the general public's reaction to seeing a prisoner in chains. Not only can it be alarming but prisoners can also react in a hostile manner towards anybody who shows the slightest sign of disgust. In Gary's case this was not to be an issue. He was a beaten man, chained to a prisoner officer on whose face was also written sadness and concern. He was clearly no threat to anybody.

I had got to know Gary's family well over the past couple of months and I had formed an impression of a normal, caring, hardworking family who desperately wanted Gary to reform. However, they were also concerned about how Gary might react to news of his father's death. They all lived up to my expectations and Gary was also able to allay any fears that he might react badly.

We all sensed a feeling of warmth and welcome from his family as we were greeted by some of the nicest people I had met in many years. Gary's father was a pillar of the local community and was well respected. We were thanked for our efforts to try to get Gary there on time.

His visit to his father's bedside was very traumatic but he handled the situation in a very responsible and adult manner. It was Lisa's first experience of death and she was also visibly shaken. Although Gary was frustrated with the conditions placed on him during the escort, he could see that the three of us were handling the situation as well as we could.

I thanked Lisa and Nick for their input and suggested to the Governor that they should be particularly commended for their performance. I received no response.

I had conducted at least two dozen 'death bed escorts' during my career but this particular one had affected me deeply. I felt that the level of security that had been ordered was out of proportion to the risk imposed by the prisoner or his family. The intelligence offered by the security department was inaccurate to the extreme.

I had taken a short break following the visit to the hospital, but my mind was pre-occupied with the thoughts of the impending funeral, which I was informed would be the following Friday.

I hoped that Nick and Lisa might be able to attend the funeral but unfortunately, they were not available.

Gary and his family had specifically requested that I should be one of the officers who escorted him to the funeral but I felt very uneasy about the prospect. I was barely coping with my own feelings and shared with other staff that I felt pressured into accepting this duty.

I simply did not want to go, but felt I had to. In hindsight, my panic was about not having the ability to make things right for Gary and his family on this sad occasion.
It was also about the changes that were occurring throughout the jail that prevented myself (and other officers) completing operational duties with a sufficient level of dignity, humanity and respect.

In short, the security conditions for escorts, accompanied paroles or indeed any appointments to places outside of the prison had become inflexible and in some cases unworkable within an efficient therapeutic community.

In the past, there had been occasions when security needed to be lowered according to local conditions and this was one of them.

Funeral escorts were particularly difficult to conduct under conditions of top security and the forthcoming funeral would be a testing time for me and the other staff who were attending. I hoped that the arrangements for the funeral would have been made before I returned to work, but absolutely nothing had been done.

It was inconceivable that something so important could have been left until the last minute. I had to run around, chasing paperwork and trying to recruit staff for the escort at very short notice. If I could have taken a step back at this point and assessed my own condition, both mentally and physically, it would have been obvious that I was approaching burnout.

I had been feeling physically sick at the prospect of attending the funeral and felt like running away from all of my responsibilities, but I felt I couldn't because so many people would be let down, particularly Gary who had been on an emotional roller coaster over the past ten days.

At the last minute a driver was found, and a nice guy, Bob Askew, an officer from C wing agreed to accompany me. He had recently transferred to Grendon from HMP Weare, in Weymouth.

I was relieved that an experienced and very capable officer would be present, and he was also a man who could empathise with Gary. However, he had not had an easy introduction to the Grendon regime, having to witness several ludicrous investigations into trivial matters and perhaps feeling very uneasy about the managements understanding of the therapeutic value of staff/prisoner relationships.

He was certainly a caring, understanding officer but he would not take any unnecessary risks, which was good.

I doubted my own ability to remain objective and asked him if he would be happy to take charge of the escort. Ordinarily the officer who had the most years in service would have been in charge (which of course was me) but I told him that I was not happy to take on that responsibility.

I joked 'I feel like running away from everything. Can you imagine the headlines in the News of the World? Prison Officer escapes during a funeral escort'.

He laughed at the suggestion, but little did he realise how real that feeling was within me.

I decided to appeal to the Governor for a reduction in the level of security at the church.

Simply applying one set of handcuffs would suffice and at least that would allow me to drape a jacket discreetly over the cuffs. Gary could also put his arm around his mother to support her and it would even have been possible for him to assist with the carrying of his father's coffin, which the family wanted so much to happen.

I knew that I could trust Gary one hundred percent. I knew he would not run away from his dad's funeral. I made an appeal on behalf of myself and my colleague (in the furtherance of therapy) based on over twenty years of experience at Grendon and with well over thirty funeral escorts under my belt.

It was an emotional appeal and the Governor listened sympathetically. He also had the experience and ability to grant the small gesture that would allow us to conduct the escort with more humanity and dignity.

He said, 'I have listened to your case Joe, which I fully understand but before I make a final decision I must consult an expert'.

I knew that our fate was sealed when he rang the security department. I knew the cause was beaten because this so-called expert had also been responsible for several recent decisions that showed no interest in the value of the therapeutic communities.

The answer I got was negative!

My mouth became dry and my heart was beating heavily as I left the Governor's office and made my way back to C wing. There were tears in my eyes as I walked along the corridor and I felt angry that this regime had been undermined so badly.

I passed a couple of prisoners who were waiting outside the canteen and one spoke to me 'You look like shit Joe, are you ok'? He asked.

I tried to smile but it must have appeared false. My lips quivered as I replied 'Thanks, you don't look so smart yourself you twat. I'll be fine once I've taken the tablets'. We laughed together - I couldn't let him see how much hurt existed inside of me.

I was repeating to myself over and over 'I'm a prison officer, a support to others; I shouldn't be feeling like this - get a grip on it'. But the more I tried to control my feelings the stronger they became.

I let myself onto the wing and went straight into the staff office, followed closely by the wing therapist and probation officer. As I stared out of the office window I began to shake from head to foot and the tears began to flow. I felt out of control.

Within a few moments, Bob Askew came into the office and the door was closed. I cried bucketsful and explained 'I couldn't make tomorrow right for Gary and his family. I therefore didn't want to attend the funeral in the morning'.

All the staff understood my anxieties and they must have realised how deep the feelings went? I had coped with much worse in the past but this reaction was way out of my control.

Although it was obvious to everybody that my emotions were in turmoil, I was encouraged to 'be strong for Gary and his family'.

It's true, I had done so well at the hospital, even though it had been traumatic and his family wanted me to be there. With this support and encouragement, I began to convince myself again that I was the only man for the job. I felt I had to pull myself together for Gary's sake.

Bob said 'Gary will be pleased you are going. He will know you have done your best to help him. Let's go and tell him that it's alright for tomorrow'.

We went onto the landing and approached Gary's cell. I began to explain the arrangements for the morning. Then without warning I again broke down in floods of tears. 'I'm sorry mate, I tried to make things better for you and your mum but nobody wants to listen', I sobbed.

Can you imagine this surreal moment? A prisoner is faced with a prison officer who is crying and asking for forgiveness because he cannot provide a dignified escort to his dad's funeral. How many times has this happened in any jail?

In an amazing gesture, Gary put his arm around my shoulders and said quietly 'It's ok mate, I know you did your best for me and my family. I'm just happy you'll be there'.

Gary's comments made me even more determined to go, even though emotionally I was falling apart.

The wing Governor was informed of my condition and fully realised that I was over involved emotionally. In my present state of mind, it was impossible for me to be objective. However, he was more amused than concerned by my behaviour, which made me even more determined to get through it. I was an absolute liability and in truth Bob Askew would face a lot of pressure tomorrow.

He rang me at home that evening to check that I was ok. 'Don't worry mate, I'll be fine', I said cheerfully. How could I tell him that I felt unable to cope?

In hindsight, all of the signs and symptoms of my behaviour signified that I was heading for a severe mental breakdown.

We had to get to Liverpool by 9.30 am so we decided to unlock Gary at 5 am and leave by 5.30 am. Four hours was a comfortable time for this journey.

We arrived together. I went down to the wing to unlock Gary while Bob collected the paperwork, the handcuffs and the escort vehicle.

The night staff delayed the unlocking of Gary's cell door, which only served to heighten the anxiety that he was already feeling. He had not slept at all during the night and had shared a cell with another man from Liverpool who had supported him through many depressive periods.

As Gary emerged from his cell he was in confrontation mode and an argument developed with one of the night staff. The officer seemed unable to make any allowances for the circumstances and appeared to relish the wind up. I hated this arrogant streak in some prison officers.

We had a signed agreement that Gary would change into his funeral clothes when he arrived at the church. He was wearing a pair of jeans and a T shirt and carried a black shirt on a hanger. In the jails reception area, another argument developed as the night staff insisted he changed into the shirt before leaving the prison.

I argued that we had an agreement to change him on our arrival in Liverpool.

'How are you going to do that, if you're not allowed to remove the handcuffs'? The officer smirked. I simply replied, 'We will find a way'.

Gary could pay his last respects to his father and through an ingenious method of cuffing, we managed to change him into his funeral clothes and attended the church service on time. He remained cuffed to me and had his hands cuffed together throughout the entire service.

I had insisted on being cuffed to him, which in hindsight had been a wrong decision. Bearing in mind how I had been behaving in the few days before the escort, I was soon experiencing some powerful emotions that I couldn't move away from!

As we greeted Gary's mother at the entrance to the church the only way he could put his arms around her was to lift the cuffs over her head. The pair cried on each other's shoulders and I felt the urge to put my arm around his mother's shoulders in a gesture of comfort, rather than stand like a statue next to them. His family appreciated my gesture but it was a wrong move for me as my emotions were laid bare, and once again tears began to flow.

As the service progressed Gary was shaking and crying uncontrollably and I was literally locked into his every move.

I even had to blow his nose for him because he was unable to do it for himself. I was angry with the Governor for insisting on this punitive level of physical security.

There was simply no need for it.

As we followed his father's coffin out of the church, Gary attempted to walk beside his mum and support her. But due to the handcuffing arrangements I was ceremoniously dragged behind the group of mourners, side stepping to avoid tripping over but stumbling into the congregation as we slowly made our way up the aisle. It was a nightmare experience made worse by the fact that I was overwhelmed by my own emotions. I had never been through any experience such as this in my entire career.

His family was very understanding and applauded the efforts that we had made to try to make the occasion as dignified as we could, but I knew that memories of Mr B's funeral would forever be tarnished for this family by the vision of their son shackled like an animal.

Perhaps there are those of you who feel that convicted criminals deserve everything that they get. Why should they be treated humanely?

I have always viewed the wider picture and considered the unseen victims who are the prisoner's family. Grendon could always pride itself on its ability to be unique and different. It is a pride that on this day it did not deserve to hold.

I don't think we were ever more grateful to be on a return journey to the prison. We were pleased and rightfully proud to have done our best of a very bad job. Gary and his family expressed their gratitude.

The journey back to the jail was horrendous, taking us a total of 6 hours to complete. The traffic was nose to tail on several occasions and to make matters worse Gary had a stomach upset, so we had to stop at several service areas to use the toilet.

In a twenty-year career which includes over a hundred and ten secure escorts, I have always used public conveniences for prisoners. It is always a demanding situation and you hope that the public are not unduly alarmed. If there is a smile on the faces of the prisoners and escorting staff, this goes a terrific way to relieve the anxieties of the public.

Over the years, the relationship between Grendon officers and their escorts has been such that smiles were easy to adopt because often a personal officer, who has a good relationship with the prisoner, would be involved in the operation.

This was the case for me and Gary, and although I didn't expect him to smile following his father's funeral he made a significant effort to relax the public as we made our way to the toilets.

We passed a group of open mouthed school kids and Gary exclaimed 'Look kids, all of this is because I stole a packet of Smarties. Make sure you don't break the rules as you grow up'.

We attached the six foot 'closeting chain' which went under the toilet door.

I recalled a previous escort in a comparable situation when a member of public announced 'Fuck me mate, if that's the size of the chain, how big is your dog'?

We were soon on our way again and we eventually arrived safely back in Grendon at 1930 hours, very tired and exhausted.

We had put a great deal of effort into ensuring that the escort was conducted professionally. Although, it could be argued that my emotional breakdown, witnessed by the prisoner, his family and the entire congregation was not at all professional. However, I had no control over this, which was an indication of how ill I was becoming.

We made tough decisions that appeared to be right at the time.

The last thing I expected was the reaction I got from a female Principal Officer as I was climbing out of the escort vehicle in the prison yard. This was the same officer I had confronted during the previous big spin.

'I'll see you later' she snarled.

I was still cuffed to Gary at this point and he reacted to her provocation. 'Why don't you fucking leave him alone, he's done well; I've just come back from my dad's funeral'.

She ignored the comment and continued to rebuke me as we entered the reception area.

Another rule of good management in prisons is that you do not criticise a colleague in front of other staff and particularly prisoners, especially if that prisoner is likely to react aggressively.

'I want a paper on my desk before you go off duty, explaining everything that happened today.' she stormed.

'No problem' I snapped. 'You'll get it, but not today, and do me a favour, suspend me on full pay for six months while you are at it please'. I begged.

I arrived home that evening extremely distressed and unable to sleep. The events of the day rolled over and over in my mind. I needed all the willpower I could muster to get myself into work next day and was spoiling for a fight with anybody who wanted one.

I felt that perhaps Peter Bennett might want to enquire into my state of mind after the events of the last couple of days. Instead, this was ignored in preference for an official investigation into my 'inappropriate behaviour' during the escort.

I welcomed any investigation, so that I might argue the case for a review of future escort procedures, particularly those that involve the use of double cuffing.

Grendon occasionally takes long term prisoners for a visit to the family (in their home). This is a therapeutic visit so that they can talk to family members away from the prison environment, to begin to prepare them for the outside world. In the past I had accompanied many 'lifers' without the use of cuffs, but the current rules are that they must remain cuffed at all times. However, if the prisoner wishes to use the toilet at the family home, one set of cuffs is removed and the six foot 'closeting chain' is applied to give them freedom of movement.

Following this incident my illness continued to worsen and as a reaction to this and a catalogue of other frustrations at work I finally suffered a significant mental breakdown.

An independent medical examiner described me as 'suffering from a severe depressive illness with anxiety features'. He anticipated that I would be away from work for a period of 3 to 6 months at least, in fact, I never returned to Grendon and was eventually medically retired from the prison service.

At the time of my medical retirement I was filled with a mixture of sadness and anger. I knew I would miss the relationships that I had with the prisoners and my fellow officers, but not for one moment have I missed those prison service managers who seemed to revel in my downfall.

14 years later, I can look back on all of this and see that it was my reluctance to face changes that ultimately caused the problems. It had been a mistake to go back into the prison service at all. However, as painful as it all became, I am proud of my own achievements over the years and proud to have been a part of Grendon Prisons history.

As far back as February 1997, Dr. Peter Lewis who was then Director of Therapy at Grendon stated 'In the last 6 months we have seen the creation of a new therapeutic community at Aylesbury Prison which looks to the support of the Association of Therapeutic Communities in prison, who have been helpless in witnessing the annihilation of two therapeutic communities for young offenders within the last 6 months. So how will Grendon fare in the future'?

He suspected that 'Grendon will never be fed enough for healthy growth and development'.

The slow drip feed has continued to the present day but it is my belief that it has never been quite enough. In my opinion, Grendon is being therapeutically starved whilst security and operational development sucks the life out of its unique communities.

As Grendon has now reached full accreditation of its therapeutic regime, there will always be jobs for psychologists and other professionals and in truth Grendon prison will continue to help prisoners to reform, to a certain degree.

Bearing in mind how happy I had been when I first walked through the gates of Grendon prison twenty-seven years ago, it feels tragic that my final memory is that of being escorted out of the same gates in floods of tears.

Grendon had lost its appeal for me, but the fresh staff joining the prison service will still benefit from their experience there and many prisoners will derive great benefit from their time in therapy.

I was left to recover successfully from my illness and embark on another career, which I suspected would not be a million miles removed from prison work, but as one chapter of my life ends, I can look back at what I have learned from this experience so far?

Chapter 17

As my work with criminal's progresses I try to understand what it is that makes an individual commit such horrendous acts against other human beings. Is there a common theme throughout? In short, the answer is no!

There are many theories, but for me the most obvious place to start to examine probable causes is in the development of the human mind.

From the moment of birth an infant begins to relate to others and by examining the development of the mind from this very early stage, I believe we can come to learn what it is that promotes these relationships and what are the possible consequences for the development of our individual personalities, for good or bad.

There is a structure that will enable us to organise all our life experiences and it exists in all of our minds. However, in some people, I believe, it becomes disorganised and muddled.

Sigmund Freud referred to the human mind as having three distinct aspects and he named them as the Id, Ego and Super Ego. These include our biological make-up (any physical disabilities etc.) our individual experiences and our relationships with others. Studying these helps us to better understand how our emotions and behaviour might be affected.

There is a great disagreement between experts about what is more important to study. Should we consider the mind as a "closed system" through psychiatry, or perhaps the mind as an "open system" affected by our contact with others, through psychology?

As I stated previously, I believe that the best way to understand criminal behaviour is to look at both aspects.

In the early years in Grendon prison there were both psychologists and psychiatrists available.
It is my opinion that a model of treatment based solely on psychology is flawed.

It is logical to begin to examine the foetus's life and possible experiences within the womb. The level at which any conflict operates may be relatively conscious or deeply conscious.

Sometimes it's not easy to say why we have done something wrong.

It has been suggested that an unborn baby is not totally psychologically fused with the mother. Therefore, some experiences from the outside world do seem to penetrate the womb and affect the unborn child.

Often, looking at an offender's family background, years before he/she is born, can determine what chances this person will have of avoiding problems in later life.

The more disturbed the family is, the more likely it will be for problems to be passed from generation to generation, until somebody decides to change the pattern.

Using Ultra-Sound scanning techniques, the foetus can be observed reacting to external events.

In 1997, the British Medical Association reported that an unborn child would curl up and suck its thumb in response to parents arguing. After it was born the baby would take up the same position in its cot during further arguments.

So, although the womb is still a safe place for an infant to be, the evidence supports the theory that the human mind develops well before birth.

From the moment of birth, the infant must begin to relate to others, in an environment full of new sounds, sights and smells and from this point the three aspects of the human mind begins to develop.

A newborn baby is not a passive object. It moves, cries and later will smile, walk and seek the company of others. It is motivated by forces that are related to the basic needs of food, sleep and contact with others (and later in life sex).

These are all aspects of any animal's physical survival and the motivation to satisfy the basic urges and desires comes directly from the part of the mind that is referred to as the Id.

An infant is initially controlled completely by the Id and the memory of how its instincts are responded to (or not) forms the basis of the child's good (or bad) memories. Therefore, being "a deprived child" can logically affect our behaviour as an adult.

The Id is the foundation stone of the mind on which all other stones are laid. It is the unconscious part of us, which feels all our basic drives. It is the source of our instincts and psychic energy. Any internal disturbance can only be released through discharge or satisfaction. So, we are able to find an instincts source, object and aim.

The source is the amount of emotional excitement in the body and its aim is the removal of the excitement. This can be achieved in the infant's own body, but as a rule an external object is required.

For instance - The Facial expression and cries of a baby soon informs the mother that the baby is in a particularly emotional state. It is a state of excitement that relates to the need for food, warmth or physical comfort. The "good Mother" will feed clothe and comfort her baby in response to that show of emotion and the baby is then satisfied.

Feelings or emotions provide information to the individual about the state of their own drive or motivational systems. In computer terms, they provide a "read out" about specific actions and their consequences.

Emotions also provide others (through the bodies responses) with a read out about an individual state.

This external read out is called a "communication".

Such a system is crucial to our growth and survival and to the healthy development of our mind because we are not simple ready programmed beings.

We can learn and adapt ourselves to our environment. Therefore, the way in which we handle our basic drives begins to be determined (in infancy) by the response of our mother or mother substitutes and eventually by significant others in our lives.

Each learning phase needs to be negotiated at the appropriate critical time to allow satisfactory progress to the next phase.

Our mind develops according to the success of our negotiations.

Our stored memories of the results will influence our future reactions to similar situations. There remains a chance of a regression or reversal to more primitive levels of behaviour when difficulties at an earlier phase are not resolved.

In simple terms, if a child attempts to build a tower of bricks and the very bottom brick (representing the Id) is not perfectly balanced; the tower will eventually fall.

Each subsequent brick represents a phase in the development of our mind and good balance is required at each phase to ensure a strong healthy development. Some people will become unbalanced at a very early stage in life.

Quite often I view my work as "Therapeutic Bricklaying" or even re-pointing, helping offenders to address the imbalance in their minds and in their relationships with others. It would be unrealistic to expect all our basic urges and desires to be fulfilled and satisfied without consequence to the individual or others.

Freud referred to the early development phase as "the oral phase" the infants wishes will appear to be satisfied almost magically. A cry for food will result in the appearance of mother's breast or a bottle.

It may even be encouraged to believe in the never-ending power of its wishes, but to move to the next phase the mind needs to develop a method of balancing the needs and demands of the Id with the realities and opportunities of the outside world. For instance -it may not always be possible to feed a child as soon as they need it and they must learn to wait.

The Ego exists as a mediator between our basic urges and the realistic fulfilment of such urges.

The Ego is concerned with rational thinking, corresponding to consciousness, external perceptions and voluntary movement. It is there to correct the balance during the building of our personal structure.

There is a direct connection between our Ego and the cortical functions, which are mostly waking functions.

These functions are suspended in sleep, which is why our basic urges and desires (our unconscious instincts) are often realised during dreams. Men and women will dream of having sex with someone that they have admired from afar, with strangers or even members of their own family without any difficulty whatsoever. The Ego controls our defence mechanisms, but they are also relaxed during sleep and fatigue or under the influence of drugs or alcohol.

On awaking (if such dreams are remembered) we will be disturbed by our thoughts and actions because the Ego is also fully awake and triggers rational thinking linked to our conscience.

Without a conscience, we can do almost anything we want to whenever we want to and regardless of the consequences to others or ourselves.

As we grow older memories fade but the human mind retains all the information we have gathered since the day we were born. All our basic urges and desires remain as strong as ever. If the Ego is impaired or it deteriorates at any stage in our lives, the Id will seek instant gratification (as it did in the newborn infant) with disastrous consequences for all concerned.

I have worked with many people who have suffered an impairment or deterioration of their Ego to varying degrees.

The Ego is the referee between the Id and reality but to perform its task, it has to heed the third psychic level, which is the Super Ego.

Our minds develop the Super Ego from internalised representations and standards of parental figures from infancy onwards, with contributions from later relationships, teachers and other admired or feared figures. Through childhood and adolescence, we might experience Policemen as purely authority figures that exist only to uphold the law and catch criminals. We will therefore log this information in our Super Ego for future reference.

Not all operations of the Super Ego are conscious.

So, we may think things out for ourselves as adults but often, in trivial ways, we operate according to less conscious dictates. For Example, a Policeman may approach in a friendly manner but our unconscious Super Ego refers to information that represents the Policeman as a hostile figure.

Difficulties arise when impulses are repressed which may then give rise to the symptoms, in this case, on meeting the Policeman, a feeling of fear and panic, rather than a healthy communication with him.

So, the human mind is influenced by social experience. For example, poor housing and employment contribute to poor family relationships, which creates emotional disturbance.

A criminal's pattern of thinking is most often influenced by a deterioration of the Ego as a response to external (bad) influences.

To understand the process more fully I considered the nature and nurturing of the criminals behaviour by studying criminal psychology in 1997.

Criminal Psychology is related to Forensic Psychology although it is more general. It questions the notion that criminals are either mentally ill or naturally evil (mad or bad)

Experts in this field of applied psychology including many that I have worked with at Grendon (notably Dr Bernard Marcus) believe that the motivation for criminal behaviour is neither of these extreme stereotypes but instead, a complex combination
of inner and external influences.

Criminal activities are extremely varied. Therefore, consideration of the differences in individuals, play a large part in the Psychologists approach to understanding crime.

An individual's differences are based on their nature (what they are born with) and nurture (what they learn and experience) and of course their interaction between the two.

The traditional approach at Grendon was not just to study the criminal but also his family, which included adopted criminals and even twins reared together or apart. Unfortunately, this work has deteriorated to a level that is almost non-existent and today the emphasis is more on the individual intelligence or personality.

Elevated levels of extroversion (outgoing tendencies) and neuroticism (emotional or heightened emotional behaviour) are associated with criminal behaviour.

The men at Grendon were encouraged to relate their individual life stories in the group work and a common theme was present in many cases.

The men can recall the periods when their criminal behaviour began, and in most cases, it existed during the primary school years and progressively worsened. Their lifestyles and family relationships differed greatly. Although many came from broken homes there was no single factor that could be attributed to the start of their offending behaviour.

Social and interpersonal difficulties were a symptom rather than a cause and, during therapy, offenders came to understand the internal forces that influenced their decision to commit crimes, which was deep rooted in their psyche.

When being assessed for therapy the prisoners completed a battery of tests and questionnaires and among these was the Minnesota Multiphasic Personality Inventory (MMPI) which covered a wide range of human functioning. It had questions relating to social and family relationships, self-image, feelings of anxiety and depression and so on.

The general picture showed the men to be neurotic, depressed and unable to relate properly to other people.

I would describe the average criminal to be a resentful, constricted and apprehensive person, who feels disillusioned and embittered. His/her distrustful, suspicious style of life alienates people and impairs the efficiency of his/her social interactions".

Successful socialisation through the group therapy experience gives an offender the ability to empathise with and place a value on other human beings and their property.

Victim awareness is a common goal for criminals working in-group psychotherapy, often realising that they themselves were victims, who in turn set out (often sub-consciously) to create other victims.

In group work, the sharing of common experiences through a deeper interaction with other offenders brings about a realisation that, as criminals choose to offend, they can also choose not to, once the Ego has regained control over the Id.

The therapy introduces social, ethical and moral values not always obvious in the criminal's real world and if most our society owns these values this is a very powerful intervention.

The group should not be a comfortable place to be if it is running well and some of the group members will attack the values. Grendon prison challenges this tendency to corrupt and an individual can learn about the dangers of corruption and how to manage them in this context.

There have been various pioneering projects that have used psychotherapy as the focus for treating criminal behaviour. Most have existed in institutions such as Special Hospitals or Prisons, suggesting that greater emphasis be placed on working with the criminal behaviour once the damage has been done, rather than treating the causes and symptoms of criminal behaviour before it reaches this stage.

Most criminals I have met or worked with have suffered abusive and degrading lives, witnessing scenes of violence between parents or becoming the chosen object of redirected anger.
Many of them live in deprived areas and crime is very much a way of life. As they grow older they become a role model for their children and the old familiar pattern is repeated.

Group therapy helps to examine the issue of deprivation, restoring good relationships and bonding. It helps to improve self-esteem and prisoners develop more understanding and awareness of the needs of others. Most learning theories argue that criminal behaviour is determined by environmental consequences, those that nurture negative behaviour i.e. - dysfunctional families, poor and deprived neighbourhoods or delinquent peer groups.

In my experience, criminal behaviour will remain in the nature of offenders but can be treated by increasing Ego strength and nurturing positive social/interpersonal skills.

Most of the prisoners who have been successful following a period of group therapy have learned to develop good relationships with others, thereby developing acceptable social (as opposed to anti-social) behaviour.

Despite the many success stories, there are also those which are not. Sadly, this means that there will be future victims and in extreme cases deaths occur, which inevitably leads to strong criticisms of the Grendon regime.

People such as me are branded as "liberal minded do gooders" who tend to give prisoners the soft option. But I will strongly argue that my personal methods, as well as the regime at Grendon Prison, are far from soft options.

As far as I am concerned, the soft option is to lock a person behind a cell door for twenty-three hours a day without challenging their behaviour and allowing them to plot future crimes with other like-minded people.

I believe there are always lessons to be learned. However, no matter how much information is gathered by the authorities it is sometimes impossible to predict the outcome of any individual scenario.

I have never been an academic and this concluding chapter has been a bit of a mechanical engineers attempt to understand what I have taken from the past 40 years. The truth is, I don't really know what I have done or how I have done it, but I do know it has worked, often!

And so, as my long and varied career ends I can look back and feel proud, as a prison officer, to have been allowed to dig deep below the surface and challenge the long-held traditions of our prison service and the "nick culture" that impedes successful rehabilitation. It has been an exhausting journey, but one with few regrets!

Printed in Great Britain
by Amazon